More Joy of
MICROWAVING

**THE MICROWAVE
COOKING
INSTITUTE®**

Prentice Hall Press

New York London Toronto Sydney Tokyo

The joy of microwaving keeps growing. The happy result is *More Joy of Microwaving*, a new collection of superb recipes, appetizing presentation ideas and practical, helpful tips for microwave owners.

Today's cooks want mouth-watering, eye-pleasing meals and snacks. They know microwave ovens offer convenient, speedy preparation. Increasingly, they recognize the importance of healthy, nutritious foods for their active life-styles. *More Joy of Microwaving* responds to these interests, with special emphasis on leaner, lighter ingredients and more healthful dietary fiber. Irresistible treats for special occasions complete the collection.

Leaf through this book. You'll be inspired by the beautiful photographs. These luscious dishes include many of our own favorites, and many submitted by creative cooks who have delighted in *The Joy of Microwaving*. All recipes have been tested and retested by the Microwave Cooking Institute's staff of home economists. Explicit, step-by-step, how-to photos ensure that your results will live up to the promise on each glorious page.

From appetizers, soups and breads to main dishes, side dishes and desserts, *More Joy of Microwaving* is just what you've been waiting for — the definitive microwave cookbook, beautiful enough to grace your coffee table, but too useful to ever leave the kitchen!

 Prentice Hall Press
Gulf + Western Building
One Gulf + Western Plaza
New York, NY 10023

CREDITS:
Design, Photography & Production: Cy DeCosse Incorporated

Material in *More Joy of Microwaving* is compiled from the following books, authored by Barbara Methven and available from the publisher:

- Basic Microwaving
- Recipe Conversion for Microwave
- Microwaving Meats
- Microwave Baking & Desserts
- Microwaving Meals in 30 Minutes
- Microwaving on a Diet
- Microwaving Fruits & Vegetables
- Microwaving Convenience Foods
- Microwaving for Holidays & Parties
- Microwaving for One & Two
- The Microwave & Freezer
- 101 Microwaving Secrets
- Microwaving Light & Healthy
- Microwaving Poultry & Seafood
- Microwaving America's Favorites
- Microwaving Fast & Easy Main Dishes
- More Microwaving Secrets
- Microwaving Light Meals & Snacks

CY DE COSSE INCORPORATED
Chairman: Cy DeCosse
President: James B. Maus
Executive Vice President: William B. Jones

PRENTICE HALL PRESS and colophon are registered trademarks of Simon & Schuster, Inc.

Library of Congress Cataloging-in-Publication Data

More Joy of Microwaving/Microwave Cooking Institute. — 1st ed
p. cm.

Includes index. 1. Microwave Cookery. I. Microwave Cooking Institute.
TX832.M662   1988   641.5'882-dc19   88-12040
ISBN 0-13-511536-1

Manufactured in the United States of America

10 9 8 7 6 5 4 3 2 1

First Edition

Contents

Garlic Shrimp
Crab Meat Rounds
Hot Beef-Bacon & Cheese Dip

Gloria's Clam Topper

Gloria Sanchez
Bethel, Connecticut

3 tablespoons butter or
  margarine
1 medium onion, chopped
½ medium green pepper,
  chopped
1 clove garlic, minced
1 teaspoon dried oregano
  leaves
1 teaspoon dried parsley
  flakes
⅛ to ¼ teaspoon dried crushed
  red pepper
2 cans (6½ oz. each) minced
  clams, drained (reserve
  3 to 6 tablespoons liquid)
1 tablespoon lemon juice
½ cup seasoned dry bread
  crumbs
2 to 3 oz. Romano cheese,
  grated

1 cup

In 9-inch pie plate, combine butter, onion, green pepper, garlic, oregano, parsley and red pepper. Microwave at High for 4 to 6 minutes, or until onion and green pepper are tender, stirring once. Stir in clams, 3 tablespoons reserved liquid and lemon juice. Stir in bread crumbs. Add additional reserved liquid, 1 tablespoon at a time, until desired consistency. Sprinkle with grated cheese. Reduce power to 70% (Medium High). Microwave for 3 to 4 minutes, or until hot and cheese melts, rotating plate once or twice. Serve with crackers or Melba toast rounds.

Crab Meat Rounds

Sandra Rea
Baton Rouge, Louisiana

2 cans (6 oz. each) crab
  meat, rinsed, drained and
  cartilage removed
½ cup thinly sliced green
  onions
⅓ cup mayonnaise

2 tablespoons snipped fresh
  parsley
½ cup finely shredded
  Cheddar cheese
36 Melba toast rounds
  Paprika (optional)

3 dozen appetizers

In small mixing bowl, combine crab meat, onions, mayonnaise and parsley. Mix well. Stir in cheese. Set aside. Line 12-inch platter with 2 layers of paper towels. Spoon half of crab mixture onto 18 toast rounds. Arrange on prepared platter. Microwave at High for 1½ to 3 minutes, or until hot and cheese melts, rotating platter once or twice. Repeat with remaining ingredients. Garnish each appetizer with paprika.

Garlic Shrimp

Mrs. Pearl Lakey
Seymour, Missouri

It is very important to add oil in slow, thin stream for perfect mayonnaise.

Garlic Mayonnaise:

1¼ cups olive oil, divided
2 cloves garlic
1 egg
1 teaspoon dry mustard
½ teaspoon salt
3 tablespoons lemon juice

Shrimp Mixture:

3 tablespoons olive oil
2 teaspoons lemon juice
2 cloves garlic, each cut into
    4 pieces
1 bay leaf
¼ teaspoon salt
¼ teaspoon dried thyme leaves
⅛ teaspoon pepper
½ lb. medium shrimp, shelled
    and deveined

4 servings.

In blender bowl, combine ¼ cup olive oil, garlic, egg, dry mustard and salt. Blend at medium high speed until well mixed. With blender running, slowly add ½ cup olive oil in very thin stream. Slowly add lemon juice, stopping to scrape sides, if needed. With blender running, add remaining ½ cup olive oil in very thin stream, stopping to scrape sides, if needed. Mixture should be smooth and thick. Chill several hours to blend flavors.

In 1-quart casserole, combine all Shrimp Mixture ingredients, except shrimp. Cover. Microwave at 70% (Medium High) for 3½ to 5½ minutes, or until garlic is light golden, stirring once. Remove garlic. Add shrimp. Stir to coat. Re-cover. Microwave at 70% (Medium High) for 2 to 4 minutes, or until shrimp are opaque, stirring once or twice. Let stand, covered, for 2 minutes. Remove bay leaf. Serve with Garlic Mayonnaise.

Hot Crab Fondue ▲

Sandra J. Robinson
Sicklerville, New Jersey

2 pkgs. (8 oz. each) cream
    cheese
2 jars (5 oz. each) sharp
    pasteurized process
    cheese spread
½ cup half-and-half

1 teaspoon Worcestershire
    sauce
⅛ teaspoon garlic powder
⅛ teaspoon cayenne
2 cans (6 oz. each) crab
    meat, rinsed, drained and
    cartilage removed

About 4 cups

In 2-quart casserole, combine all ingredients, except crab meat. Microwave at 70% (Medium High) for 3 to 6 minutes, or until mixture is smooth, stirring 2 or 3 times with whisk. Stir in crab meat. Microwave at 70% (Medium High) for 1 to 2 minutes, or until heated through. Serve with rye and pumpernickel bread cubes for dipping.

The Mountain

Janice L. Gritz
New York, New York

A combination of two favorite dips, piled high and full of color.

1	lb. lean ground beef
1	jar (8 oz.) hot salsa or jalapeño relish, divided
¼	teaspoon salt
¼	teaspoon onion powder
¼	teaspoon garlic powder
⅛	teaspoon pepper
1	can (16 oz.) refried beans
1½	cups shredded Cheddar cheese
1½	cups shredded Monterey Jack cheese

Chopped tomatoes
Sliced green onions
Sliced black olives
Dairy sour cream
Guacamole
Tortilla or corn chips

10 to 12 servings

How to Microwave The Mountain

Crumble beef into 2-quart casserole. Stir in ½ cup salsa, salt, onion powder, garlic powder and pepper. Cover.

Microwave at High for 4 to 6 minutes, or until beef is no longer pink, stirring once or twice to break apart. Drain.

Stir in remaining ½ cup salsa and beans. On 12-inch platter, mound mixture into rounded shape, about 9 inches.

Mix cheeses together. Sprinkle over meat and bean mixture, covering completely.

Microwave at 50% (Medium) for 7 to 10 minutes, or until cheese melts, rotating platter after every 2 minutes.

Sprinkle tomatoes, onions and olives in center of cheese. Alternate dollops of sour cream and guacamole around edge of platter. Serve with tortilla chips.

Swedish Meatballs ▲

Recipe was developed by Nancy and her father.

Nancy M. Heider
Larson, Wisconsin

Meatballs:
- ¼ cup finely chopped onion
- 1 tablespoon butter or margarine
- ½ lb. lean ground beef
- ¼ lb. ground pork
- ¼ lb. ground veal
- ⅓ cup unseasoned dry bread crumbs
- ¼ cup milk
- 1 egg, beaten
- ½ teaspoon ground cardamom
- ½ teaspoon ground allspice
- ½ teaspoon ground nutmeg
- ½ teaspoon salt
- ¼ teaspoon dried dill weed
- ⅛ teaspoon pepper

Gravy:
- 1 envelope (1.8 oz.) oxtail soup mix
- 1¼ cups cold water

About 4 dozen appetizers

In small bowl, combine onion and butter. Cover with plastic wrap. Microwave at High for 1 to 2 minutes, or until onion is tender. In medium mixing bowl, combine onion mixture and remaining meatball ingredients. Mix well. For fine-textured meatballs, mix ingredients in food processor. Shape into 48 meatballs, about ¾ inch each. Place in 10-inch square casserole. Set aside.

In 4-cup measure, blend soup mix and water with whisk. Microwave at High for 4 to 6 minutes, or until mixture thickens and bubbles, blending with whisk after every 2 minutes. Set aside. Cover meatballs with wax paper. Microwave at High for 5 to 9 minutes, or until meatballs are firm and cooked through, stirring once or twice. Drain. Pour gravy over meatballs. Stir to coat. Microwave at High for 30 seconds to 1 minute, or until hot.

Oodles o' Oysters

Mrs. Tally Orange
Paw Paw, Michigan

- 1 cup butter or margarine
- 1½ teaspoons celery salt
- ½ teaspoon onion powder
- ¼ teaspoon garlic powder
- 5 to 6 cups oyster crackers
- ½ cup grated Parmesan cheese

5 to 6 cups

Place butter in large mixing bowl. Microwave at High for 2 to 3 minutes, or until butter melts. Stir in celery salt, onion powder and garlic powder. Add crackers. Stir to coat. Mix in cheese. Pour onto baking sheet. Cool completely. Store in covered container.

Broccoli Dip ▲

A popular and versatile hot dip.

Marge Clayton
Highland, Illinois

- 1 pkg. (10 oz.) frozen chopped broccoli
- 1 small onion, chopped
- 1 can (10¾ oz.) condensed cream of mushroom soup
- 2 pkgs. (4 oz. each) Neufchâtel garlic cheese spread
- 1 jar (4½ oz.) sliced mushrooms, drained
- 1 pkg. (2¾ oz.) sliced almonds
- 1 teaspoon Worcestershire sauce
- ½ teaspoon salt
- ¼ teaspoon pepper
- ¼ teaspoon hot pepper sauce

4 cups

In 1½-quart casserole, combine broccoli and onion. Cover. Microwave at High for 5 to 6 minutes, or until broccoli is defrosted and onion is tender, stirring 2 or 3 times. Drain thoroughly. Stir in remaining ingredients. Re-cover. Reduce power to 70% (Medium High). Microwave for 5 to 6 minutes, or until mixture is heated through, stirring after every 2 minutes. Serve with assorted crackers.

Spinach Dip: Follow recipe above, substituting frozen chopped spinach for broccoli. Press defrosted spinach to remove excess moisture. Continue as directed.

Hot Beef-Bacon & Cheese Dip

Teresa A. Bratton
Portsmouth, Ohio

- 3 slices bacon
- 1 pkg. (3 oz.) cream cheese
- 1 pkg. (2½ oz.) smoked sliced beef, finely chopped
- ½ cup finely shredded Cheddar cheese
- 2 tablespoons milk
- 2 green onions, thinly sliced

1 cup

Arrange bacon on roasting rack. Cover with paper towel. Microwave at High for 2½ to 4 minutes, or until brown and crisp. Cool slightly. Crumble. Place bacon in small mixing bowl or serving dish. Stir in remaining ingredients, except onions. Microwave at 70% (Medium High) for 3 to 4 minutes, or until cheese melts, stirring once. Top with onions. Serve hot with assorted crackers.

Crab & Avocado Dip

1 large ripe avocado
   Lemon juice
1 pkg. (3 oz.) cream cheese
1 tablespoon sliced green onion
1 small clove garlic, minced
1 can (2 oz.) crab meat, rinsed,
   drained and cartilage
   removed; or ½ cup shredded
   seafood sticks
1 teaspoon lime juice
¼ teaspoon Worcestershire
   sauce
   Dash cayenne

6 to 8 servings

Cut avocado in half lengthwise and remove pit. With small spoon, scoop out pulp, leaving ¼-inch shell. Chop avocado pulp and set aside. Brush surfaces of avocado shells with lemon juice. Set aside.

In small mixing bowl, place cream cheese, green onion and garlic. Microwave at High for 15 to 30 seconds, or until cheese softens. Mix in chopped avocado pulp and remaining ingredients. Stuff crab mixture evenly into avocado shells. Place one shell on plate. Microwave at High for 30 seconds to 1 minute, or until dip is warm. Repeat with second avocado shell if needed. Serve dip with corn or tortilla chips, or assorted crackers.

TIP: Dip is conveniently served in its own natural container. Microwave one avocado shell, and refrigerate second shell until more warm dip is needed.

Cucumber Dip ▶

1 large cucumber (about 12 oz.), peeled and seeded
2 teaspoons water
1 teaspoon dried mint flakes
1 teaspoon lime juice
1 pkg. (3 oz.) cream cheese
1 container (8 oz.) plain low-fat yogurt
¼ cup shredded carrot
1 tablespoon snipped fresh parsley
¾ teaspoon seasoned salt
⅛ teaspoon cayenne

About 2 cups

Shred cucumber onto several layers of paper towel. Set aside to drain. In small mixing bowl, combine water, mint flakes and lime juice. Microwave at High for 30 to 45 seconds, or until hot.

Add cream cheese. Microwave at High for 15 to 30 seconds, or until cream cheese softens. Add cucumber and remaining ingredients. Mix well. Cover and chill for at least 2 hours to blend flavors. Serve with vegetables for dipping.

Hummus

¼ cup fresh lemon juice, divided
¼ cup plus 2 tablespoons water, divided
2 tablespoons sesame seed
1 teaspoon vegetable oil
¼ teaspoon sesame oil
½ cup chopped onion
1 clove garlic, minced
1 can (15 oz.) garbanzo beans, rinsed and drained
Snipped fresh parsley (optional)

About 1⅔ cups

In blender, combine 1 teaspoon lemon juice, 2 tablespoons water, the sesame seed, vegetable oil and sesame oil. Process until smooth. Place mixture in 1-quart casserole. Add remaining lemon juice, remaining ¼ cup water and the onion and garlic. Mix well. Cover. Microwave at High for 3½ to 5½ minutes, or until onion is very tender.

Place mixture in blender. Add garbanzo beans. Process until smooth. Cover with plastic wrap. Chill for at least 1 hour before serving. Add water, if desired, for thinner consistency. Garnish with parsley. Serve as dip or spread with crackers or pita bread wedges.

Platter Presentations

Pretty and practical, these presentations give you flair without fuss. Assemble and microwave attractive appetizers directly on the serving platter. No hasty last-minute garnishing. Most of the eye-pleasing arrangements can be made at your leisure, before the final microwaving.

Baked Brie Platter

1 tablespoon butter or margarine
2 tablespoons sliced almonds
1 wheel (8 oz.) Brie cheese (4½ × 1¼ inches)
  Apple wedges
  Red and green grapes
  Crackers
  Bread sticks

4 to 6 servings

In center of 12-inch platter, microwave butter at High for 45 seconds to 1 minute, or until melted. Add almonds, stirring to coat. Microwave at High for 6 to 8 minutes, or just until almonds begin to brown, stirring 2 or 3 times.

Move almonds to edge of platter. Place Brie in center. Spoon almonds onto top of Brie. Microwave at 50% (Medium) for 2 to 3½ minutes, or until Brie feels soft. To serve, arrange fruits, crackers and bread sticks on platter around Brie.

TIP: Frost grapes by brushing with egg white and sprinkling with granulated sugar. Let dry before arranging on platter.

Fresh Vegetable Platter ▲

2 cups fresh cauliflowerets (about 1½ lbs.)
2 cups fresh broccoli flowerets (about 1 lb.)

8 oz. fresh Brussels sprouts, trimmed
8 oz. fresh baby carrots
2 tablespoons water

4 to 6 servings

Arrange vegetables in single layer on 12-inch round platter. Drizzle with water. Cover platter with vented plastic wrap. Microwave vegetables at High for 6 to 8 minutes, or until colors brighten, rotating platter once or twice. Drain through vent in plastic wrap. Refrigerate for at least 4 hours. Serve vegetables with cheese dip, if desired.

Cheesy Seafood Snack Dip

- 2 pkgs. (8 oz. each) cream cheese, cut into 1-inch cubes
- ¾ cup cocktail sauce
- 1 can (6 oz.) crab meat, rinsed, drained and cartilage removed
- 1 can (4¼ oz.) medium shrimp, rinsed and drained
- 2 tablespoons sliced green onion

6 to 8 servings

Arrange cream cheese cubes in single layer on 12-inch round platter. Microwave at 50% (Medium) for 1½ to 3 minutes, or until cheese softens, rotating platter once or twice. Spread cream cheese into even layer on platter, to within 1 inch of edges. Top evenly with cocktail sauce. Sprinkle with remaining ingredients. Serve dip with assorted crackers.

Mexican Snack Dip

- 2 pkgs. (8 oz. each) cream cheese, cut into 1-inch cubes
- 1 cup refried beans
- ¾ cup taco sauce
- 1 cup shredded Cheddar cheese
- ½ cup seeded chopped tomato
- ¼ cup sliced black olives
- 2 tablespoons sliced green onion

6 to 8 servings

Arrange cream cheese cubes in single layer on 12-inch platter. Microwave at 50% (Medium) for 1½ to 3 minutes, or until cheese softens, rotating platter once or twice.

Spread cream cheese into even layer on platter, to within 1 inch of edges. Spread refried beans in even layer over cream cheese, to within ½ inch of edges. Top with taco sauce. Sprinkle with remaining ingredients. Serve snack platter with corn or tortilla chips.

Chicken & Broccoli Bites

1   boneless whole chicken
      breast (about 12 oz.)
⅓   cup teriyaki sauce
1   tablespoon vegetable oil
½   teaspoon grated orange peel
⅛   teaspoon ground cinnamon
⅛   teaspoon ground coriander
⅛   teaspoon pepper
12 oz. fresh broccoli

4 servings

How to Microwave Chicken & Broccoli Bites

Remove and discard chicken skin. Pound chicken breast between 2 sheets of plastic wrap to about ¼-inch thickness. Cut into about 1¼-inch square pieces.

Place chicken pieces in small mixing bowl. Set aside. In 1-cup measure, combine teriyaki, oil, orange peel, cinnamon, coriander and pepper. Mix well.

Pour over chicken pieces. Toss to coat. Cover and refrigerate for at least 2 hours. Drain chicken, discarding marinade.

Arrange chicken pieces in single layer in 9-inch square baking dish. Set aside. Cut broccoli into flowerets. Reserve stalk for future use in other recipes.

Skewer 1 broccoli floweret with wooden pick. Place pick into chicken piece so broccoli portion is on top. Picks will stand upright.

Cover dish with plastic wrap. Microwave at High for 4½ to 6 minutes, or until chicken is firm and no longer pink and broccoli is tender-crisp, rearranging once.

Pea-Pod-wrapped Shrimp ▲

12 fresh pea pods, 3½ inches or
    longer
12 medium shrimp, shelled and
    deveined
3   tablespoons soy sauce
1   tablespoon vegetable oil
2   teaspoons lime juice
¼   teaspoon chili powder
¼   teaspoon ground ginger
1   clove garlic, minced

                    12 appetizers

How to Microwave Pea-Pod-wrapped Shrimp

Remove strings from pea pods. Arrange pods on plate. Sprinkle with water. Cover with plastic wrap. Microwave at High for 1 to 1½ minutes, or just until pea pods are flexible. Cool slightly.

Wrap 1 pea pod around middle of each shrimp. Secure with wooden pick. Place wrapped shrimp in 9-inch round cake dish. Set aside.

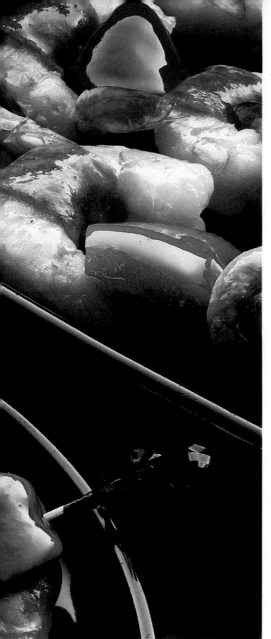

◄ Shrimp & Pepper Kabobs

- 4 thin slices hard salami
- 12 medium shrimp, shelled and deveined
- 6 wooden skewers (6-inch)
- ½ small red pepper, cut into 6 chunks
- ½ small green pepper, cut into 6 chunks
- 6 fresh mushrooms
- 2 tablespoons butter or margarine
- ¼ teaspoon onion powder
- ⅛ teaspoon dry mustard
  Dash dried thyme leaves

6 kabobs

Cut each slice of salami into 3 equal strips. Wrap 1 salami strip around middle of each shrimp. On each of 6 wooden skewers, thread a salami-wrapped shrimp, a red pepper chunk, another wrapped shrimp, a green pepper chunk and a mushroom. Place on roasting rack. Set aside.

In 1-cup measure, place remaining ingredients. Microwave at High for 45 seconds to 1 minute, or until butter melts. Stir. Brush on kabobs. Microwave at High for 3½ to 5 minutes, or until shrimp are opaque, rearranging kabobs and brushing with butter mixture once.

Shrimp Cocktail

- 1 pkg. (12 oz.) frozen uncooked large shrimp
- ¼ teaspoon dried dill weed
- ⅛ teaspoon pepper
- 1½ cups alfalfa sprouts
- ½ cup sliced celery
- 2 tablespoons chopped onion
- ¾ cup cocktail sauce
- ¼ cup plus 2 tablespoons chopped avocado
  Fresh lemon wedges (optional)

6 servings

Place shrimp in 1½-quart casserole. Sprinkle with dill weed and pepper. Cover. Microwave at 70% (Medium High) for 9 to 15 minutes, or until shrimp are opaque, stirring 2 or 3 times. Drain. Chill for at least 3 hours.

In each of 6 small (6 to 8 oz.) narrow glass bowls, evenly layer the sprouts, celery and onion. Divide shrimp among the 6 bowls, hanging shrimp over edges of bowls with tails facing inside. Spoon cocktail sauce over sprout mixture. Top with avocado. Serve with fresh lemon wedge.

Combine remaining ingredients in 1-cup measure. Mix well. Pour over shrimp. Stir gently to coat. Cover with plastic wrap. Let stand at room temperature for 15 minutes.

Remove shrimp from marinade and arrange on platter or plate. Discard marinade. Microwave shrimp at 70% (Medium High) for 4 to 5½ minutes, or until shrimp are opaque, rotating platter once or twice.

19

Cheesy Bacon Skins

4 slices bacon
¼ cup sour cream
1 tablespoon sliced green
   onion
1 teaspoon prepared
   horseradish
8 Potato Skins (below)
½ cup shredded Cheddar
   cheese

4 servings

Layer 3 paper towels on a plate. Arrange bacon slices on paper towels and cover with another paper towel. Microwave bacon at High for 3 to 6 minutes, or until brown and crisp. Cool and crumble. Set aside.

In small bowl, combine sour cream, onion and horseradish. Mix well. Divide mixture into 8 equal portions. Spread 1 portion onto each potato skin. Sprinkle skins evenly with crumbled bacon and shredded cheese. Microwave at 50% (Medium) for 3½ to 7 minutes, or until skins are hot and cheese is melted, rotating plate once. Serve with additional sour cream, if desired.

How to Prepare Potato Skins

Pierce 2 baking potatoes (8 to 10 oz. each) with fork. Arrange on roasting rack, or wrap each potato in paper towel. Microwave at High for 5 to 10 minutes, or until potatoes are tender, turning over and rearranging once. Let stand for 10 minutes.

Cut each potato lengthwise into 4 equal wedges. Carefully cut center away from each wedge, leaving ¼-inch shell. Reserve centers for use in other recipes.

Heat ½ inch vegetable oil conventionally in deep 10-inch skillet over medium-high heat. Fry potato skins until deep golden brown, 8 to 10 minutes. Drain on paper towels. Arrange potato skins cut-side-up on paper-towel-lined plate. Set aside.

Pizza Potato Skins ▲

¼ cup pizza sauce
¼ cup finely chopped
   pepperoni
1 tablespoon finely chopped
   onion
1 tablespoon finely chopped
   green pepper (optional)
8 Potato Skins (opposite)
½ cup shredded mozzarella
   cheese

Toppings:
   Chopped tomato
   Chopped green pepper
   Sliced black or pimiento-
      stuffed green olives
   Sour cream

4 servings

In small bowl, combine pizza
sauce, pepperoni, onion and
green pepper. Mix well. Divide
mixture into 8 equal portions.
Spread 1 portion onto each
potato skin. Sprinkle skins evenly
with cheese. Microwave at 50%
(Medium) for 3½ to 7 minutes, or
until skins are hot and cheese is
melted, rotating plate once. Before serving, add one or more of
the toppings.

Cream Cheese &
Shrimp-topped Skins ▼

1 pkg. (3 oz.) cream cheese
1 can (4¼ oz.) small shrimp,
   rinsed and drained
⅛ teaspoon cayenne
8 Potato Skins (opposite)
¼ cup shredded Cheddar
   cheese
¼ cup shredded Monterey Jack
   cheese
2 tablespoons sliced green
   onion or chopped green
   pepper
   Lemon wedges
   Cocktail sauce

4 servings

In small mixing bowl, microwave
cream cheese at High for 15 to
30 seconds, or until softened.
Stir. Gently mix in shrimp and
cayenne. Divide mixture into 8
equal portions. Spread 1 portion
onto each potato skin. Sprinkle
skins evenly with cheeses and
onion. Microwave at 50% (Medium) for 3½ to 7 minutes, or until
skins are hot and cheeses are
melted, rotating plate once.
Serve with lemon wedges and
cocktail sauce.

Herb Chicken
Potato Skins ▲

1 can (5 oz.) chunk chicken,
   drained
2 tablespoons Italian dressing
2 tablespoons grated
   Parmesan cheese
2 tablespoons finely chopped
   green pepper (optional)
¼ teaspoon dried marjoram
   leaves
⅛ teaspoon garlic powder
⅛ teaspoon pepper
8 Potato Skins (opposite)
½ cup shredded Monterey Jack
   cheese
   Sour cream
   Sliced green onions

4 servings

In small mixing bowl, combine
chicken, Italian dressing, Parmesan cheese, green pepper,
marjoram, garlic and pepper.
Mix well. Divide mixture into 8
equal portions. Spread 1 portion
onto each potato skin. Sprinkle
skins evenly with Monterey Jack
cheese. Microwave at 50% (Medium) for 3½ to 7 minutes, or until skins are hot and cheese is
melted, rotating plate once. Before serving, top with sour cream
and green onions.

Cheesy Mexican Popcorn

8 cups popped popcorn
¼ cup plus 2 tablespoons
   butter or margarine
1 teaspoon chili powder
¼ teaspoon seasoned salt
¼ teaspoon ground cumin
⅛ teaspoon cayenne
½ cup grated American cheese
   food

8 cups

Place popcorn in large bowl.
Set aside. Place butter in 2-cup
measure. Add chili powder, seasoned salt, cumin and cayenne.
Microwave at High for 1½ to 1¾
minutes, or until butter melts. Stir
in cheese. Spoon evenly over
popcorn. Using 2 large spoons,
toss until popcorn is evenly
coated with cheese mixture.

Sour Cream Chive Popcorn

8 cups popped popcorn
¼ cup butter or margarine
1½ teaspoons freeze-dried
   chives
2 tablespoons sour cream
   sauce mix*

8 cups

Place popcorn in large bowl. Set
aside. Place butter in 2-cup measure. Add chives. Microwave at
High for 1¼ to 1½ minutes, or
until butter melts. Stir in sour
cream sauce mix. Spoon evenly
over popcorn. Using 2 large
spoons, toss until popcorn is
evenly coated with butter mixture.

*Half of 1 envelope (1.25 oz.).
Save remaining half of envelope
for another recipe of Sour Cream
Chive Popcorn.

Herb Parmesan Popcorn

8 cups popped popcorn
¼ cup plus 2 tablespoons
   butter or margarine
½ teaspoon Italian seasoning
¼ teaspoon garlic salt
½ cup grated Parmesan cheese

8 cups

Place popcorn in large bowl. Set
aside. Place butter in 2-cup measure. Add Italian seasoning and
garlic salt. Microwave at High for
1½ to 1¾ minutes, or until butter
melts. Stir in cheese. Spoon
evenly over popcorn. Using 2
large spoons, toss until popcorn
is evenly coated with seasoned
cheese mixture.

Crunchy Snack Mix ▶

½ cup butter or margarine
1 package (.4 oz.) ranch salad
  dressing mix, buttermilk
  recipe
3 cups oyster crackers
1 can (12 oz.) mixed nuts
2 cups small pretzel twists

7 to 8 cups

In large mixing bowl, microwave
butter at High for 1½ to 1¾ minutes, or until butter melts. Stir in
salad dressing mix. Add remaining ingredients. Toss to coat.
Microwave at High for 4 to 6 minutes, or until mixture is very hot
and butter is absorbed, stirring
once. Spread on paper-towel-
lined baking sheet. Cool completely. Store in covered container.

Seasoned Sticks & Stones

1 can (9 oz.) shoestring
  potatoes
1 cup dry roasted peanuts
⅓ cup butter or margarine
2 teaspoons dried parsley
  flakes
1½ teaspoons chili powder
¼ teaspoon garlic powder
¼ teaspoon cayenne

8 cups

In large bowl, combine shoestring potatoes and peanuts. Set
aside. In 1-cup measure, microwave butter and seasonings at
High for 1½ to 1¾ minutes, or
until butter melts. Mix well. Pour
melted butter mixture over shoestring potatoes and peanuts.
Toss to coat. Microwave at High
for 4 to 6 minutes, or until shoestring potatoes are hot, tossing
with two forks after first 2 minutes
and then after every minute. Let
cool slightly. Serve warm.

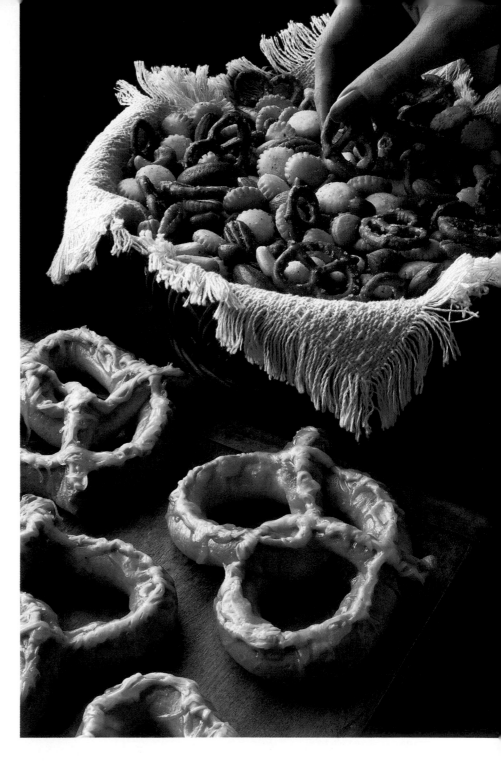

Hot Soft Pretzels ▲

4 soft pretzels
  Prepared mustard

¼ cup finely shredded Cheddar
  cheese

4 servings

Place pretzels on wax-paper-lined plate. Squeeze or spoon mustard
evenly on tops of pretzels. Sprinkle cheese evenly on tops of pretzels.
Press lightly, if necessary, so cheese adheres to mustard. Microwave
at 70% (Medium High) for 1½ to 2¼ minutes, or until pretzels are warm
and cheese is melted, rotating plate once.

Beverages

◄ Mexican Hot Chocolate

- ⅔ cup sugar
- ½ cup cocoa
- 2 teaspoons ground cinnamon
- ½ cup hot water
- 4 cups milk
- 1 teaspoon vanilla
  Prepared whipped topping
  Sliced almonds

4 to 6 servings

In 3-quart casserole, combine sugar, cocoa and cinnamon. Add hot water. Mix well. Cover. Microwave at High for 2 to 3 minutes, or until mixture is hot, stirring once. Blend in milk.

Re-cover. Microwave at High for 8 to 11 minutes, or until mixture is hot but not boiling, stirring 2 or 3 times. Add vanilla. Serve hot, topped with whipped topping and almonds.

◄ Hot Pineapple Punch

- 1 can (46 oz.) pineapple juice
- 1 small orange, thinly sliced
- ¼ cup butter or margarine
- 1 to 2 tablespoons sugar
- 1 teaspoon rum extract
- ½ teaspoon ground cardamom
  Toasted coconut (optional)

10 to 12 servings

In 8-cup measure, combine all ingredients, except coconut. Cover with plastic wrap. Microwave at High for 10 to 15 minutes, or until mixture is hot, stirring once or twice. Sprinkle each serving with toasted coconut before serving.

◄ Hot Bloody Mary

- 1¾ cups tomato juice
- 2 teaspoons lemon juice
- ¾ teaspoon Worcestershire sauce
- ¼ teaspoon celery salt
- ⅛ teaspoon red pepper sauce
- 2 tablespoons vodka
  Fresh ground pepper
  Celery stalks

2 servings

In 4-cup measure, combine tomato and lemon juices, Worcestershire sauce, celery salt and red pepper sauce. Cover with plastic wrap. Microwave at High for 3 to 4½ minutes, or until mixture is hot, stirring once. Stir in vodka. Divide evenly between 2 mugs. Top each drink with pepper and celery stalk.

Hearty Health Broth

- 1 can (10½ oz.) condensed beef broth
- 1 cup water
- ½ cup tomato juice
- ½ cup carrot juice
- ½ teaspoon onion powder
  Dash dried thyme leaves
  Dash pepper

4 servings

In 1½-quart casserole, combine all ingredients. Cover. Microwave at High for 7 to 10 minutes, or until mixture is hot, stirring twice. Serve in mugs. Garnish with celery stalk or whole green onion, if desired.

◀ Peachy Iced Tea

◀ Peachy Iced Tea

    6 cups hot water
    1 can (5½ oz.) apricot nectar
    2 tablespoons lemon juice
    1 to 2 tablespoons packed
       brown sugar
    1 teaspoon grated lemon peel
    4 tea bags
 1½ cups sliced frozen peaches

8 servings

In 2-quart measure, combine water, apricot nectar, lemon juice, brown sugar and lemon peel. Cover with plastic wrap. Microwave at High for 11 to 14 minutes, or until mixture is hot but not boiling, stirring once. Add tea bags. Set aside.

Place peaches in 1-quart casserole. Cover. Microwave at 50% (Medium) for 3½ to 5 minutes or until peaches are defrosted, stirring once. Let stand for 3 to 5 minutes to complete defrosting. In food processor or blender, process peaches until smooth.

Remove and discard tea bags. Stir peach mixture into tea. Chill at least 2 hours. Serve over ice. Garnish tea with lemon slice, if desired.

Cardamom-Spice Coffee ▲

 1½ cups hot water
  ⅛ teaspoon ground allspice
  ⅛ teaspoon ground
     cardamom
   1 tablespoon instant coffee
     crystals
  ½ cup milk
   2 teaspoons sugar
     Prepared whipped topping

2 servings

Pour ¾ cup hot water into each of 2 large coffee mugs. Sprinkle evenly with allspice and cardamom. Microwave at High for 2½ to 4 minutes, or until water mixture is hot. Stir 1½ teaspoons of coffee crystals into each mug. Set aside.

In 1-cup measure, combine milk and sugar. Microwave at High for 1¼ to 1¾ minutes, or until milk is hot but not boiling, stirring once. Pour milk mixture evenly into coffee mugs. Top with dollop of whipped topping. Sprinkle with additional cardamom, if desired.

Gingered Orange Tea ▲

   1 medium orange
   4 cups hot water
   1 tablespoon crystallized ginger
   4 tea bags

4 to 6 servings

Remove peel from orange. Set orange aside. Using thin blade of knife, cut away any white membrane from peel. Cut peel into thin strips. Cut orange in half. Squeeze halves and reserve juice.

In 2-quart measure, combine orange peel strips and juice. Add water and ginger. Cover with plastic wrap. Microwave at High for 8 to 10 minutes, or until mixture is hot, stirring once. Add tea bags and let steep for 3 to 5 minutes. Remove and discard tea bags. To serve, strain tea into cups. Serve tea iced, if desired.

Lemon & Spice Tea

   4 cups hot water
   2 teaspoons lemon juice
   1 teaspoon grated lemon peel
   6 whole cloves
   6 whole allspice
   4 tea bags
     Honey

4 servings

In 2-quart measure, combine water, lemon juice, lemon peel, cloves and allspice. Cover with plastic wrap. Microwave at High for 8 to 10 minutes, or until hot, stirring twice. Add tea bags. Let steep for 3 to 5 minutes. Remove and discard tea bags. To serve, strain tea into cups. Add honey to taste.

Strawberry Margaritas ▼

     2 cups frozen unsweetened
         strawberries
  1½ cups water
     ½ cup sugar
     1 can (6 oz.) frozen limeade
         concentrate
     ¾ cup tequila
     ¼ cup triple sec (orange
         liqueur)

                        4 to 6 servings

Place strawberries in 1-quart
casserole. Cover. Microwave at
50% (Medium) for 3½ to 5½ minutes, or until defrosted, stirring
once. Place in food processor or
blender. Process until smooth.
Set aside.

In 2-quart measure, combine
water and sugar. Microwave at
High for 2 to 3½ minutes, or until
water is hot and sugar is dissolved, stirring once. Set aside.

Remove lid from limeade can.
Place can in microwave oven.
Microwave at High for 30 to 45
seconds, or until limeade is defrosted. Pour into sugar mixture.
Add strawberries, tequila and
triple sec. Mix well.

Freeze margarita mixture for at
least 6 hours, or until slushy, stirring occasionally. Dip rim of
glass in water or lime juice, then
in sugar, before filling with frozen
margarita mixture.

Refreshing Lime Cooler

     1 can (12 oz.) frozen limeade
         concentrate
     1 cup water
     1 cup sugar
    28 fresh or frozen strawberries
         Club soda or mineral water

                            28 cubes

Remove lid from limeade can.
Place can in microwave oven.
Microwave at High for 1 minute.
Set aside. In 1-quart measure,
combine water and sugar. Microwave at High for 2 to 3 minutes,
or until mixture is hot and sugar
is dissolved, stirring once or twice.
Add limeade and mix well.

Divide mixture evenly between
2 ice cube trays. Place 1 strawberry in each cube compartment.
Freeze for 5 to 6 hours, or until
cubes are firm. Loosen edges
of cubes with spatula. To serve,
place 2 or 3 cubes in each glass.
Pour club soda over cubes, and
mix slightly.

Tangy Raspberry Shake ▲

     1 cup frozen unsweetened
         raspberries
     ¾ cup buttermilk
     ½ cup milk
     1 tablespoon honey
     2 tablespoons sweetened
         lemonade-flavored drink mix

                          2 servings

Place raspberries in 1-quart
casserole. Cover. Microwave at
50% (Medium) for 2 to 3 minutes,
or until defrosted, stirring once.
Place in blender or food processor. Add remaining ingredients.
Process until smooth and frothy.
Serve cold.

Tangy Blueberry Shake: Follow
recipe above, except substitute
1 cup frozen blueberries for
raspberries.

Sunny Tea ▲

¼ cup instant lemon-flavored
    tea powder
2 tablespoons packed brown
    sugar
½ teaspoon ground cinnamon

¼ teaspoon ground nutmeg
5 cups hot water
1 can (6 oz.) frozen pineapple-
    orange juice concentrate,
    defrosted

Serves 6

In 2-qt. casserole combine tea, brown sugar, cinnamon and nutmeg.
Gradually stir in water. Add concentrate; cover. Microwave at High 8
to 10 minutes, or until heated, stirring after half the cooking time. Garnish with lemon slices, if desired.

Hot Punch ▲

1 jar (32 oz.) cranberry-apple
    drink
¼ cup packed brown sugar
1 tablespoon lemon juice
4 whole cloves
2 cinnamon sticks
1 cup red wine, optional

Serves 6

In 2-qt. casserole combine all
ingredients except wine; cover.
Microwave at High 6 to 8
minutes, or until heated, stirring
after half the cooking time and
adding wine when 2 minutes
cooking time remain.

Mocha Chocolate ▲

½ cup instant cocoa mix
¼ cup instant coffee crystals
4 cups hot water

Serves 4

Combine instant cocoa and coffee. Measure water into 2-qt. measure; cover. Microwave at High 5 to 8 minutes, or until almost boiling. Stir in cocoa and coffee mixture. Pour into serving cups. Garnish with whipped topping and shaved chocolate curls, if desired.

Hot Beef Broth ▲

2 cans (10½ oz. each) condensed beef broth
1¾ cups hot water
1½ teaspoons lemon juice
1 teaspoon Worcestershire sauce
½ teaspoon prepared horseradish
2 to 4 tablespoons sherry, optional
4 green onions

Serves 4

In 2-qt. casserole combine broth, water, lemon juice, Worcestershire sauce and horseradish; cover. Microwave at High 6 to 8 minutes, or until heated, stirring after half the cooking time. Mix in sherry. Pour into serving cups. Serve with whole green onions.

◄ Fruit Punch in Watermelon Bowl

1 large oblong watermelon
1 large cantaloupe
3 cups sugar
3 cups hot water
2 qts. strawberries, divided
1 cup cranberry cocktail juice
   Juice of 5 oranges
   Juice of 5 lemons
2 qts. carbonated water
2 to 3 cups crushed ice

Serves 20

How to Microwave Fruit Punch in Watermelon Bowl

Cut slice from bottom of watermelon to keep it from tipping. Cut off top third. Scoop balls; remove seeds. Cover and refrigerate balls. Remove remaining pulp from bottom with large spoon to form bowl.

Cut scallops or a saw-tooth design using a small glass or bowl as guide for a decorative edge. Drain shell. Refrigerate.

Scoop balls from cantaloupe. Cover; refrigerate. Combine sugar and hot water in 2-qt. casserole; cover. Microwave at High 9 to 12 minutes, or until boiling. Uncover. Microwave at High 4 minutes. Cool.

Remove hulls from 1-qt. strawberries. In 5-qt. casserole combine hulled strawberries, cranberry, orange and lemon juices and cooled syrup. Chill.

Rub rims of 20 glasses with orange or lemon rind, then dip in additional sugar. Place a whole strawberry on each rim. Chill until sugar is hardened.

Pour carbonated water, ice and juice mixture into watermelon bowl just before serving. Serve in sugar-frosted glasses. Combine watermelon and cantaloupe balls to serve separately.

Irish Coffee ▲

¼ cup packed light brown
    sugar
2 tablespoons plus 1
    teaspoon instant coffee
    crystals
5½ cups hot water
1¼ to 1½ cups Irish whiskey
    Sweetened whipped cream

Serves 6 to 8

In 2-qt. measure or bowl
combine brown sugar, coffee
crystals and hot water; cover.
Microwave at High 5 to 8
minutes, or until very hot. Stir to
dissolve brown sugar. Stir in
whiskey. Pour into individual
cups. Top with sweetened
whipped cream.

Cappuccino for Two ▲

2 to 3 teaspoons packed light
    brown sugar
2 teaspoons instant coffee
    crystals
1⅓ cups hot water
¼ cup orange liqueur
    Sweetened whipped cream

Serves 2

In 2-cup measure combine
brown sugar, coffee crystals,
and hot water. Cover.
Microwave at High 2 to 4
minutes, or until hot. Stir to
dissolve sugar. Stir in liqueur.
Pour into individual cups. Top
with sweetened whipped cream.

Cappuccino for Eight

2 to 3 tablespoons packed
    light brown sugar
2 tablespoons instant coffee
    crystals
4 cups hot water
¾ cup orange liqueur
    Sweetened whipped cream

Serves 8

In 1½- to 2-qt. measure or bowl
combine brown sugar, coffee
crystals and hot water. Cover.
Microwave at High 4 to 6½
minutes, or until hot. Stir to
dissolve sugar. Stir in liqueur.
Pour into individual cups. Top
with sweetened whipped cream.

Soups

Confetti Soup

◄ Strawberry Soup

Barb Gray
Ballwin, Missouri

Serve very cold as a first course soup.

- 1 quart ripe strawberries, washed and hulled
- 2 tablespoons lemon juice
- 1½ cups hot water
- ½ cup sugar
- 1 tablespoon quick-cooking tapioca
- ½ cup sweet white wine
  Dairy sour cream or yogurt (optional)

6 to 8 servings

In food processor or blender bowl, combine strawberries and lemon juice. Process until smooth. Pour into 2-quart casserole. Stir in hot water, sugar and tapioca. Cover. Microwave at 70% (Medium High) for 12 to 17 minutes, or until tapioca is translucent, stirring 2 or 3 times. Stir in wine. Chill for at least 4 hours. Garnish with dollop of sour cream, if desired.

Cream of Tomato Soup ▲

Jeanne L. Wingert
Mondovi, Wisconsin

- 2 tablespoons butter or margarine
- 1 tablespoon finely chopped onion
- 3 tablespoons all-purpose flour
- 1 teaspoon salt
- 1 teaspoon sugar
- ¼ teaspoon dried marjoram leaves
  Dash pepper
- 1 can (16 oz.) stewed tomatoes, puréed
- 2 cups milk

4 servings

In 1-quart casserole, combine butter and onion. Microwave at High for 2 minutes. Stir in flour, salt, sugar, marjoram and pepper. Blend in tomatoes. Microwave at High for 3 to 6 minutes, or until mixture thickens and bubbles, stirring twice. Set aside. Place milk in 2-cup measure. Microwave at High for 2 to 3 minutes, or until hot. Blend hot milk into tomato mixture, stirring with whisk. Microwave at High for 2 to 4 minutes, or until heated through.

Chilled Carrot Soup

Captain John F. Vandegrift, Sr.
Groves, Texas

- 1 cup chopped carrots
- 1 large potato, peeled and chopped
- 1 medium leek, white part only, chopped
- 1 can (14½ oz.) ready-to-serve chicken broth
- 1 tablespoon fresh lemon juice
- ¼ teaspoon salt
- ¼ teaspoon dried summer savory leaves
- ⅛ teaspoon ground nutmeg
- ⅛ teaspoon pepper
- 1 cup half-and-half

3 to 4 servings

In 1½-quart casserole, combine all ingredients, except half-and-half. Mix well. Cover. Microwave at High for 20 to 25 minutes, or until vegetables are very tender, stirring twice. Let stand, covered, for 5 minutes. Pour into blender or food processor bowl. Process until smooth. Return vegetable mixture to casserole. Blend in half-and-half. Re-cover. Chill for at least 4 hours.

Cold Cherry Soup

2 cups frozen pitted dark sweet
   cherries
⅓ cup sugar
⅛ teaspoon ground cinnamon
¼ cup white wine
1 cup buttermilk
1 tablespoon sour cream

4 to 6 servings

Cold Peach Soup: Follow recipe
above, except substitute 2 cups
frozen sliced peaches for cherries. Microwave at High for 10 to
15 minutes, or until peaches are
tender, stirring once or twice.

How to Microwave Cold Cherry Soup

Combine all ingredients, except buttermilk and sour cream,
in 1½-quart casserole. Mix well.
Microwave at High for 7 to 10 minutes, or until mixture bubbles and
sugar dissolves, stirring once.

Remove cherries with slotted
spoon, reserving cooking liquid.
In blender or food processor,
process cherries until smooth.
Blend in cooking liquid and buttermilk. Chill for at least 1 hour.

Blend 1 teaspoon chilled soup
and the sour cream in small
bowl. Spoon soup into individual
dishes. Top each serving with sour
cream mixture. Using wooden
pick, make a swirl design in each
sour cream topping.

Creamy Italian ▶ Summer Squash Soup

¼ cup chopped onion
2 tablespoons olive or vegetable oil
1 clove garlic, minced
½ teaspoon Italian seasoning
1 medium zucchini, thinly sliced
1 medium summer squash, thinly sliced
¼ cup all-purpose flour
½ teaspoon salt
⅛ teaspoon pepper
1½ cups milk
¾ cup ready-to-serve chicken broth
½ cup seeded chopped tomato

4 servings

In 2-quart casserole, combine onion, oil, garlic and Italian seasoning. Cover. Microwave at High for 3 to 3½ minutes, or until onion is tender. Stir in zucchini and summer squash. Re-cover. Microwave at High for 6 to 9 minutes, or until squash is very tender, stirring 2 or 3 times.

Sprinkle flour, salt and pepper over squash. Stir to coat. Blend in milk and chicken broth until smooth. Microwave at High for 7½ to 11 minutes, or until mixture thickens and bubbles around edges, stirring 2 or 3 times. Stir in tomato. Let stand for 3 minutes. Sprinkle with grated Parmesan cheese before serving, if desired.

Ginger Carrot Soup

2 cups sliced carrots (½-inch slices)
1 cup peeled cubed potato (¾-inch cubes)
1 small onion, chopped
½ cup water
3 tablespoons butter or margarine
2 tablespoons soy sauce
1 teaspoon instant chicken bouillon granules
1 teaspoon packed brown sugar
1 teaspoon grated fresh gingerroot
½ teaspoon ground coriander
1¼ cups milk
Yogurt or sour cream
Fresh parsley sprigs

4 servings

In 1½-quart casserole, combine all ingredients except milk, yogurt and parsley. Cover. Microwave at High for 17 to 22 minutes, or until vegetables are very tender, stirring once or twice. Let stand, covered, for 10 minutes.

Place vegetable mixture in food processor or blender. Process until smooth. Return to casserole. Blend in milk. Cover. Microwave at High for 2 to 3 minutes, or until soup is hot. Garnish each serving with yogurt and a fresh parsley sprig, if desired. Soup may be served chilled.

Cauliflower-Blue Cheese Soup

Clara C. Carli
North Arlington, New Jersey

1½ cups sliced zucchini,
    ¼ inch thick
1½ cups fresh cauliflowerets,
    1-inch pieces
¼ cup water
2½ cups half-and-half, divided
3 tablespoons all-purpose
    flour
1 tablespoon instant chicken
    bouillon granules
2 egg yolks, beaten
⅓ cup crumbled blue cheese
    (2 oz.)

3 to 4 servings

In 2-quart casserole, combine zucchini, cauliflower and water. Cover. Microwave at High for 5 to 6 minutes, or until zucchini is tender-crisp, stirring once. Set aside. Place ½ cup half-and-half in 4-cup measure. Stir in flour and bouillon. Blend in remaining 2 cups half-and-half. Stir flour mixture into vegetables. Reduce power to 70% (Medium High). Microwave, uncovered, for 9 to 14 minutes, or until mixture thickens and bubbles, stirring after every 3 minutes.

Beat small amount of hot mixture into egg yolks. Return egg yolk mixture to soup, stirring constantly. Stir in blue cheese. Reduce power to 50% (Medium). Microwave for 2 minutes, or until heated through.

Country Potato-Cheese Soup

Susanne Adams
Livingston, Montana

2½ cups cubed potatoes,
    ¼-inch cubes
1 cup chopped carrots
½ cup chopped celery
½ cup chopped onion
1 cup hot water, divided

2 teaspoons instant chicken
    bouillon granules
½ teaspoon salt
⅛ teaspoon pepper
1 cup milk
1 cup shredded Cheddar
    cheese

4 to 6 servings

In 2-quart casserole, combine potatoes, carrots, celery, onion, ¼ cup water, bouillon, salt and pepper. Cover. Microwave at High for 10 to 13 minutes, or until vegetables are tender, stirring once. Pour into food processor or blender bowl. Process until coarsely puréed. Return vegetable mixture to casserole. Blend in remaining ¾ cup water and the milk. Stir in cheese. Re-cover. Microwave at High for 1½ to 3½ minutes, or until cheese melts, stirring once or twice.

Smoky Bean Soup

Sharon Allen
Wichita, Kansas

1 cup dried Great Northern
    beans, rinsed and sorted
1 cup dried pinto beans,
    rinsed and sorted
6 cups hot water
2 bay leaves
1 large onion, chopped
1 clove garlic, minced
1 teaspoon salt
½ teaspoon dried thyme leaves
½ teaspoon pepper
1 to 1½ teaspoons liquid
    smoke
¼ cup packed brown sugar,
    optional
1 ham hock
    or ham bone
1 can (8 oz.) tomato sauce

8 to 10 servings

In 5-quart casserole, combine
Great Northern and pinto beans,
water, bay leaves, onion, garlic,
salt, thyme, pepper and liquid
smoke. Cover. Microwave at
High for 10 to 15 minutes, or
until boiling. Let stand, covered,
for 1 hour. Stir in brown sugar.
Add ham hock. Re-cover.
Microwave at High for 5
minutes. Reduce power to 50%
(Medium). Microwave for 1 hour,
turning ham hock over and
stirring after every 20 minutes.
Remove ham hock. Cut ham
from bone. Return ham to soup.
Discard bone. Stir in tomato
sauce. Re-cover. Microwave at
50% (Medium) for 45 minutes
to 1¼ hours, or until beans are
tender, stirring once. Remove
bay leaves.

Variation:
Follow recipe above,
substituting 1½ to 2 cups
cubed fully cooked ham for
ham hock.

Cheesy Vegetable Soup ▲

Darlene A. Withrow
Marinette, Wisconsin

2 cups frozen broccoli,
    cauliflower and carrot
    mixture
1 cup peeled cubed potato,
    ¼-inch cubes
½ cup chopped onion
½ cup chopped celery
1 can (14½ oz.) ready-to-serve
    chicken broth
1 can (10¾ oz.) condensed
    cream of mushroom soup
½ lb. pasteurized process
    cheese spread, cut into
    ½-inch cubes

4 to 6 servings

In 2-quart casserole, combine frozen vegetable mixture, potato,
onion and celery. Cover. Microwave at High for 7 to 10 minutes, or
until vegetables are tender, stirring once. Mash vegetables slightly if
desired. Mix in remaining ingredients. Re-cover. Microwave at High
for 6 to 9 minutes, or until cheese melts and mixture can be stirred
smooth, stirring twice.

Creamy Leek Soup

1 medium leek
3 tablespoons butter or
   margarine
1½ cups milk
1 can (10¾ oz.) condensed
   cream of potato soup

1 teaspoon instant chicken
   bouillon granules
⅛ teaspoon pepper
   Dash ground nutmeg

4 servings

Trim ends and cut leek in half lengthwise. Rinse under cold water to remove dirt. Slice leek crosswise into ½-inch pieces. In 2-quart casserole, place leek slices and butter. Cover. Microwave at High for 8 to 10 minutes, or until leeks are tender, stirring 2 or 3 times.

Add milk, potato soup, chicken bouillon granules and pepper. Mix well. Re-cover. Microwave at High for 4 to 7 minutes, or until soup is hot, stirring once or twice. Before serving, sprinkle with nutmeg.

Creamy Leek and Shrimp Soup: Follow recipe above, except add 1 can (4¼ oz.) large canned shrimp, rinsed and drained, with milk and remaining ingredients.

Beet Soup ▲

½ cup finely shredded apple
¼ cup finely chopped onion
1 tablespoon butter or
   margarine
1 tablespoon cornstarch
½ teaspoon grated orange peel
   (optional)
⅛ teaspoon ground cloves
1 can (14½ oz.) ready-to-serve
   beef broth
1 can (16 oz.) diced beets,
   rinsed and drained

4 servings

In 1½-quart casserole, combine apple, onion and butter. Cover. Microwave at High for 3 to 5 minutes, or until onion is tender, stirring once. Stir in cornstarch, orange peel and cloves. Blend in beef broth. Microwave, uncovered, at High for 11 to 18 minutes, or until mixture is thickened and slightly translucent, stirring 2 or 3 times. Stir in beets. Cover. Let stand for 2 minutes.

Avocado Soup

2 cans (14½ oz. each) ready-
   to-serve chicken broth
½ cup half-and-half
½ teaspoon salt
⅛ teaspoon ground cumin
2 avocados, peeled and
   seeded
2 tablespoons chopped onion
2 tablespoons lime juice

4 to 6 servings

In 2-quart casserole, combine
broth, half-and-half, salt and
cumin. Cover. Microwave at High
for 5 to 9 minutes, or just until
mixture is hot, stirring once. In
food processor or blender, place
avocados, onion and lime juice.
Process until smooth. Blend a
small amount of avocado mixture
into hot broth mixture. Add remaining avocado mixture and
blend with whisk until smooth.
Serve immediately. Garnish each
serving with avocado and lime
slices, if desired.

Mexican Corn Chowder ▲

½ cup chopped onion
⅓ cup chopped green pepper
2 tablespoons butter or
   margarine
1 clove garlic, minced
¼ teaspoon ground cumin
⅛ teaspoon chili powder
1 can (10¾ oz.) condensed
   chicken broth
1 cup water
1 pkg. (10 oz.) frozen corn
1 medium tomato, seeded and
   chopped
2 tablespoons canned
   chopped green chilies
1 teaspoon dried parsley flakes
½ teaspoon salt

4 servings

In 2-quart casserole, combine onion, green pepper, butter, garlic, cumin
and chili powder. Cover. Microwave at High for 5 to 7 minutes, or until
vegetables are tender, stirring once or twice. Add remaining ingredients.
Re-cover. Microwave at High for 8 to 12 minutes, or until soup is hot,
stirring once or twice.

New England Clam Chowder

Kandace A. Beale
Kersey, Pennsylvania

2 cups cubed potatoes,
   ¼-inch cubes
¾ cup thinly sliced celery
1 medium onion, chopped
2 cans (6½ oz. each) minced
   clams, drained (reserve
   liquid)
1 teaspoon salt
1 teaspoon dried parsley
   flakes
¼ teaspoon dried thyme leaves
¼ teaspoon pepper
1 medium carrot, grated
2 cups milk, divided
¼ cup all-purpose flour
3 tablespoons butter or
   margarine

4 to 6 servings

In 2-quart casserole, combine potatoes, celery, onion, reserved clam liquid, salt, parsley, thyme and pepper. Mix well. Cover. Microwave at High for 5 minutes. Stir in carrot. Re-cover. Microwave at High for 4 to 6 minutes, or until vegetables are tender. In 2-cup measure, blend ¼ cup milk and flour until smooth. Stir flour mixture, remaining 1¾ cups milk and butter into potato mixture. Microwave, uncovered, at High for 5 to 6 minutes, or just until mixture begins to thicken, stirring twice. Stir in clams. Microwave at High for 2 minutes, or until slightly thickened and hot.

Navy Bean Soup

Alva D. Chastain
Annapolis, Maryland

Serve this hot and hearty soup with bread sticks or French bread.

- 1 lb. dried navy beans, rinsed and sorted
- 1 large onion, chopped
- 6 cups hot water
- 1 ham hock or ham bone
- 1 medium carrot, grated
- 1 tablespoon dried celery flakes
- 1 teaspoon salt
- ¼ teaspoon pepper
- ¼ teaspoon dried oregano leaves
- ⅛ teaspoon dried thyme leaves
- 1 can (16 oz.) whole tomatoes, cut up
- 1 cup milk, optional

6 to 8 servings

How to Microwave Navy Bean Soup

Combine beans, onion and water in 5-quart casserole. Cover. Microwave at High for 10 to 15 minutes, or until boiling. Let stand, covered, for 1 hour.

Add ham hock, carrot, celery flakes, salt, pepper, oregano and thyme. Re-cover. Microwave at High for 5 minutes. Reduce power to 50% (Medium). Microwave for 1 hour, turning ham hock over and stirring after every 20 minutes. Remove ham hock from soup.

Cut ham from bone. Return ham to soup. Discard bone. Stir in tomatoes. Re-cover. Microwave at 50% (Medium) for 1½ to 2 hours, or until beans are tender, stirring once. Blend in milk. Mash beans if thicker soup is desired.

Sherried Leek Soup

John R. Fuhrbach
Amarillo, Texas

- ¼ cup butter or margarine, cut up
- 3 to 4 medium leeks, cut in half lengthwise and thinly sliced
- 1 can (10¾ oz.) condensed chicken broth, divided
- ½ teaspoon salt
- ¼ to ½ teaspoon pepper
- 2 cups peeled cubed potatoes, ¼-inch cubes
- 1½ cups milk
- ½ cup whipping cream
- ¼ cup sherry

6 to 8 servings

In 2-quart casserole, combine butter, leeks, ¼ cup broth, salt and pepper. Cover. Microwave at High for 7 to 13 minutes, or until leeks are tender, stirring once. Set aside. In 1-quart casserole, combine potatoes and ¼ cup broth. Cover. Microwave at High for 6 to 8 minutes, or until potatoes are tender, stirring once.

Beat potatoes and remaining broth with electric mixer or in food processor bowl until smooth. Add to leek mixture. Blend in milk and cream. Re-cover. Reduce power to 70% (Medium High). Microwave for 7 to 10 minutes, or until heated through, stirring after every 3 minutes. Stir in sherry.

Lentil Soup

Edith H. Hancock
Lakewood, New Jersey

- 1 small onion, finely chopped
- 1 clove garlic, minced
- 1 tablespoon olive oil
- 1¼ cups dried lentils, rinsed and sorted
- 6 cups hot water
- 2 medium carrots, thinly sliced
- 1 large stalk celery, finely chopped
- 1 medium potato, cut into ½-inch cubes
- 1 can (8 oz.) tomato sauce
- ½ cup cubed fully cooked ham or pork, ¼-inch cubes
- ½ teaspoon dried marjoram leaves
- Salt

6 to 8 servings

In 3-quart casserole, combine onion, garlic and olive oil. Cover. Microwave at High for 2 to 3 minutes, or until onion is tender. Stir in remaining ingredients, except salt. Re-cover. Microwave at High for 5 minutes. Reduce power to 70% (Medium High). Microwave for 45 minutes to 1 hour, or until lentils are tender, stirring 2 or 3 times. Stir in salt to taste.

Confetti Soup

Nancy Olson
Belgrade, Minnesota

3 tablespoons butter or
   margarine
1 cup cubed carrots, ¼-inch
   cubes
1 cup cubed rutabaga, ¼-inch
   cubes
½ cup chopped onion
½ cup chopped celery
1 cup fresh broccoli flowerets
   or cauliflowerets
¼ cup all-purpose flour
½ teaspoon salt
½ teaspoon pepper
¼ teaspoon sugar
4 cups milk
1 cup shredded pasteurized
   process American cheese
1 cup frozen corn
½ cup cubed fully cooked
   ham, ¼-inch cubes
½ cup frozen peas

5 to 6 servings

In 3-quart casserole, combine
butter, carrots, rutabaga, onion,
celery and broccoli. Cover.
Microwave at High for 9 to 14
minutes, or until vegetables are
tender, stirring 3 times. Stir in
flour, salt, pepper and sugar.
Blend in milk. Reduce power to
70% (Medium High). Microwave,
uncovered, for 15 to 18 minutes,
or until mixture is slightly thickened, stirring after every 4
minutes. Stir in cheese, corn,
ham and peas. Microwave at
70% (Medium High) for 3 to 5
minutes, or until heated through
and cheese melts, stirring once.

Puerto Rican Bean Soup ▲

Gail Rosario
Albuquerque, New Mexico

1½ cups uncooked broken
    spaghetti
1 lb. fully cooked Polish
   sausage, cut into ¼-inch
   cubes
1 medium onion, chopped
½ medium green pepper,
   chopped
1 tablespoon chili powder
1 teaspoon salt
1 teaspoon garlic powder
½ teaspoon dried basil leaves
½ teaspoon dried oregano
   leaves
2 cans (15 oz. each) kidney
   beans, drained
4 cups hot water
1 can (8 oz.) tomato sauce

6 to 8 servings

Prepare spaghetti as directed on package. Rinse and drain. Set
aside. In 3-quart casserole, combine sausage, onion, green
pepper, chili powder, salt, garlic powder, basil and oregano. Cover.
Microwave at High for 6 to 8 minutes, or until vegetables are
tender, stirring twice. Stir in spaghetti and remaining ingredients.
Microwave, uncovered, at High for 8 to 9 minutes, or until heated
through, stirring twice.

Meats

Braised Pork Chops with Winter Vegetables

Rolled Burgundy Steak

1 to 1¼-lb. boneless beef top round steak, about ½ inch thick

Marinade:

¼ cup burgundy wine
2 tablespoons Worcestershire sauce
1 tablespoon vegetable oil
½ teaspoon dried summer savory leaves
¼ teaspoon dried tarragon leaves
¼ teaspoon coarsely ground pepper
⅛ teaspoon garlic powder

Filling:

1 cup chopped fresh mushrooms
½ cup shredded zucchini
½ cup herb-seasoned stuffing mix
⅛ teaspoon salt

4 servings

How to Microwave Rolled Burgundy Steak

Trim steak and pound to about ¼-inch thickness. Place in nylon cooking bag. Set aside. In 1-cup measure, combine all marinade ingredients. Mix well.

Pour marinade over steak. Secure bag with nylon tie or string. Refrigerate for at least 4 hours, or overnight. Remove meat from marinade, and lay on flat surface. Set aside. Discard marinade. Reserve bag.

Beef

Petite Fillets with Piquant Topping

2 tablespoons sliced shallots	½ teaspoon Worcestershire sauce
1 tablespoon snipped fresh parsley	⅛ teaspoon salt
1 small clove garlic, minced	Dash pepper
1 tablespoon butter or margarine	4 beef tenderloin steaks (4 to 5 oz. each), about 1 inch thick
2 tablespoons currant jelly	
1½ teaspoons coarse brown mustard	

4 servings

In 1-quart casserole, combine shallots, parsley, garlic and butter. Microwave at High for 2 minutes. Stir in remaining ingredients except steak. Cover. Microwave at High for 1 to 2 minutes, or until jelly melts, stirring once. Set aside.

Preheat a microwave browning grill at High as directed by manufacturer. Add steaks. Let stand for 1½ minutes. Turn steaks over. Microwave at High for 3 to 4 minutes, or until beef is medium rare. Spoon topping over each steak. Serve on toasted French bread slices, if desired.

Combine mushrooms and zucchini in 1-quart casserole. Cover. Microwave at High for 3 minutes. Drain thoroughly, pressing to remove excess moisture. Return to casserole, and stir in stuffing mix and salt.

Spoon filling over steak to within ½ inch of edges, pressing lightly so filling adheres to meat. Starting with narrow end, roll up steak, enclosing filling. Tie steak in several places with string. Return steak to bag. Secure bag loosely with nylon tie or string.

Place bag in 9-inch square baking dish. Microwave at High for 5 minutes. Microwave at 50% (Medium) for 15 to 20 minutes longer, or until beef is tender, turning over once. Let bag stand, closed, for 5 to 10 minutes. To serve steak, cut into slices.

Beef Tenderloin with Carrots & Leeks

2 slices bacon, cut into 1-inch pieces
3 tablespoons all-purpose flour
1 teaspoon instant beef bouillon granules
½ teaspoon bouquet garni seasoning
¾ cup water
½ cup white wine
½ teaspoon bouquet sauce
2 cups frozen baby carrots
1 cup thinly sliced leeks
1½ lbs. beef tenderloin, cut into ¾-inch pieces

4 to 6 servings

Place bacon in 2-quart casserole. Microwave at High for 2 to 3 minutes, or until brown and crisp, stirring once. Stir in flour, bouillon and bouquet garni seasoning. Blend in water, wine and bouquet sauce. Stir in carrots and leeks. Cover. Microwave at High for 14 to 18 minutes, or until mixture is thickened and carrots are tender, stirring twice. Stir in beef pieces. Re-cover. Microwave at High for 2 to 6 minutes, or until beef is desired doneness, stirring once.

Burgundy Beef with Peppers

1 pkg. (1.8 oz.) oxtail soup and recipe mix
1 cup water
½ cup burgundy wine
½ teaspoon dried marjoram leaves
⅛ teaspoon garlic powder
⅛ teaspoon pepper
2 lbs. boneless beef sirloin steak, about 1 inch thick, cut into ¼-inch strips
8 oz. fresh mushrooms, cut in half
1 medium green pepper, cut into ¼-inch strips

6 to 8 servings

How to Microwave Burgundy Beef with Peppers

Blend soup mix and water in 3-quart casserole. Cover. Microwave at High for 4 to 6 minutes, or until mixture is thickened, beating once with whisk.

Stir in wine, marjoram, garlic powder, pepper and beef strips. Re-cover. Microwave at 70% (Medium High) for 9 to 12 minutes, or until beef is tender and no longer pink, stirring once or twice.

Stir in mushrooms and green pepper. Re-cover. Microwave at 70% (Medium High) for 7 to 9 minutes, or until vegetables are tender, stirring once.

51

Orange Beef & Bok Choy ▶

- ¼ cup teriyaki sauce
- 2 tablespoons orange juice
- 2 tablespoons sliced green onion
- 1 clove garlic, minced
- 1 teaspoon vegetable oil
- ¼ teaspoon sesame oil (optional)
- ¼ teaspoon sugar
- ¾- lb. boneless beef sirloin steak, about 1-inch thick, cut into thin strips
- 2 cups sliced bok choy, stems and leaves, 1-inch slices
- 1 can (8 oz.) sliced water chestnuts, rinsed and drained
- 1½ teaspoons cornstarch
- ½ small orange, quartered and thinly sliced

4 servings

In 2-quart casserole, combine teriyaki sauce, orange juice, onion, garlic, oils and sugar. Microwave at High for 1 minute or until mixture is warm. Add beef strips. Let stand for 15 minutes.

Add bok choy and water chestnuts. Microwave at High for 5 to 8 minutes, or until beef is no longer pink, stirring twice. Drain liquid from beef mixture and place in 2-cup measure. Add small amount of reserved liquid to cornstarch. Blend. Add back to reserved liquid, stirring to combine. Microwave at High for 1 to 2 minutes, or until mixture is thickened and translucent, stirring every minute. Pour over beef mixture. Toss to coat. Garnish with orange slices. Serve with hot cooked rice, if desired.

Braised Beef & Cabbage Dinner ▲

- 1½- lb. boneless beef top round steak, ½ to ¾ inch thick
- 2 tablespoons all-purpose flour
- 2 teaspoons instant beef bouillon granules
- ½ teaspoon fennel seed
- ¼ teaspoon pepper
- 1 cup tomato juice
- 1 lb. cabbage, cut into ½-inch slices
- 1 small onion, thinly sliced
- 1 large tomato, peeled, seeded and chopped

4 servings

Trim steak and pound to about ¼-inch thickness. Cut into serving-size pieces. Set aside. In nylon cooking bag, place flour, beef bouillon granules, fennel and pepper. Add steak pieces. Shake to coat evenly. Pour tomato juice over steak. Add cabbage and onion.

Secure bag loosely with nylon tie or string. Place bag in 9-inch square baking dish. Microwave at High for 5 minutes. Microwave at 50% (Medium) for 35 to 45 minutes longer, or until beef is tender, turning bag over once. Add tomato. Let bag stand, closed, for 5 minutes.

Italian Style Stuffed Shells ▲

12 uncooked jumbo pasta shells
½ lb. lean ground beef
1 tablespoon sliced green onion
1 tablespoon snipped fresh parsley, divided
¾ teaspoon Italian seasoning, divided

½ cup low-fat cottage cheese
¼ cup grated Parmesan cheese
1 egg, beaten
¼ teaspoon salt
¼ teaspoon pepper, divided
1 can (8 oz.) tomato sauce
¼ teaspoon sugar

4 servings

Prepare shells as directed on package. Rinse and drain. Set aside. Crumble ground beef into 1-quart casserole. Add onion, 2 teaspoons parsley and ½ teaspoon Italian seasoning. Cover. Microwave at High for 2 to 4 minutes, or until meat is no longer pink, stirring once to break apart. Drain. Add cheeses, egg, salt and ⅛ teaspoon pepper. Mix well. Stuff shells evenly with ground beef mixture.

Place shells in 9-inch round baking dish. Set aside. In 1-cup measure, combine tomato sauce, sugar, the remaining 1 teaspoon parsley, ¼ teaspoon Italian seasoning and ⅛ teaspoon pepper. Mix well. Pour evenly over stuffed shells. Cover with plastic wrap. Microwave at High for 6 to 8 minutes, or until filling is hot, rearranging shells once.

Meatloaf with Broccoli Sauce

Meatloaf:
1 lb. lean ground beef
1 cup cooked brown rice
¼ cup finely chopped onion
1 egg, beaten
2 tablespoons milk
½ teaspoon salt
¼ teaspoon pepper
⅛ teaspoon garlic powder
⅛ teaspoon ground nutmeg

Sauce:
1 cup chopped fresh broccoli
2 tablespoons butter or margarine
1 tablespoon all-purpose flour
¼ teaspoon salt
¾ cup milk
¼ cup shredded Swiss cheese (optional)

6 servings

In medium mixing bowl, combine all meatloaf ingredients. Mix well. Shape into 6½ × 3½-inch loaf, and place on roasting rack. Cover with wax paper. Microwave at High for 13 to 17 minutes, or until meatloaf is firm and internal temperature in center registers 150°F, rotating rack once or twice. Set aside, covered.

In 1-quart casserole, combine broccoli and butter. Cover. Microwave at High for 2½ to 3 minutes, or until broccoli is tender-crisp. Stir in flour and salt. Blend in milk. Microwave, uncovered, at High for 3 to 4½ minutes, or until sauce thickens and bubbles, stirring twice. Stir in cheese until melted. Slice meatloaf and spoon sauce over slices.

Beef & Bulgur Stuffed Peppers

1½ cups plus 2 tablespoons water, divided
½ cup bulgur or cracked wheat
½ lb. lean ground beef
⅓ cup shredded carrot
2 tablespoons finely chopped onion
½ teaspoon dried basil leaves
½ cup shredded Monterey Jack cheese
⅓ cup frozen corn
½ teaspoon salt
⅛ teaspoon pepper
4 large red or green peppers

4 servings

Place 1½ cups water in 4-cup measure. Microwave at High for 4 to 5 minutes, or until boiling. Stir in bulgur. Cover with plastic wrap. Let stand about 30 minutes or until bulgur softens. Drain, pressing to remove excess moisture. Set aside.

Crumble ground beef into 1-quart casserole. Add carrot, onion and basil. Cover. Microwave at High for 3 to 4 minutes, or until meat is no longer pink, stirring once to break apart. Drain. Stir in bulgur, cheese, corn, salt and pepper. Mix well. Set aside.

Cut ½-inch slice from top of peppers, reserving tops. Remove seeds and membrane. Remove thin slice from bottom of each pepper to allow peppers to stand upright. Fill peppers evenly with bulgur mixture. Place upright in 9-inch round baking dish. Add remaining 2 tablespoons water around peppers. Top peppers with reserved tops. Cover with plastic wrap. Microwave at High for 10 to 15 minutes, or until peppers are tender, rotating dish once. Let stand, covered, for 5 minutes.

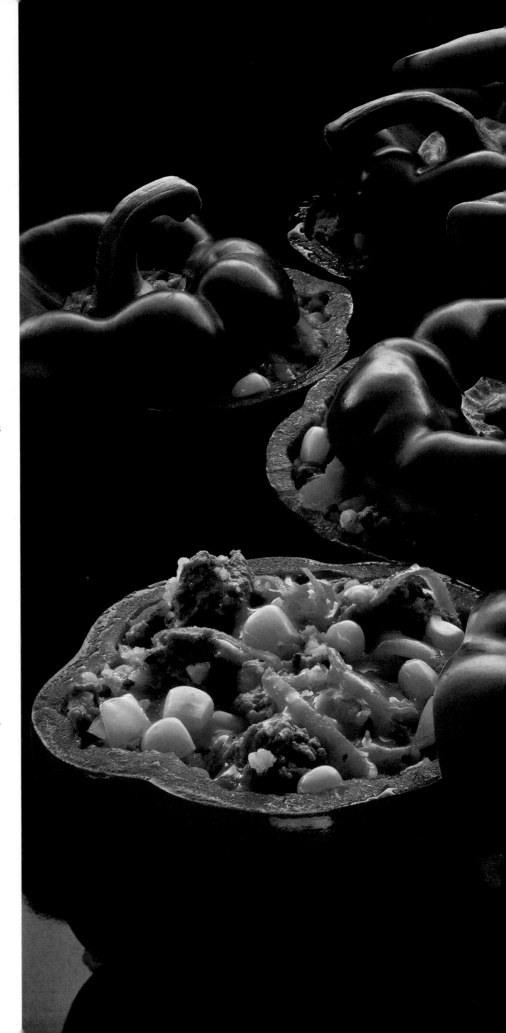

American Lasagna

Gloria Struhelka
Pewaukee, Wisconsin

12 uncooked lasagna noodles

Sauce:

½ lb. lean ground beef
1 clove garlic, minced
1 can (16 oz.) whole tomatoes, drained and chopped
1 can (6 oz.) tomato paste
¾ teaspoon Italian seasoning
½ teaspoon salt
½ teaspoon dried oregano leaves
¼ teaspoon sugar
¼ teaspoon pepper

2 cups small curd cottage cheese
2 eggs
¾ cup grated Parmesan cheese, divided
2 cups shredded mozzarella cheese

6 to 8 servings

How to Microwave American Lasagna

Prepare lasagna noodles as directed on package. Rinse. Let stand in warm water while preparing sauce.

Crumble beef into 1-quart casserole. Add garlic. Cover. Microwave at High for 2 to 3 minutes, or until beef is no longer pink, stirring once to break apart. Drain. Stir in remaining sauce ingredients. Re-cover. Microwave at High for 5 minutes, stirring after half the time. Set aside.

Combine cottage cheese, eggs and ¼ cup Parmesan cheese in food processor or blender bowl. Process until smooth. Set aside. Place lasagna noodles on paper towels to drain.

Layer 4 noodles, half of mozzarella cheese, half of cottage cheese mixture and half of sauce in 10-inch square casserole. Repeat once. Top with remaining 4 noodles. Sprinkle with remaining ½ cup Parmesan cheese.

Cover with vented plastic wrap. Microwave at High for 5 minutes. Rotate casserole half turn. Reduce power to 70% (Medium High).

Microwave for 10 to 14 minutes, or until temperature in center registers 150°F, rotating casserole twice. Let stand, covered, for 10 minutes. Garnish with dried parsley flakes, if desired.

Cheesy Broccoli-stuffed Meatloaf

1½ lbs. lean ground beef
1 egg, slightly beaten
¼ cup plus 2 tablespoons
    seasoned dry bread
    crumbs, divided
¼ cup finely chopped onion,
    divided
¾ teaspoon salt, divided
½ teaspoon dried basil leaves
⅛ teaspoon pepper
1 cup frozen broccoli cuts
½ cup shredded cheese
    (Monterey Jack, Cheddar
    or mozzarella)
1 tablespoon butter or
    margarine
¼ teaspoon bouquet sauce

6 servings

How to Microwave Cheesy Broccoli-stuffed Meatloaf

Combine beef, egg, ¼ cup bread crumbs, 2 tablespoons onion, ½ teaspoon salt, the basil and pepper in medium mixing bowl. Mix well. Set aside. In 1-quart casserole, combine broccoli and remaining 2 table-spoons onion. Cover.

Microwave at High for 2 to 3 minutes, or until hot. Cool slightly. Cut broccoli into bite-size pieces. Stir in remaining 2 tablespoons bread crumbs, remaining ¼ teaspoon salt and the cheese. Set aside.

Place butter in custard cup. Microwave at High for 45 seconds to 1 minute, or until butter melts. Stir in bouquet sauce. Set aside.

58

Press half of beef mixture into 8 × 4-inch loaf dish, forming an indentation in center and about 1-inch thickness on sides. Spoon broccoli mixture into center indentation.

Top with remaining beef mixture, pressing evenly and sealing edges. Brush butter mixture lightly over top of loaf. Cover with wax paper. Place dish on saucer in microwave oven. Microwave at High for 5 minutes. Rotate dish half turn. Brush with remaining butter mixture. Re-cover.

Microwave at 70% (Medium High) for 11 to 15 minutes, or until bottom center of loaf appears cooked and internal temperature in center of loaf registers 150°F, rotating dish once or twice. Let stand, covered, for 5 minutes.

Mediterranean Layered Casserole

1 lb. ground beef, or
  ½ lb. ground lamb plus
  ½ lb. ground beef
2 teaspoons instant minced
  onion
⅓ cup tomato sauce
½ teaspoon ground cinnamon

½ teaspoon salt, divided
¼ teaspoon pepper, divided
1 pkg. (4.75 oz.) cream-style
  potatoes mix
1⅓ cups milk
1 cup water

1 cup ricotta cheese
¼ cup grated Parmesan cheese
1 egg, slightly beaten
2 teaspoons dried parsley
  flakes

6 servings

How to Microwave Mediterranean Layered Casserole

Crumble beef into 1-quart casserole. Add onion. Cover. Microwave at High for 4 to 7 minutes, or until beef is no longer pink, stirring once to break apart. Drain.

Stir in tomato sauce, cinnamon, ¼ teaspoon salt and ⅛ teaspoon pepper. Set aside.

Combine potatoes and sauce packet, milk and water in 9-inch square baking dish. Cover with plastic wrap. Microwave at High for 5 minutes. Stir. Microwave, uncovered, at High for 8 to 13 minutes, or until potatoes are tender and sauce thickens, stirring once.

Layer beef mixture over potatoes. Set aside. In small mixing bowl, combine ricotta and Parmesan cheeses, egg, remaining ¼ teaspoon salt, remaining ⅛ teaspoon pepper and the parsley. Mix well.

Spread cheese mixture evenly over beef layer. Cover with wax paper.

Microwave at High for 6 to 9 minutes, or until center is hot and cheese mixture appears set, rotating dish once. Let stand, covered, for 5 to 10 minutes.

Calzone

A restaurant favorite that can be frozen, too.

*Nancy J. Klein
Eugene, Oregon*

1 lb. loaf frozen bread dough
½ lb. lean ground beef
½ lb. Italian sausage
1 cup sliced fresh mushrooms
½ cup chopped green pepper
¼ cup sliced black olives
¼ cup chopped onion
2 teaspoons Italian seasoning
2 tablespoons catsup
2 cups mozzarella cheese

4 servings

Grease 8 × 4-inch loaf dish. Butter frozen dough on all sides. Place in prepared dish. Microwave at 50% (Medium) for 2 minutes, rotating dish after half the time. Let stand for 5 minutes. Turn dough over. Microwave at 50% (Medium) for 1 to 2 minutes, or until soft to the touch and slightly warm. Cover with plastic wrap. Let rise in warm place until doubled, about 1 hour.

In 2-quart casserole, crumble beef and sausage. Stir in mushrooms, green pepper, olives, onion and Italian seasoning. Cover. Microwave at High for 4 to 6 minutes, or until meat is no longer pink, stirring once to break apart. Drain. Stir in catsup. Set aside.

Preheat conventional oven to 400°F. Lightly oil baking sheet. Set aside. Punch down dough. Divide into 4 equal pieces. Roll or stretch each piece into 8 × 6-inch oval. Place one-fourth of meat mixture in center of each oval. Top with one-fourth of cheese. Fold half of dough over meat and cheese. Seal edges. Repeat with remaining dough. Place on prepared baking sheet. Brush calzones with oil. Bake until lightly browned, 10 to 15 minutes.

How to Microwave in a Cooking Bag

Coat bag by placing 1 tablespoon flour in bag before microwaving. Shake to distribute flour, then proceed with recipe. Additional flour listed with ingredients is needed for thickening.

Secure bag loosely with nylon ties provided or string, to allow some steam to escape. DO NOT use metal twist ties: arcing may occur during microwaving.

Use oven mitts or pot holders when handling nylon cooking bags during or after microwaving. Bags retain heat from food.

Beef & Broccoli

½ cup water
⅓ cup sliced green onions
¼ cup soy sauce
3 tablespoons honey
1 tablespoon sherry
1 tablespoon all-purpose flour
¼ teaspoon grated fresh gingerroot
¼ teaspoon instant beef bouillon granules
⅛ teaspoon garlic powder
2 lbs. boneless beef top round steak (½ inch thick), thinly sliced
1 cup diagonally sliced carrots (¼-inch slices)
3 cups broccoli flowerets and thinly sliced stalks (about ¾ lb.)

6 servings

In nylon cooking bag, place water, onions, soy sauce, honey, sherry, flour, gingerroot, bouillon and garlic powder. Shake bag gently to mix. Add beef strips. Secure bag. Refrigerate for at least 4 hours. Place bag in 9-inch square baking dish. Add carrots to bag. Secure bag loosely. Microwave at High for 5 minutes. Microwave at 50% (Medium) for 30 to 40 minutes longer, or until meat is tender, adding broccoli during last 5 minutes. Let bag stand for 5 to 8 minutes before serving.

Veal

Walnut-Tarragon Veal Cutlets ▶

- 1 egg, beaten
- 1 tablespoon lemon juice
- ⅔ cup unseasoned dry bread crumbs
- ¼ cup finely chopped walnuts
- 1 tablespoon dried parsley flakes
- ¾ teaspoon salt
- ½ teaspoon dried tarragon leaves
- ¼ teaspoon pepper
- ¾ lb. veal cutlets, about ¼ inch thick
  Lemon slices (optional)

4 servings

How to Microwave Walnut-Tarragon Veal Cutlets

Line a 12-inch round platter with 2 layers of paper towels. Set aside. In 9-inch pie plate, blend egg and lemon juice. Set aside.

Mix bread crumbs, walnuts, parsley, salt, tarragon and pepper on sheet of wax paper. Dip veal in egg mixture, then in crumb mixture, pressing lightly to coat both sides.

Place cutlets on paper towel-lined platter. Microwave at 70% (Medium High) for 7 to 10 minutes, or until veal is firm rotating platter twice.

Saucy Veal & Mushrooms ▲

1 envelope (.87 oz.) white sauce mix
2 tablespoons snipped fresh parsley
½ teaspoon salt
⅛ teaspoon pepper
⅔ cup milk

8 oz. fresh mushrooms, thinly sliced
1½ lbs. veal round steak, about ½ inch thick, cut into ¼-inch strips
¼ cup dairy sour cream

6 to 8 servings

In 2-quart casserole, combine sauce mix, parsley, salt and pepper. Blend in milk. Beat well with whisk. Microwave at High for 3½ to 4½ minutes, or until mixture is very thick, stirring after every minute. Gently stir in mushrooms. Microwave at High for 2 minutes. Stir. Add veal strips. Stir. Cover. Microwave at 50% (Medium) for 15 to 20 minutes, or until veal is no longer pink, stirring once or twice. Stir in sour cream. Let stand, covered, for 5 to 10 minutes.

Cut lemon into thin slices. Cut each slice through the center, leaving one edge of peel intact. Twist slice into 'S' shape. Garnish veal with lemon twist.

Lemon Breaded Veal with Caper Sauce

1 egg, beaten
½ cup unseasoned dry bread crumbs
2 teaspoons dried parsley flakes, divided
¾ teaspoon grated lemon peel, divided
½ teaspoon paprika
¼ teaspoon salt
¼ teaspoon pepper
¾ lb. veal scallops, about ¼ inch thick
2 teaspoons cornstarch
⅔ cup ready-to-serve chicken broth
2 tablespoons vermouth
1 teaspoon butter or margarine
¼ teaspoon sugar
1 tablespoon drained capers

4 servings

Pour egg into 9-inch pie plate. Set aside. In shallow dish, mix bread crumbs, 1 teaspoon parsley, ½ teaspoon lemon peel, the paprika, salt, and pepper. Dip veal in egg, then in crumb mixture, pressing lightly to coat both sides. Place scallops on roasting rack. Microwave at 70% (Medium High) for 7 to 10 minutes, or until veal is firm, rotating rack twice. Cover to keep warm. Set aside.

In 2-cup measure, combine remaining 1 teaspoon parsley and ¼ teaspoon lemon peel. Stir in cornstarch. Blend in broth, vermouth, butter and sugar. Microwave at High for 2½ to 4 minutes, or until mixture is thickened and translucent, stirring every minute. Add capers. To serve, pour sauce over veal.

Veal with Marsala Sauce ▲

1 cup sliced fresh mushrooms
⅓ cup ready-to-serve chicken broth
¼ cup sweet Marsala wine
2 tablespoons snipped fresh parsley
¼ teaspoon salt

1 lb. boneless veal shoulder steak, about ½ inch thick, cut into 4 serving-size pieces
1 tablespoon all-purpose flour
2 tablespoons milk
¼ teaspoon bouquet sauce

4 servings

In 9-inch square baking dish, combine mushrooms, broth, wine, parsley and salt. Cover with plastic wrap. Microwave at High for 4 to 5 minutes, or until mushrooms are tender, stirring once. Add veal pieces. Turn to coat with broth mixture. Re-cover. Microwave at 70% (Medium High) for 5 to 6 minutes, or until veal is medium done, rearranging pieces once. Remove veal from broth mixture. Cover veal to keep warm. Set veal and broth aside.

Place flour in small mixing bowl. Blend in milk and bouquet sauce until mixture is smooth. Add to broth mixture. Mix well. Microwave at High for 3 to 5 minutes, or until sauce thickens and bubbles, stirring every minute. To serve, pour sauce over veal.

Saucy Dijon Veal

- 1 pkg. (10 oz.) frozen asparagus cuts
- ¾ to 1-lb. boneless veal round steak, cut into ¾-inch pieces
- 3 tablespoons all-purpose flour
- ½ teaspoon salt
- ¼ teaspoon bouquet garni seasoning
- ½ cup julienne carrot (1½ × ¼-inch strips)
- ½ cup chopped onion
- 1 tablespoon butter or margarine
- 1 cup fresh mushroom halves
- ½ cup ready-to-serve chicken broth
- ⅓ cup white wine
- 2 teaspoons Dijon mustard

4 to 6 servings

Unwrap asparagus and place on plate. Microwave at High for 4 to 6 minutes, or until defrosted. Drain and set aside. Place veal pieces in large plastic food-storage bag. Add flour, salt and bouquet garni seasoning. Shake to coat meat. Set aside.

In 2-quart casserole, combine carrot, onion and butter. Cover. Microwave at High for 5 to 6 minutes, or until vegetables are tender, stirring once. Add veal and any excess flour mixture. Stir in mushrooms, broth, wine and mustard. Re-cover. Microwave at 70% (Medium High) for 13 to 16 minutes, or until veal is no longer pink, stirring twice. Add asparagus. Re-cover. Microwave at 70% (Medium High) for 4 minutes. Let stand, covered, for 10 minutes. Serve over hot cooked egg noodles, if desired.

Pork

Quick Creole Chops

4 pork chops (4 to 5 oz. each)
   ½ inch thick
2 tablespoons all-purpose flour
1 cup sliced zucchini, ¼ inch
   thick
½ cup red or green pepper
   pieces, 1-inch pieces
1 can (16 oz.) stewed
   tomatoes
¼ cup chili sauce
1 teaspoon sugar
¼ teaspoon dried thyme leaves
⅛ teaspoon cayenne

4 servings

Place chops in large plastic food storage bag. Add flour. Shake to coat. Arrange chops in 9-inch square baking dish with bone-side toward center of dish. Add any excess flour to dish. Top with zucchini and red pepper. Set aside.

In small mixing bowl, blend remaining ingredients. Pour over chops and vegetables. Cover with wax paper. Microwave at 70% (Medium High) for 20 to 28 minutes, or until pork near bone is no longer pink and sauce thickens, rotating dish once or twice. Let stand, covered, for 5 minutes.

To reheat: Place one serving on plate. Cover with wax paper. Microwave at 70% (Medium High) for 3½ to 4½ minutes, or until heated through.

Braised Pork Chops with Sweet Peppers

- 1 medium onion, thinly sliced
- 1 clove garlic, minced
- 1 tablespoon olive oil
- 2 tablespoons all-purpose flour
- ½ teaspoon salt
- ⅛ teaspoon cayenne
- 4 butterflied pork chops, about ½ inch thick (6 to 8 oz. each)
- ⅓ cup ready-to-serve chicken broth
- 2 teaspoons lime juice
- 1 teaspoon Worcestershire sauce
- 1 medium red pepper, cut into ½-inch strips

4 servings

How to Microwave Braised Pork Chops with Sweet Peppers

Combine onion, garlic and oil in 9-inch square baking dish. Cover with plastic wrap. Microwave at High for 3 to 4 minutes, or until onion is tender-crisp. In large plastic food storage bag, combine flour, salt and cayenne.

Add chops. Shake to coat. Arrange coated chops over onion and garlic. In 1-cup measure, combine broth, lime juice and Worcestershire sauce. Mix well.

Pour over chops. Cover with plastic wrap. Microwave at 70% (Medium High) for 10 minutes. Turn chops over. Stir sauce.

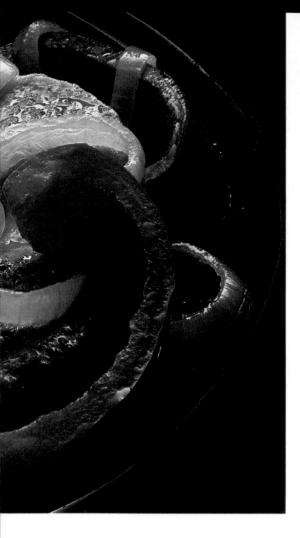

Arrange red pepper strips on chops. Cover with plastic wrap. Microwave at 70% (Medium High) for 10 to 13 minutes, or until pork is no longer pink, rotating dish once. Let stand, covered, for 3 minutes.

Fruited Pork Ragout

1 cup julienne rutabaga (2 × ½-inch strips)
1 medium onion, cut into 8 pieces
1 cup ready-to-serve chicken broth
1 can (17 oz.) apricot halves, drained (reserve ⅓ cup syrup)
¼ cup all-purpose flour

½ teaspoon fennel seed, crushed
½ teaspoon salt
1½ lbs. boneless pork loin, cut into 1-inch pieces
½ teaspoon bouquet sauce
1 medium cooking apple, cut into ½-inch cubes (about 1 cup)
½ cup raisins

6 servings

In 3-quart casserole, combine rutabaga, onion, broth and ⅓ cup apricot syrup. Cover. Microwave at High for 8 to 11 minutes, or until vegetables are tender-crisp, stirring twice. In large plastic food storage bag, combine flour, fennel and salt. Add pork pieces. Shake to coat. Add to vegetables. Stir in bouquet sauce, apple and raisins. Re-cover. Microwave at High for 5 minutes. Mix well. Microwave at 70% (Medium High) for 20 to 25 minutes, or until pork is tender and no longer pink, stirring twice. Stir in apricots. Let stand, covered, for 5 minutes.

71

Herbed Pork & Peppers

1 medium onion, cut in half lengthwise and then into ½-inch strips
⅓ cup white wine
1 tablespoon vegetable oil
1 clove garlic, minced
½ teaspoon dried thyme leaves
½ teaspoon dried parsley flakes
¼ teaspoon salt
¼ teaspoon bouquet sauce
2 butterflied pork chops (about ¾ lb.), cut into ¼-inch strips
2 cups green, red or yellow pepper chunks (1-inch chunks)
1 teaspoon cornstarch

4 servings

In 2-quart casserole, combine all ingredients, except pork, peppers and cornstarch. Cover. Microwave at High for 4 to 5 minutes, or until onion is tender-crisp, stirring once. Cool slightly. Add pork strips. Re-cover. Refrigerate for 30 minutes to 1 hour. Add peppers. Mix well. Re-cover. Microwave at 70% (Medium High) for 6 to 11 minutes, or until pork is no longer pink, stirring once or twice.

Drain liquid from pork and peppers into a 2-cup measure. Cover pork and peppers to keep warm. Add a small amount of reserved liquid to cornstarch. Blend. Add back to reserved liquid, stirring to combine. Microwave at High for 1½ to 2 minutes, or until mixture is thickened and translucent, stirring every minute. Pour over pork and peppers. Toss to coat. Serve with hot cooked rice or noodles, if desired.

Braised Pork Chops with Winter Vegetables ►

¾ cup julienne carrot
(2 × ¼-inch strips)
¾ cup julienne rutabaga
(2 × ¼-inch strips)
¾ cup julienne turnip
(2 × ¼-inch strips)
1 small onion, thinly sliced
¼ cup plus 3 tablespoons
ready-to-serve beef broth,
divided
4 pork loin chops (5 to 6 oz.
each), about ½ inch thick
1 tablespoon snipped fresh
parsley
2 teaspoons packed brown
sugar
¼ teaspoon dried rosemary
leaves, crushed
¼ teaspoon salt
Dash pepper

4 servings

In 9-inch square baking dish, combine carrot, rutabaga, turnip and onion. Pour 3 tablespoons broth over vegetables. Cover with plastic wrap. Microwave at High for 8 to 10 minutes, or until vegetables are tender-crisp, stirring once. Arrange pork chops over vegetables, bone side toward center of dish. Set aside, covered.

In 1-cup measure, combine remaining ¼ cup broth, the parsley, brown sugar, rosemary, salt and pepper. Mix well. Pour evenly over pork chops. Re-cover. Microwave at 70% (Medium High) for 12 to 16 minutes, or until pork near bone is no longer pink, rotating dish once or twice. Let stand, covered, for 5 minutes. With slotted spoon, lift meat and vegetables to serving plate.

Plum-sauced Pork Medallions

1½ lbs. pork tenderloins,
trimmed, diagonally sliced
½ inch thick
1 bay leaf
1 can (16½ oz.) whole purple
plums, in heavy syrup
¼ cup port wine
¼ cup raisins
1½ teaspoons instant beef
bouillon granules
½ teaspoon caraway seed
¼ teaspoon salt
⅛ teaspoon pepper

6 servings

Place tenderloin slices in 9-inch square baking dish. Add bay leaf. Set aside. Drain plums and reserve ¼ cup syrup. Remove and discard pits from plums, and place plums in food processor or blender. Process until smooth.

Place processed plums in small mixing bowl. Add reserved syrup, and remaining ingredients. Mix well. Pour over pork slices. Cover with wax paper. Microwave at 70% (Medium High) for 18 to 23 minutes, or until pork is firm and cooked through, stirring sauce and rearranging pork, 2 or 3 times. Let stand, covered, for 5 minutes. Arrange on serving plate. Spoon sauce over pork.

Teriyaki Orange Ribs

1 tablespoon all-purpose flour
4 lbs. pork spareribs, trimmed
    and cut into serving-size
    pieces
½ cup teriyaki sauce
2 tablespoons frozen orange
    juice concentrate
1 clove garlic, minced
¼ teaspoon ground ginger
⅛ teaspoon cayenne

4 servings

Place flour in nylon cooking bag. Shake to coat. Add ribs. In 1-cup measure, blend teriyaki sauce, orange juice concentrate, garlic, ginger and cayenne. Pour over ribs. Secure bag with string or nylon tie. Place bag on plate. Refrigerate for at least 8 hours or overnight.

Place ribs in bag in 10-inch square casserole. Microwave at High for 5 minutes. Microwave at 70% (Medium High) for 25 to 35 minutes, or until pork is tender, turning ribs over and rearranging twice. Let stand, covered, for 10 minutes.

To reheat: Place one serving on plate. Cover with wax paper. Microwave at 70% (Medium High) for 2½ to 4 minutes, or until heated through.

Pork Enchiladas

1 lb. ground pork
⅓ cup chopped onion
1 can (10 oz.) enchilada
    sauce, divided
2 tablespoons canned
    chopped green chilies
½ teaspoon ground cumin
6 corn tortillas, 6-inch
1 cup shredded Cheddar
    cheese
2 tablespoons sliced
    green onion

4 to 6 servings

Crumble pork into 1½-quart casserole. Add chopped onion. Cover. Microwave at High for 5 to 7 minutes, or until pork is no longer pink, stirring twice to break apart. Drain. Stir in ¼ cup enchilada sauce, the chilies and cumin. Set aside.

Soften tortillas conventionally as directed on package. Place one-sixth of pork mixture in center of each tortilla. Roll up, enclosing filling. Arrange enchiladas seam-side down in 9-inch square baking dish. Pour remaining enchilada sauce over enchiladas. Sprinkle with cheese and sliced green onion. Microwave at 70% (Medium High) for 5 to 7 minutes, or until heated through and cheese melts, rotating dish once or twice.

To reheat: Place one serving on plate. Microwave at 70% (Medium High) for 2 to 3 minutes, or until heated through.

Lamb

◄ Summer Lamb Stew

2 tablespoons all-purpose flour	2 lbs. boneless lamb shoulder, cut into ¾-inch pieces
2 teaspoons sugar	1 can (28 oz.) whole tomatoes, cut up
1 clove garlic, minced	
½ teaspoon dried marjoram leaves	4 cups trimmed fresh spinach leaves
½ teaspoon salt	1 cup sliced summer squash, ⅛ inch thick
⅛ teaspoon cayenne	

4 to 6 servings

In 3-quart casserole, combine flour, sugar, garlic, marjoram, salt and cayenne. Mix well. Add lamb pieces. Toss to coat. Stir in tomatoes. Cover. Microwave at High for 5 minutes. Stir. Re-cover. Microwave at 50% (Medium) for 40 to 55 minutes, or until lamb is tender, stirring 2 or 3 times. Gently stir in spinach and summer squash. Re-cover. Microwave at High for 2 minutes. Let stand, covered, for 5 minutes.

Lamb Chops with Minty Pear Sauce

4 lamb loin chops (4 to 5 oz. each)	½ teaspoon salt
	½ teaspoon dried mint flakes
1 can (16 oz.) pear halves, drained and cut into ½-inch strips (reserve syrup)	½ teaspoon grated orange peel
	1 tablespoon cornstarch
	1 tablespoon cold water
1 teaspoon packed brown sugar	

4 servings

Arrange chops in 9-inch square baking dish with bone-side toward center of dish. Set aside. Add water to pear syrup to equal ¾ cup. In small mixing bowl, combine pear syrup, brown sugar, salt, mint and orange peel. Mix well. Pour over chops. Cover with wax paper. Microwave at High for 5 minutes. Baste chops with cooking liquid. Re-cover. Microwave at 50% (Medium) for 10 to 13 minutes, or until lamb is medium doneness, basting once. Remove chops to serving plate. Cover. Set aside. In small bowl, blend cornstarch and water until smooth. Blend into cooking liquid. Microwave, uncovered, at High for 2 to 4 minutes, or until mixture is thickened and translucent, stirring once. Stir in pear slices. Microwave at High for 30 seconds to 1 minute, or until hot. Serve sauce over chops.

Spinach-stuffed Lamb

Judith Hackler
Elkins Park, Pennsylvania

5-lb. boneless leg of lamb,
  rolled and tied
1 tablespoon curry powder
1 teaspoon pepper
1 teaspoon minced fresh garlic
½ teaspoon ground ginger
½ lb. fresh spinach, trimmed,
  stems removed

Stuffing:
⅓ cup butter or margarine
2 cups soft raisin bread
  crumbs (4 to 5 slices)
¼ cup sliced green onions
1 tablespoon snipped fresh
  parsley
¼ teaspoon pepper

10 to 12 servings

How to Microwave Spinach-stuffed Lamb

Untie lamb and lay flat on work surface. Remove any large fat deposits. In small bowl, combine curry powder, pepper, garlic and ginger. Mix well. Rub over inside of lamb surface. Layer spinach over lamb. Set aside.

Place butter in small mixing bowl. Microwave at High for 1½ to 1¾ minutes, or until butter melts. Stir in remaining ingredients. Spread stuffing mixture over spinach. Re-roll lamb, enclosing spinach and stuffing.

Tie securely. Place on roasting rack. Microwave at High for 8 minutes. Turn lamb over. Reduce power to 50% (Medium). Microwave for 37 to 57 minutes, or until internal temperature in center registers 135 to 140°F for medium doneness, turning lamb over after half the time. Let stand, tented with foil, for 10 minutes before carving.

Gyros Loaf

Delicious served warm or cold.

Betty Newlin Harwood
Elgin, Illinois

Gyros Loaf:

2 slices white bread, torn into
  small pieces
¼ cup water
½ lb. ground lamb
½ lb. lean ground beef
1 egg, beaten
¼ cup finely chopped onion
1½ teaspoons dried parsley
  flakes
1½ teaspoons dried oregano
  leaves
1½ teaspoons dried mint flakes
¾ teaspoon salt
⅛ teaspoon pepper
1 clove garlic, minced

Yogurt-Cucumber Sauce:

1 container (8 oz.) plain
  low-fat yogurt
1 small onion, sliced and
  separated into rings
½ cup peeled, seeded and
  finely chopped cucumber
1 tablespoon snipped fresh
  parsley, optional
1½ teaspoons lemon juice
¼ teaspoon salt

6 to 8 pita breads, 6-inch,
  cut in half
  Lettuce, optional
  Chopped tomatoes,
  optional

6 to 8 servings

In large mixing bowl, combine bread and water. Let stand for 3 minutes. Mix. Stir in remaining loaf ingredients. Shape into loaf. Place in 8 × 4-inch loaf dish. Place on saucer in microwave oven. Microwave at 70% (Medium High) for 19 to 24 minutes, or until internal temperature in center registers 150°F, rotating dish twice. Let stand for 10 minutes. Drain thoroughly. Slice. Set aside.

In small mixing bowl, blend all sauce ingredients. Place slices of Gyros Loaf in each pita bread. Serve with lettuce and tomatoes. Spoon Yogurt-Cucumber Sauce over each pita.

Grape Leaves with Lamb Filling

Filling:
- 1 lb. ground lamb
- ¼ cup finely chopped onion
- ¼ cup chopped green pepper
- 1 clove garlic, minced
- 1 cup cooked rice
- ¼ cup raisins
- 2 tablespoons snipped fresh parsley
- 2 tablespoons pine nuts
- 2 tablespoons catsup
- ½ teaspoon bouquet garni seasoning
- ½ teaspoon salt
- ¼ teaspoon ground allspice
- ⅛ teaspoon cayenne

- 1 jar (8 oz.) grape leaves, rinsed and drained
- 2 tablespoons water
- 1 small lemon, sliced

Sauce:
- 1 can (8 oz.) tomato sauce
- ½ teaspoon sugar
  Dash salt
  Dash ground cinnamon

6 servings

How to Microwave Grape Leaves with Lamb Filling

Crumble ground lamb into 2-quart casserole. Add onion, green pepper and garlic. Cover. Microwave at High for 4 to 7 minutes, or until lamb is no longer pink, stirring once to break apart. Drain. Add remaining filling ingredients. Mix well.

Lay one grape leaf flat with vein-side-up. Spoon about 1 table-spoon filling onto center of leaf. Fold in point of leaf, then sides. Roll up leaf, enclosing filling. Repeat with remaining filling to form 2½ to 3 dozen grape leaves. Reserve any extra grape leaves.

Place filled leaves in 10-inch square casserole. Sprinkle with water. Top filled leaves with lemon slices, then with damp reserved grape leaves. Microwave at High for 8 to 12 minutes, or until leaves are hot, rotating dish once. Set aside.

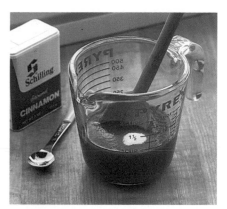

Combine all sauce ingredients in 2-cup measure. Microwave at High for 2 to 2½ minutes, or until mixture is hot and bubbly, stirring once. Spoon sauce onto plate and arrange filled grape leaves over sauce. Garnish with additional lemon slices, if desired.

Poultry

Lime & Cumin Cornish Game Hens

Chicken

Country-style Chicken

2 medium baking potatoes,
   quartered
1 medium yam or sweet
   potato, peeled and cut into
   1-inch pieces
1 medium onion, cut into
   8 pieces
⅔ cup ready-to-serve chicken
   broth, divided
2½ to 3-lb. broiler-fryer chicken,
   cut into 8 pieces, skin
   removed
2 tablespoons snipped fresh
   parsley
½ teaspoon salt
¼ teaspoon dried marjoram
   leaves
¼ teaspoon dried thyme
   leaves
¼ teaspoon pepper

Gravy:
3 tablespoons all-purpose
   flour
½ cup milk
½ teaspoon bouquet sauce

4 servings

How to Microwave Country-style Chicken

Combine baking potatoes, yams, onion and ⅓ cup broth in 10-inch square casserole. Cover. Microwave at High for 7 to 10 minutes, or just until vegetables are tender, stirring once.

Arrange chicken over vegetables. Combine parsley, salt, marjoram, thyme and pepper with remaining ⅓ cup broth. Pour over chicken. Re-cover.

Microwave at 70% (Medium High) for 22 to 27 minutes, or until chicken near bone is no longer pink and juices run clear, rearranging chicken twice.

Lift chicken and vegetables with slotted spoon to platter. Cover. Set aside. Strain cooking liquid into 4-cup measure. Skim fat, if desired.

Add water to equal 1 cup. In small bowl, blend flour, milk and bouquet sauce with whisk. Blend into cooking liquid.

Microwave at High for 4 to 6 minutes, or until mixture thickens and bubbles, stirring 2 or 3 times with whisk. Serve with chicken and vegetables.

Quick Chicken & Rice

1 pkg. (4.6 oz.) rice and
    sauce mix with peas
1⅓ cups hot water
1 cup frozen cut green beans
2½ to 3-lb. broiler-fryer chicken,
    cut into 8 pieces, skin
    removed
2 teaspoons dried parsley
    flakes
½ teaspoon paprika
¼ teaspoon seasoned salt
⅛ teaspoon pepper

4 servings

In 10-inch square casserole, combine rice and sauce mix, water and green beans. Mix well. Arrange chicken over rice mixture. In small bowl, combine parsley, paprika, seasoned salt and pepper. Sprinkle evenly on chicken. Cover. Microwave at High for 15 to 20 minutes, or until chicken near bone is no longer pink and juices run clear, rearranging chicken once or twice. Let stand, covered, for 5 to 10 minutes.

To reheat: Place one serving on plate. Cover with wax paper. Microwave at High for 2½ to 3½ minutes, or until heated through.

Creamy Chicken & Vegetables

1 pkg. (16 oz.) frozen broccoli cuts with cauliflower
2 bone-in whole chicken breasts (10 to 12 oz. each) split in half, skin removed
½ teaspoon onion powder Seasoned salt (optional)
1 can (10¾ oz.) condensed cream of mushroom soup
½ cup dairy sour cream
1 teaspoon dried parsley flakes
¼ teaspoon dried thyme leaves
2 tablespoons butter or margarine
⅓ cup finely crushed cheese crackers

4 servings

Arrange vegetables in 9-inch square baking dish. Place chicken breast halves over vegetables. Sprinkle with onion powder and seasoned salt. Cover with plastic wrap. Microwave at High for 15 to 20 minutes, or until chicken near bone is no longer pink and juices run clear. Drain. In small mixing bowl, combine soup, sour cream, parsley and thyme. Mix well. Spoon evenly over chicken and vegetables. Re-cover. Microwave at High for 3 to 5 minutes, or until mixture is hot. Place butter in small bowl. Microwave at High for 45 seconds to 1 minute, or until butter melts. Stir in cracker crumbs. Sprinkle evenly over chicken. Microwave, uncovered, at High for 1 minute.

To reheat: Place one serving on plate. Cover with wax paper. Microwave at High for 2 to 3½ minutes, or until heated through.

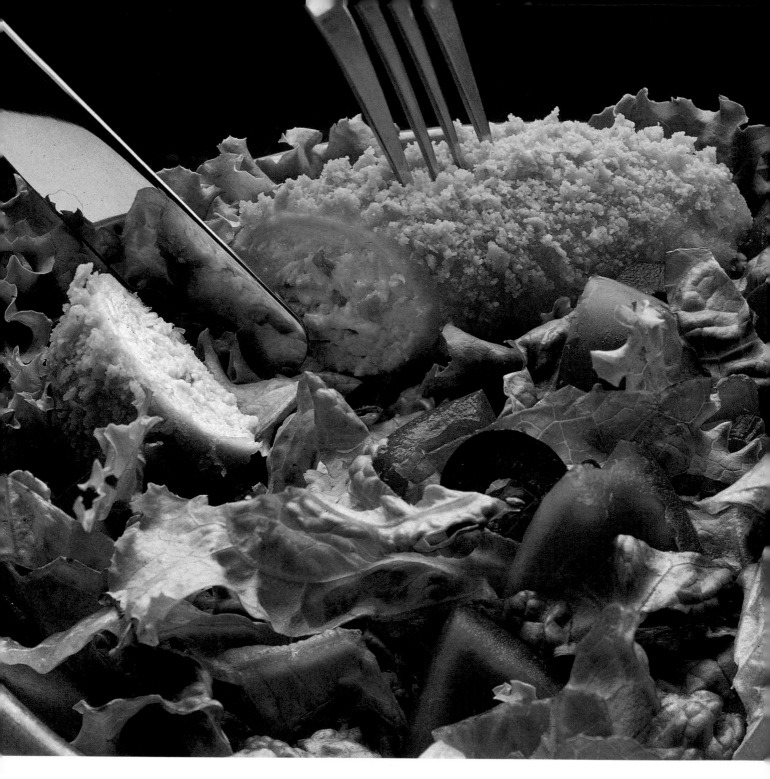

Chicken Viejo

Serve on lettuce with chopped tomatoes, sliced black olives and taco sauce.

Patricia Johnson
Mission Viejo, California

2 boneless whole chicken breasts (10 to 12 oz. each) skin removed, cut in half

¼ cup butter or margarine, divided

2 tablespoons sharp pasteurized process cheese spread

1 tablespoon sliced green onion

1 tablespoon canned chopped green chilies, drained

½ teaspoon salt

1 cup Cheddar cheese crackers

2 teaspoons Mexican seasoning, optional

4 servings

How to Microwave Chicken Viejo

Pound each chicken breast half between two sheets of plastic wrap to ¼-inch thickness. Set aside. Place 2 tablespoons butter in small bowl. Microwave at 30% (Medium Low) for 15 to 30 seconds, or until softened.

Stir in cheese spread, onion, chilies and salt. Spread one-fourth of cheese mixture at one end of each chicken breast half.

Fold in sides and roll up, enclosing filling. Secure with wooden picks. Set aside. Place remaining 2 tablespoons butter in 9-inch pie plate. Microwave at High for 45 seconds to 1 minute, or until butter melts. Set aside.

Place crackers in food processor or blender bowl. Process until fine crumbs. Place crumbs in shallow dish. Stir in Mexican seasoning.

Dip each stuffed breast in melted butter, then in crumbs to coat, pressing lightly.

Place seam-side down on roasting rack. Microwave at 70% (Medium High) for 8 to 10 minutes, or until chicken is firm and no longer pink, rotating rack 2 or 3 times. Remove wooden picks.

89

Gourmet Stuffed Chicken Breasts

2 boneless whole chicken
  breasts (10 to 12 oz. each),
  skin removed
1 tablespoon chopped onion
1 teaspoon snipped
  fresh parsley
¼ teaspoon dried crushed
  sage leaves
¼ teaspoon salt
  Dash ground nutmeg
⅓ cup whipping cream

Sauce:
1 tablespoon butter or
  margarine
1 tablespoon all-purpose flour
⅛ teaspoon salt
  Dash ground nutmeg
½ cup ready-to-serve
  chicken broth
2 tablespoons whipping cream
1 tablespoon sliced almonds

2 servings

How to Microwave Gourmet Stuffed Chicken Breasts

Use sharp knife to cut along membrane while lifting and pulling tenderloin away from chicken breast. Cut tenderloin into 1-inch pieces.

Place tenderloin pieces, onion, parsley, sage, salt and nutmeg in a food processor or blender. Process until mixture is finely chopped. With machine running, add whipping cream. Process until mixture is smooth, stopping to scrape sides of container, if necessary. Set aside.

Pound each chicken breast to about ¼-inch thickness between sheets of plastic wrap to prevent spattering. Spread processed chicken mixture evenly down centers of chicken breasts.

Fold in sides of chicken breasts and roll up, enclosing filling. Wrap each chicken breast loosely in plastic wrap, leaving ends untucked. Place seam-side-down on plate. Microwave at 50% (Medium) for 11 to 16 minutes, or until internal temperature registers 170°F, rotating plate once. Set aside.

Place butter in 2-cup measure. Microwave at High for 45 seconds to 1 minute, or until melted. Stir in flour, salt and nutmeg. Blend in remaining sauce ingredients.

Microwave at High for 2¼ to 3 minutes, or until mixture thickens and bubbles, stirring twice. Carefully unwrap chicken breasts. Pour sauce over chicken and sprinkle with sliced almonds to serve.

Honey Lemon Chicken Breasts

2 bone-in whole chicken breasts (12 to 16 oz. each), split in half, skin removed
2 tablespoons honey
1 tablespoon lemon juice
1 tablespoon packed brown sugar
1 tablespoon soy sauce
1 tablespoon snipped fresh parsley
¼ teaspoon bouquet sauce
¼ teaspoon grated lemon peel
4 thin lemon slices

4 servings

How to Microwave Honey Lemon Chicken Breasts

Score chicken breasts diagonally at 1-inch intervals, in diamond pattern, using a sharp knife. Set aside. In 9-inch square baking dish, combine remaining ingredients, except lemon slices. Stir to dissolve sugar.

Add chicken breasts scored-side-down. Coat with honey mixture. Cover. Refrigerate for 30 minutes. Arrange breast halves scored-side-up on roasting rack, with meaty portions toward outside. Cover with wax paper.

Microwave at High for 13 to 15 minutes, or until chicken near bone is no longer pink and juices run clear, rotating rack 2 or 3 times and basting with honey mixture once. Before serving, garnish with lemon slices.

Golden Cheddary Chicken

2 boneless whole chicken
  breasts (12 to 16 oz. each),
  split in half, skin removed

4 slices Cheddar cheese
  (3 × 1 × ⅛-inch strips)

2 teaspoons butter or
  margarine

⅔ cup Cheddar cheese
  croutons, coarsely crushed

1½ teaspoons dried parsley
  flakes

⅛ teaspoon pepper

4 servings

Tuck thin ends under each chicken breast half to form a uniform shape. Arrange chicken in 9-inch square baking dish. Cover with wax paper. Microwave at High for 8 to 12 minutes, or until chicken is firm and no longer pink in center, rotating dish once. Place a strip of cheese over top of each chicken piece. Loosely cover with wax paper. Set aside.

In small mixing bowl, microwave butter at High for 30 seconds to 1 minute, or until melted. Stir in croutons, parsley and pepper. Sprinkle over cheese-topped chicken. Press lightly so crouton mixture adheres to cheese. Serve with long-grain white or wild rice, if desired.

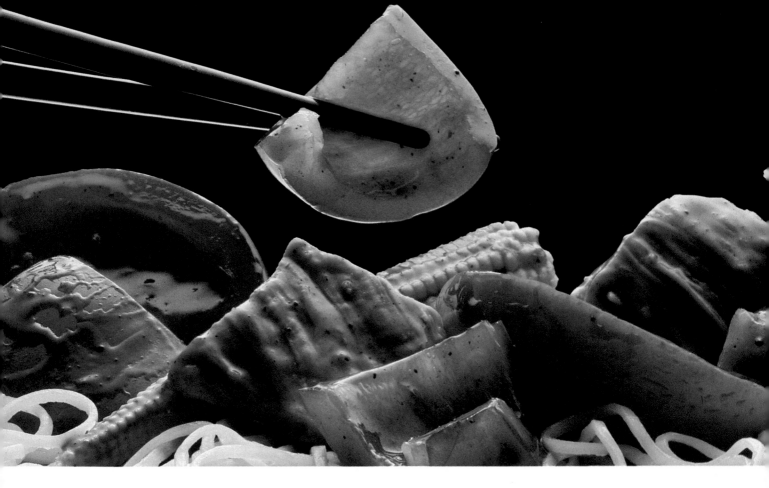

Chinese Chicken with Vegetables

2 lbs. boneless whole chicken breasts, skin removed, cut into 1-inch pieces
2 tablespoons soy sauce
1 large green pepper, cut into 1-inch pieces
2 teaspoons cornstarch
1 teaspoon sugar
¼ teaspoon ground ginger
¼ teaspoon chili powder
⅛ teaspoon cayenne
1 tablespoon water
1 tablespoon Hoisin sauce
1 large tomato, cut into 12 wedges
1 jar (7 oz.) whole baby corn, drained

6 to 8 servings

How to Microwave Chinese Chicken with Vegetables

Combine chicken pieces and soy sauce in 2-quart casserole. Cover. Microwave at High for 6 to 9 minutes, or until chicken is no longer pink, stirring after every 2 minutes.

Remove chicken with slotted spoon to bowl. Cover. Set aside. Add green pepper to cooking liquid in casserole. Re-cover. Microwave at High for 3 to 4 minutes, or until green pepper is tender-crisp.

94

Add green pepper to chicken. Re-cover. Set aside. Reserve cooking liquid in casserole. In small bowl, combine cornstarch, sugar, ginger, chili powder, cayenne and water. Mix well.

Blend cornstarch mixture and Hoisin Sauce into cooking liquid. Microwave, uncovered, at High for 2 to 4 minutes, or until mixture is thickened and translucent, stirring 2 or 3 times.

Stir in chicken, green pepper, tomato and corn. Toss gently to coat. Re-cover. Microwave at High for 3 to 5 minutes, or until hot, stirring once.

Spicy Rice & Skewered Chicken

1½ lbs. boneless whole chicken breasts, skin removed, cut into ½-inch strips
½ cup finely chopped onion, divided
1 tablespoon soy sauce
1 tablespoon packed brown sugar
1 tablespoon lemon juice

1 teaspoon chili powder, divided
⅓ cup chopped celery
¼ cup chopped green pepper
1 clove garlic, minced
1 tablespoon vegetable oil
2 tablespoons chopped pimiento

2 tablespoons snipped fresh parsley, divided
½ teaspoon salt
¼ teaspoon cayenne
1 cup uncooked long-grain white rice
2 cups hot water
6 wooden skewers, 10-inch

4 to 6 servings

How to Microwave Spicy Rice & Skewered Chicken

Combine chicken, ¼ cup onion, the soy sauce, brown sugar, lemon juice and ½ teaspoon chili powder in small mixing bowl. Mix well. Cover. Set aside. In 2-quart casserole, combine remaining ¼ cup onion, the celery, green pepper, garlic and oil. Cover. Microwave at High for 3 to 4 minutes, or until vegetables are tender, stirring twice.

Add remaining ½ teaspoon chili powder, the pimiento, 1 tablespoon parsley, the salt, cayenne, rice and water. Re-cover. Microwave at High for 5 minutes. Microwave at 50% (Medium) for 15 to 25 minutes longer, or until rice is tender and liquid is absorbed. Let stand, covered, for 5 minutes.

Divide chicken into 6 equal portions. Thread 1 portion loosely onto each skewer. Arrange skewers on roasting rack. Cover with wax paper. Microwave at High for 5 to 7 minutes, or until chicken is no longer pink, turning over and rearranging skewers twice. Serve skewered chicken on rice. Before serving, sprinkle with remaining parsley.

Warm Spanish Chicken Salad

1 lb. boneless whole chicken breast, skin removed, cut into ¾-inch cubes

1 pkg. (6 oz.) seasoned long-grain white and wild rice mix

2 cups water

1 small summer squash, cut in half lengthwise and thinly sliced

1 medium tomato, peeled, seeded and cut into chunks

⅓ cup quartered pitted black olives

3 tablespoons olive oil

1 tablespoon lemon juice

1 tablespoon red wine vinegar

6 servings

In 2-quart casserole, combine chicken, rice and seasoning packet, and water. Stir. Cover. Microwave at High for 5 minutes. Microwave at 50% (Medium) for 30 to 35 minutes longer, or until rice is tender and liquid is absorbed. Stir in squash. Re-cover. Let stand for 5 minutes. Add remaining ingredients. Mix well. Serve with a slotted spoon.

◄ Caribbean Chicken Medley

1 tablespoon cornstarch
½ teaspoon dry mustard
½ teaspoon ground ginger
½ teaspoon dried cilantro leaves
1 can (8 oz.) pineapple chunks in juice, drained (reserve ¼ cup juice)
2 tablespoons soy sauce
2 tablespoons Russian dressing or catsup

1½ lbs. boneless whole chicken breasts, skin removed, cut into 1-inch pieces
1 small zucchini, cut in half lengthwise and thinly sliced
¼ cup chopped carrot
6 green onions, sliced diagonally (½-inch slices)

6 servings

In 2-quart casserole, combine cornstarch, mustard, ginger and cilantro. Blend in ¼ cup pineapple juice, the soy sauce and dressing. Add chicken, zucchini and carrot. Cover. Microwave at High for 10 to 14 minutes, or until sauce is thickened and translucent, stirring 3 times. Stir in onions and pineapple chunks. Re-cover. Microwave at High for 2 minutes, or until hot. Serve over hot cooked rice, if desired.

Chicken Almond Ding

1 lb. boneless whole chicken breast, skin removed, cut into ½-inch cubes
2 teaspoons soy sauce
2 teaspoons cornstarch
2 teaspoons vegetable oil, divided
¼ teaspoon sesame oil
¼ teaspoon salt
⅛ teaspoon garlic powder

½ cup whole blanched almonds
½ cup ready-to-serve chicken broth
1½ cups thinly sliced celery
2 tablespoons sliced green onion
2 oz. fresh pea pods, cut into ½-inch lengths
Hot cooked rice

4 servings

In 2-quart casserole, combine chicken, soy sauce, cornstarch, 1 teaspoon vegetable oil, the sesame oil, salt and garlic powder. Mix well. Let stand at room temperature for 15 minutes. In 9-inch pie plate, place remaining 1 teaspoon vegetable oil and the almonds. Toss to coat. Microwave at High for 5 to 10 minutes, or until almonds are golden brown, stirring after every 2 minutes. Set aside.

Microwave chicken mixture at High for 3 to 4 minutes, or just until chicken is no longer pink, stirring once. Add broth. Mix well. Add celery and onion. Cover. Microwave at High for 6 to 9 minutes, or until sauce is thickened and translucent and celery is tender. Add almonds and pea pods. Microwave at High for 1 minute. Let stand, covered, for 5 minutes. Serve with rice.

Lemon Chicken & Broccoli with Poppy Seed Noodles

1 lb. boneless whole chicken breast, skin removed, cut into ½-inch strips
1 tablespoon plus 2 teaspoons vegetable oil, divided
1 tablespoon sliced green onion
1½ teaspoons grated lemon peel, divided
1 teaspoon vinegar
¼ teaspoon sugar
1 pkg. (10 oz.) frozen chopped broccoli or 2 cups fresh broccoli flowerets
2 tablespoons water
2 tablespoons butter or margarine
1 teaspoon poppy seed
¼ teaspoon salt
8 oz. uncooked wide egg noodles

4 servings

In 2-quart casserole, combine chicken strips, 2 teaspoons oil, the onion, ½ teaspoon lemon peel, the vinegar and sugar. Mix well. Set aside. In 1½-quart casserole, combine broccoli and water. Cover. Microwave at High for 4 to 6 minutes, or until broccoli is hot, stirring once to break apart. Drain. Set aside.

In 1-cup measure, microwave butter at High for 45 seconds to 1 minute, or until melted. Add remaining 1 tablespoon oil and 1 teaspoon lemon peel, the poppy seed and salt. Prepare egg noodles as directed on package. Rinse and drain. Toss cooked noodles with butter mixture. Cover to keep warm. Set aside.

Microwave chicken mixture at High for 4 to 5½ minutes, or until chicken is no longer pink, stirring once or twice. Add broccoli to chicken mixture. Arrange noodles on serving platter. Top with chicken and broccoli mixture. Garnish with lemon slices, if desired.

Chicken & Zucchini Enchiladas

- ¼ cup chopped onion
- 1 clove garlic, minced
- 1 tablespoon vegetable oil
- 1 tablespoon plus 2 teaspoons all-purpose flour
- 1 teaspoon chili powder
- ½ teaspoon ground cumin
- ½ teaspoon salt
- 1 cup milk
- 1½ cups cubed zucchini (¼-inch cubes), divided
- 1 cup cut-up cooked chicken
- ½ cup shredded Monterey Jack cheese
- 6 corn tortillas (6-inch)
  Sliced green onion
  Seeded chopped tomato

4 servings

In 2-quart casserole, combine chopped onion, garlic and oil. Cover. Microwave at High for 2 to 3 minutes, or until onion is tender. Stir in flour, chili powder, cumin and salt. Blend in milk. Microwave at High for 5 to 8 minutes, or until mixture thickens and bubbles, stirring every minute. Remove ½ cup sauce. Set aside. Add 1 cup cubed zucchini, the chicken and cheese to remaining sauce.

Soften tortillas as directed on package. Spoon ⅓ cup chicken mixture down center of each tortilla. Tightly roll up tortilla, enclosing filling. Arrange enchiladas seam-side-down in 9-inch square baking dish. Pour reserved sauce over top. Sprinkle with remaining ½ cup zucchini. Cover with plastic wrap. Microwave at 70% (Medium High) for 6 to 8 minutes, or until 140°F in center, rotating dish twice. Before serving, sprinkle with sliced green onion and chopped tomato.

Chili & Chicken Burritos

- ½ cup chopped onion
- 1 clove garlic, minced
- 1 lb. boneless whole chicken breast, skin removed, cut into 1-inch pieces
- 1 cup cooked white rice
- 1 cup seeded chopped tomato
- 1 can (4 oz.) chopped green chilies
- 1 cup shredded Cheddar cheese
- ¼ teaspoon dried oregano leaves
- ¼ teaspoon salt
- 4 flour tortillas (10-inch)
  Shredded lettuce

Toppings:
  Salsa or taco sauce
  Guacamole
  Green onions
  Sour cream

4 servings

In 1-quart casserole, combine onion and garlic. Cover. Microwave at High for 2 to 3 minutes, or until onion is tender. Add chicken. Re-cover. Microwave at High for 4 to 6 minutes, or until chicken is no longer pink, stirring once. Mix in rice, tomato, chilies, cheese, oregano and salt. Set aside.

Place tortillas between 2 dampened paper towels. Microwave at High for 30 seconds to 1 minute, or just until tortillas feel warm. Spoon one-fourth of chicken mixture in center of each tortilla. Fold in one end of tortilla and then 2 sides. Roll to enclose filling. Place burritos seam-side-down in 9-inch square baking dish. Cover with dampened paper towel. Microwave at High for 6 to 7 minutes, or until burritos are hot, rotating dish once. Serve on shredded lettuce. Top as desired.

Whole Wheat Chicken & Broccoli Strata

1 pkg. (10 oz.) frozen
   chopped broccoli
4 to 5 slices whole wheat
   bread
1 cup cubed cooked chicken
   or turkey (½-inch cubes)
½ cup shredded Swiss cheese
1¼ cups milk
3 eggs, beaten
¾ teaspoon onion salt
½ teaspoon dry mustard
   Dash cayenne
½ cup shredded Cheddar
   cheese

6 servings

Unwrap broccoli and place on plate. Microwave at High for 4 to 6 minutes, or until defrosted. Drain. Set aside. Lightly grease a 10-inch pie plate. Cut each slice of bread in half diagonally. Fit bread halves around bottom and sides of pie plate, with crusts forming top edge. Top with chicken, Swiss cheese and broccoli. Set aside.

In 4-cup measure, blend milk, eggs, onion salt, mustard and cayenne. Pour evenly over broccoli mixture. Cover with plastic wrap. Refrigerate for at least 4 hours, or overnight.

Cover broccoli mixture with wax paper. Microwave at High for 5 minutes. Microwave at 70% (Medium High) for 15 to 28 minutes longer, or until knife inserted in center comes out clean, rotating pie plate twice. Sprinkle top with Cheddar cheese. Loosely cover with wax paper. Let stand for 5 minutes.

Lime & Cumin Cornish Game Hens

¼ cup dark corn syrup
2 tablespoons lime juice
½ to 1 teaspoon grated lime peel
1 teaspoon ground cumin, divided
½ teaspoon salt, divided
4 Cornish game hens (18 oz. each)
½ teaspoon dried oregano leaves
⅛ teaspoon pepper

4 servings

In 1-cup measure, combine corn syrup, lime juice, lime peel, ½ teaspoon cumin and ¼ teaspoon salt. Microwave at High for 45 seconds to 1 minute, or until hot. Stir. Set aside. Secure hens' legs together with string. Place hens in large plastic food-storage bag. Pour corn syrup mixture over hens. Secure bag and place bag in dish. Refrigerate for at least 2 hours.

Remove hens from marinade and arrange breast-side-up on roasting rack. In small bowl, combine remaining ½ teaspoon cumin, ¼ teaspoon salt, the oregano and pepper. Rub mixture on hens. Microwave at High for 22 to 32 minutes, or until legs move freely and juices run clear, rotating rack twice. Let stand, covered, for 5 minutes.

Cornish Hen & Vegetable Platter

2 Cornish game hens
  (18 oz. each)
1 tablespoon butter or
  margarine
3 tablespoons seasoned dry
  bread crumbs
2 tablespoons Italian dressing
¼ teaspoon brown bouquet
  sauce
1 medium red pepper, cut into
  1½-inch chunks
1 medium green pepper, cut
  into 1½-inch chunks
1 medium yellow squash, cut
  into 1½-inch chunks
1 small onion, cut into 8 wedges
2 tablespoons butter or
  margarine, cut up

2 servings

Gently lift and loosen skin from breast area of each Cornish hen. Set aside. In small bowl, microwave butter at High for 45 seconds to 1 minute, or until melted. Add bread crumbs, stirring to coat. Place stuffing mixture under loosened skin of hens. Secure legs together with string. Place hens breast-sides-up on 12-inch round platter. Set aside.

In small bowl, combine Italian dressing and bouquet sauce. Mix well. Brush hens lightly with mixture. Microwave hens at High for 17 to 20 minutes, or until legs move freely and juices run clear, rearranging hens once or twice, and brushing with glaze after half the time. If desired, blot platter with paper towels to absorb cooking liquids. Cover hens with foil and set aside.

Combine remaining ingredients in 1½-quart casserole. Cover and microwave at High for 6 to 7 minutes, or until vegetables are tender-crisp, stirring once. To serve, arrange vegetables around Cornish hens.

Turkey

Apricot-glazed Turkey ▶

4- lb. boneless whole turkey
½ teaspoon dried marjoram
    leaves
¼ teaspoon pepper
1 jar (12 oz.) apricot preserves
1 tablespoon butter or
    margarine

6 to 8 servings

How to Microwave Apricot-glazed Turkey

Place turkey on roasting rack. Rub with marjoram and pepper. Cover with wax paper. Microwave at High for 10 minutes.

Combine apricot preserves and butter in 2-cup measure. Microwave at High for 1 to 2 minutes, or until mixture bubbles. Brush all sides of turkey with one-third of apricot mixture. Re-cover.

Microwave at 70% (Medium High) for 35 to 45 minutes, or until internal temperature registers 175°F, in several places, turning turkey over and brushing once with apricot mixture. Let stand, tented with foil, for 10 minutes.

Place remaining apricot mixture in small bowl. Microwave at High for 1 to 1½ minutes, or until heated through. Serve with sliced turkey.

Savory Italian Turkey ▲

3 to 4-lb. bone-in turkey breast half	½ teaspoon dried oregano leaves
¾ cup Italian dressing	¼ teaspoon dried rosemary leaves

6 to 8 servings

Place turkey in large plastic food storage bag. In 1-cup measure, combine Italian dressing, oregano and rosemary. Pour over turkey. Secure bag. Place bag on plate. Refrigerate for at least 8 hours or overnight, turning bag over once.

Remove turkey from marinade. Discard marinade. Place turkey skin-side down on roasting rack. Cover with wax paper. Microwave at High for 10 minutes. Turn turkey skin-side up. Re-cover. Microwave at 50% (Medium) for 30 to 45 minutes, or until internal temperature registers 170°F in thickest portion. Let stand, tented with foil, for 10 minutes.

To reheat: Place one serving on plate. Cover with wax paper. Microwave at 70% (Medium High) for 1½ to 2 minutes, or until heated through.

Creole-sauced Turkey

1 can (8 oz.) stewed tomatoes
½ cup sliced green onions
½ cup catsup
1 tablespoon packed brown
   sugar
1 tablespoon vinegar
½ teaspoon dry mustard
½ teaspoon dried thyme leaves
¼ teaspoon salt
2 turkey tenderloins (about
   ¾ lb. each)

6 servings

In 10-inch square casserole, combine all ingredients, except turkey. Mix well. Place turkey in tomato mixture. Spoon sauce over turkey. Cover. Microwave at High for 5 minutes. Spoon sauce over turkey. Re-cover. Microwave at 70% (Medium High) for 16 to 22 minutes, or until turkey is firm and no longer pink, rotating casserole once. Let stand, covered, for 5 to 10 minutes.

To reheat: Place one serving on plate. Cover with wax paper. Microwave at 70% (Medium High) for 1½ to 2 minutes, or until heated through.

Mustard Turkey Slices

1 cup dairy sour cream
1 tablespoon Dijon or
   prepared mustard
2 teaspoons lemon juice
1 teaspoon honey
¼ teaspoon salt
¾ cup cornflake crumbs
½ teaspoon paprika
⅛ teaspoon garlic powder
1 to 1½ lbs. turkey tenderloins,
   diagonally sliced ½ inch
   thick
½ teaspoon dried parsley
   flakes

4 to 6 servings

In shallow bowl, blend sour cream, mustard, lemon juice, honey and salt. Reserve half of sour cream mixture in small bowl. Set aside. On sheet of wax paper, combine cornflake crumbs, paprika and garlic powder. Dip each turkey slice in sour cream mixture, then roll in cornflake mixture, pressing lightly to coat. Place turkey on roasting rack. Microwave at 70% (Medium High) for 10 minutes. Rearrange turkey slices. Microwave at 70% (Medium High) for 8 to 10 minutes, or until turkey is firm and no longer pink. Combine reserved sour cream mixture and parsley. Microwave at 50% (Medium) for 1½ to 2½ minutes, or until heated through, stirring once. Serve sauce with turkey.

Turkey Cutlets with Green Chili Sauce

½ cup shredded Monterey Jack cheese
½ teaspoon ground cumin, divided
½ cup cornflake crumbs
⅛ teaspoon garlic powder
8 turkey cutlets (2 oz. each), about ¼ inch thick

Sauce:

1 can (4 oz.) chopped green chilies
¼ cup seeded chopped tomato
1 tablespoon snipped fresh parsley
½ teaspoon olive oil
¼ teaspoon salt

4 servings

In small bowl, combine cheese and ¼ teaspoon cumin. Set aside. In shallow dish, combine cornflake crumbs, garlic powder and remaining ¼ teaspoon cumin. Set aside.

Top each of 4 cutlets with one-fourth of cheese mixture, spreading to within ¼ inch of edge. Top with remaining cutlets, pressing edges gently together to seal. Dip stuffed cutlets in cornflake crumb mixture, pressing lightly to coat both sides.

Arrange cutlets on roasting rack. Microwave at 70% (Medium High) for 10 to 14 minutes, or until turkey is firm and no longer pink, rotating rack once or twice. Cover with wax paper to keep warm.

Place chopped green chilies in food processor or blender. Process until smooth. Add remaining sauce ingredients. Stir to combine. Serve cutlets topped with sauce.

Olive-topped Turkey Cutlets

1 lb. turkey cutlets, about ¼ inch thick
½ cup diagonally sliced celery (½-inch slices)
8 small pimiento-stuffed green olives, cut in half
8 medium pitted black olives, cut in half
1 clove garlic, minced
¼ cup white wine

1 tablespoon olive oil
1 tablespoon snipped fresh parsley
1 teaspoon instant chicken bouillon granules
1 teaspoon lemon juice
¼ teaspoon dried rubbed sage leaves
⅛ teaspoon pepper

4 to 6 servings

Arrange cutlets in 9-inch square baking dish. Top with celery, green and black olives and garlic. Set aside. In 1-cup measure, combine remaining ingredients. Mix well. Pour over cutlets. Cover with wax paper. Marinate at room temperature for 15 minutes. Cover. Microwave at 70% (Medium High) for 9 to 15 minutes, or until turkey is firm and no longer pink, rearranging once or twice.

Turkey Fajitas

Marinade:
- 1 tablespoon lemon juice
- 1 tablespoon white wine
- 1 tablespoon vegetable oil
- 1 tablespoon sliced green onion
- 1 teaspoon soy sauce
- 1 teaspoon packed brown sugar
- 1 clove garlic, minced
- ¼ teaspoon crushed red pepper flakes
- 2 drops liquid smoke flavoring

- ¾ lb. turkey tenderloin, cut into thin strips
- ½ medium green pepper, cut into thin strips
- ½ medium onion, thinly sliced
- 4 flour tortillas (8-inch)

Toppings:
- Salsa sauce
- Guacamole
- Seeded chopped tomato

4 servings

In 1½-quart casserole, combine all marinade ingredients. Add turkey strips. Stir to coat. Cover. Refrigerate for 30 minutes. Add green pepper and onion to marinated turkey. Re-cover. Microwave at 70% (Medium High) for 6 to 11 minutes, or until turkey is firm and no longer pink, stirring 3 times.

Place tortillas between 2 dampened paper towels. Microwave at High for 30 seconds to 1 minute, or just until tortillas feel warm. Spoon one-fourth of turkey, onion and green pepper mixture down the center of each tortilla. Top as desired. Roll up tortillas to enclose filling.

Turkey Chili ▲

- 1 cup chopped green pepper
- ½ cup chopped onion
- 1 clove garlic, minced
- 1 lb. ground turkey
- 1 can (28 oz.) whole tomatoes, cut up
- 1 can (16 oz.) pinto beans, drained
- 1 can (15 oz.) kidney beans, drained
- 1 can (10¾ oz.) condensed tomato soup
- ½ cup water
- 1 tablespoon plus 1 teaspoon chili powder
- ¾ teaspoon celery salt
- ¼ teaspoon cayenne
- ¼ teaspoon pepper

6 to 8 servings

In 3-quart casserole, combine green pepper, onion and garlic. Cover. Microwave at High for 2 minutes. Crumble ground turkey over vegetables. Re-cover. Microwave at High for 4 to 7 minutes, or until turkey is firm, stirring twice to break apart.

Add remaining ingredients. Mix well. Cover with wax paper. Microwave at High for 20 to 30 minutes, or until flavors blend, stirring 2 or 3 times. Let stand, covered, for 10 minutes. Top each serving with shredded Cheddar cheese, if desired.

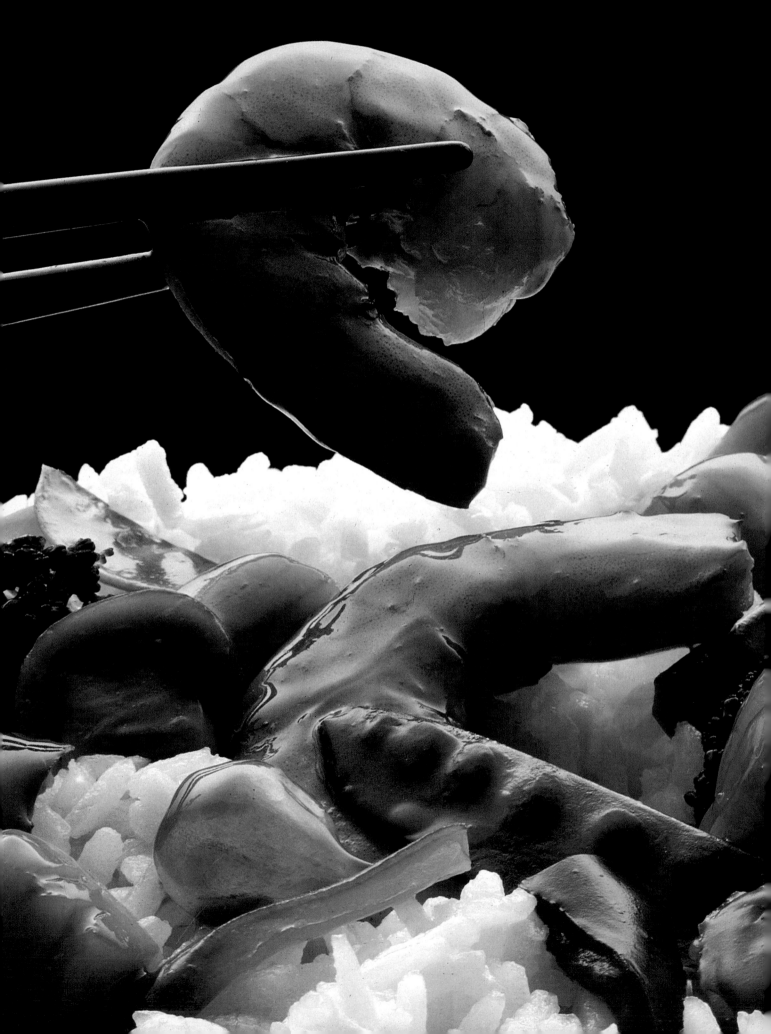

Fish & Seafood

Shrimp & Scallop Stir-fry

Shrimp & Scallop Stir-fry

Kathy Smith
Suitland, Maryland

Kathy's family prefers this delicious main dish served over brown rice.

2 cups frozen Japanese-style
   vegetables
1 pkg. (6 oz.) frozen pea pods
⅓ cup water
1 tablespoon cornstarch
3 tablespoons soy sauce
3 tablespoons sherry
1 tablespoon vegetable oil
2 teaspoons sugar
½ teaspoon ground ginger
1 lb. medium shrimp, shelled
   and deveined
½ lb. bay scallops

6 servings

In 2-quart casserole, combine Japanese-style vegetables and pea pods. Cover. Microwave at High for 4 to 5 minutes, or until vegetables are defrosted, stirring after half the time to break apart. Let stand, covered, for 5 minutes. Drain. Set aside.

In 2-cup measure, blend water, cornstarch, soy sauce, sherry, oil, sugar and ginger. Microwave at High for 3 to 4 minutes, or until mixture is thickened and translucent, stirring twice. Pour over vegetables. Stir in shrimp and scallops. Re-cover. Microwave at High for 7 to 10 minutes, or until shrimp and scallops are opaque, stirring twice. Let stand, covered, for 3 minutes. Serve over hot cooked brown or white rice.

Scampi

Harold R. Ferguson
Walnut Creek, California

Butter mixture can be spread on French bread and toasted under the broiler.

¼ cup butter or margarine
¾ cup olive oil
¼ cup snipped fresh parsley
2 tablespoons fresh lemon
   juice
2 cloves garlic, minced
½ teaspoon salt
½ teaspoon pepper
1½ lbs. medium shrimp,
   shelled and deveined

4 to 6 servings

Place butter in 10-inch square casserole. Microwave at High for 1¼ to 1½ minutes, or until butter melts. Blend in olive oil. Stir in parsley, lemon juice, garlic, salt and pepper. Add shrimp, stirring to coat with butter mixture. Cover. Reduce power to 70% (Medium High). Microwave for 6 to 9 minutes, or until shrimp are opaque, stirring twice. Let stand, covered, for 2 to 3 minutes. Place shrimp on platter or serve over hot cooked rice. Serve with butter mixture as a sauce.

Seafood-Vegetable Medley

Mrs. Lynn M. Sewell
Elwood, New Jersey

2 tablespoons butter or
   margarine
1 medium onion, thinly sliced
1 tablespoon snipped fresh
   parsley
¼ teaspoon dried tarragon
   leaves
1½ cups thinly sliced zucchini
   or summer squash
1 medium tomato, cut into
   1½-inch pieces
12 fresh mushrooms, cut in half
4 seafood sticks (1 oz. each)
   cut into 1-inch pieces
¼ lb. bay scallops
   Salt
   Pepper
4 oz. sliced Monterey Jack
   cheese, ⅛ inch thick

4 servings

How to Microwave Seafood-Vegetable Medley

Combine butter, onion, parsley and tarragon in 1½-quart casserole. Cover. Microwave at High for 3 minutes.

Stir in zucchini, tomato and mushrooms. Re-cover. Microwave at High for 4 to 5 minutes, or until zucchini is tender-crisp, stirring once.

Stir in seafood pieces and scallops. Re-cover. Microwave at High for 2½ to 3½ minutes, or until scallops are opaque, stirring once.

Lift vegetables and seafood with slotted spoon and divide among four individual (12 to 15 oz. each) casseroles. Sprinkle each with salt and pepper.

Arrange cheese slices over seafood mixture.

Place under preheated broiler 3 to 4 inches from heat, until cheese melts, 2 to 3 minutes. Serve with toasted French bread.

◀ Spicy Shrimp & Pan-fried Noodles

 1 small onion, cut into 1-inch chunks
½ medium green pepper, cut into 1-inch chunks
 1 medium carrot, thinly sliced
 3 tablespoons vegetable oil, divided
¼ cup soy sauce
½ teaspoon sesame oil
¼ teaspoon crushed red pepper flakes
¾ teaspoon sugar
 2 teaspoons cornstarch
¾ lb. large shrimp, shelled and deveined
 8 oz. uncooked angel hair pasta

4 servings

In 2-quart casserole, combine onion, green pepper, carrot and 1 tablespoon vegetable oil. Cover. Microwave at High for 4 to 6 minutes, or until vegetables are tender-crisp, stirring once. Set aside.

In medium mixing bowl, combine soy sauce, sesame oil, red pepper flakes, sugar and cornstarch. Stir to dissolve cornstarch. Add shrimp. Toss to coat. Microwave at 70% (Medium High) for 7 to 10 minutes, or until shrimp are opaque and sauce is thickened and translucent, stirring once or twice. Add shrimp mixture to vegetable mixture. Cover to keep warm. Set aside.

Prepare pasta as directed on package. Rinse and drain. In 9-inch non-stick skillet, heat remaining 2 tablespoons vegetable oil conventionally over medium-high heat. Add pasta, pressing into an even layer. Cook for about 4 to 5 minutes, or until golden brown. Invert pasta onto serving plate, browned-side-up. If necessary, reheat shrimp mixture at 70% (Medium High) for 2 minutes. Top pasta with shrimp mixture.

Scallop & Ham Bake ▲

 1 cup ricotta or cottage cheese
⅓ cup milk
 3 tablespoons grated Parmesan cheese
½ teaspoon dried marjoram leaves
¼ teaspoon salt
 1 pkg.(10 oz.) frozen peas
½ lb. bay scallops
 2 teaspoons lemon juice
 1 teaspoon dried parsley flakes
 3 cups uncooked egg noodles
½ cup cubed fully cooked ham (½-inch cubes)
Grated Parmesan cheese
Paprika

4 to 6 servings

In food processor or blender, combine ricotta cheese, milk, 3 tablespoons Parmesan cheese, the marjoram and salt. Process until smooth. Set aside. Place peas in 1-quart casserole. Microwave at High for 4 to 5 minutes, or until defrosted. Drain. Set aside.

In 2-quart casserole, combine scallops, lemon juice and parsley. Cover. Microwave at 70% (Medium High) for 3½ to 6 minutes, or until scallops are firm and opaque. Drain. Set aside.

Prepare noodles as directed on package. Rinse and drain. Add noodles, peas and ham to scallops. Stir in ricotta mixture. Cover. Microwave at High for 4 minutes. Stir. Sprinkle with Parmesan cheese and paprika. Re-cover. Microwave at High for 2 to 6 minutes, or until hot.

Oriental Orange Seafood Kabobs

- 3 tablespoons teriyaki sauce
- 1 tablespoon orange marmalade
- 12 sea scallops (about ½ lb.)
- 8 large shrimp (about ½ lb.), shelled and deveined
- 4 wooden skewers, 10-inch
- 4 thin orange slices
- 1 cup ready-to-serve chicken broth
- 1 tablespoon butter or margarine
- 1 teaspoon dried parsley flakes
- ¼ teaspoon grated orange peel
- 1 cup instant rice

4 servings

How to Microwave Oriental Orange Seafood Kabobs

Combine teriyaki sauce and orange marmalade in medium mixing bowl. Microwave at High for 30 seconds to 1 minute, or until marmalade melts, stirring once. Add scallops and shrimp. Stir to coat. Let stand for 15 minutes.

Place 1 shrimp and 1 scallop on skewer. Wrap 1 orange slice around 1 scallop and add to skewer. Add 1 more scallop and 1 more shrimp. Repeat sequence with remaining skewers.

Arrange kabobs on roasting rack. Microwave at 70% (Medium High) for 9 to 11 minutes, or until shrimp and scallops are firm and opaque, rotating rack and rearranging kabobs twice. Cover with wax paper; let stand.

Combine broth, butter, parsley and orange peel in 1-quart casserole. Cover. Microwave at High for 4 to 5 minutes, or until broth boils.

Stir in rice. Re-cover. Microwave at High for 1 minute. Let stand for 5 minutes, or until liquid is absorbed. Serve kabobs on rice.

Neptune Torte

Crepes:
- 1 tablespoon butter or margarine
- 1¼ cups milk
- 1 cup all-purpose flour
- 1 egg
- ¼ teaspoon salt

Filling:
- 2 tablespoons butter or margarine
- 2 tablespoons all-purpose flour
- 1 teaspoon dried basil leaves
- ¾ cup milk
- 2 tablespoons white wine
- 1 cup shredded Monterey Jack cheese
- 1 can (6 oz.) crab meat, rinsed, drained and cartilage removed
- 1 can (4¼ oz.) small shrimp, rinsed and drained
- 1 tablespoon sliced green onion

4 servings

How to Microwave a Neptune Torte

Place 1 tablespoon butter in small bowl. Microwave at High for 45 seconds to 1 minute, or until melted. In blender or food processor, place melted butter and remaining crepe ingredients. Process until mixture is smooth. Chill for at least 1 hour.

Heat a lightly oiled 6-inch skillet conventionally over medium heat. Pour about 3 tablespoons crepe batter into skillet. Tilt skillet in a circular motion to coat bottom with a thin layer of batter.

Cook until edges of crepe are set and begin to pull away from edges of pan. Turn and brown other side. Repeat to yield 6 crepes. Stack crepes between wax paper and set aside. Any additional crepes may be frozen for later use.

Place 2 tablespoons butter in 4-cup measure. Microwave at High for 45 seconds to 1 minute, or until melted. Stir in flour and basil. Blend in milk and wine. Microwave at High for 3 to 4 minutes, or until mixture thickens and bubbles, stirring 2 or 3 times. Stir in cheese, crab meat and shrimp.

Place 1 crepe in bottom of 9-inch pie plate. Top with ⅓ cup seafood mixture. Spread to within ½ inch of edge. Repeat layers, ending with seafood mixture.

Sprinkle top with green onion. Cover with plastic wrap. Microwave at 50% (Medium) for 7 to 9 minutes, or until hot and bubbly around edges, rotating dish 2 or 3 times. Serve torte in wedges.

Orange-sauced Roughy ▲

½ cup fresh orange juice
⅓ cup white wine or
    ready-to-serve chicken broth
2 teaspoons cornstarch
1 teaspoon sugar
    Dash dried thyme leaves
¾ lb. orange roughy fillets,
    about ½ inch thick, cut into
    serving-size pieces

4 servings

In 2-cup measure, blend all ingredients, except fish. Microwave at High for 2½ to 4½ minutes, or until sauce is thickened and translucent, stirring once or twice. Set aside.

In 9-inch square baking dish, arrange fish with thickest portions toward outside. Cover with plastic wrap. Microwave at High for 3½ to 5½ minutes, or until fish flakes easily with fork, rotating dish once. Let stand, covered, for 2 minutes. If necessary, microwave sauce at High for 1 minute, or until hot. Arrange fish on serving platter. Top with sauce.

Cajun Stuffed Sole ▲

⅓ cup chopped red or green
    pepper
2 tablespoons sliced green
    onion
2 tablespoons butter or
    margarine
1 teaspoon dried parsley flakes
¼ teaspoon cayenne
¼ teaspoon salt
⅛ teaspoon pepper
1 cup corn bread stuffing mix
1 can (8 oz.) corn, drained
2 tablespoons ready-to-serve
    chicken broth or water
4 sole fillets (8 oz. each), about
    ¼ inch thick and 10
    inches long

4 servings

In 1-quart casserole, combine red
pepper, onion, butter, parsley,
cayenne, salt and pepper. Cover.
Microwave at High for 2 to 3 minutes, or until vegetables are tender, stirring once. Add remaining
ingredients, except sole. Mix well.

Spread one-fourth of stuffing
down the center of each fillet.
Roll up fillet, enclosing stuffing.
Secure with wooden pick. Stand
stuffed fillets on end in 9-inch pie
plate. Cover with plastic wrap.
Microwave at 70% (Medium High)
for 8 to 10 minutes, or until center
of fish roll flakes easily with fork,
rotating dish once or twice. Let
stand, covered, for 3 minutes.

Cod & Tomato Bake

1 medium onion, cut into
    wedges
1 tablespoon olive oil
¼ teaspoon dried thyme leaves
1 can (16 oz.) stewed tomatoes
1 pkg. (10 oz.) frozen cod fillets

Topping:
⅓ cup crushed Cheddar cheese
    crackers
1 tablespoon grated Parmesan
    cheese
1 teaspoon dried parsley flakes

4 servings

In 9-inch square baking dish, place onion, oil and thyme. Cover with
plastic wrap. Microwave at High for 4 to 8 minutes, or until onion is tender, stirring once. Add tomatoes. Mix well. Arrange frozen cod fillets
over tomato mixture. Re-cover. Microwave at High for 8 to 11 minutes,
or until fish flakes easily with fork, rotating dish 2 or 3 times.

In small bowl, combine all topping ingredients. Mix well. Spoon mixture evenly over cod pieces. Microwave at High for 1 to 2 minutes, or
until hot.

123

◄ Citrus-sauced Shrimp & Fillets

1 tablespoon butter or margarine
¼ teaspoon grated lemon peel
¼ teaspoon grated orange peel
1 tablespoon all-purpose flour
¼ teaspoon salt
⅛ teaspoon ground nutmeg
½ cup milk
1 pkg. (10 oz.) frozen sole fillets
1 can (4¼ oz.) small shrimp, rinsed and drained
1 pkg. (10 oz.) frozen chopped spinach
2 tablespoons water

4 servings

In 9-inch square baking dish, place butter and lemon and orange peels. Cover with plastic wrap. Microwave at High for 45 seconds to 1 minute, or until butter melts. Stir in flour, salt and nutmeg. Blend in milk. Arrange frozen fish fillets in a single layer in dish. Cover with plastic wrap. Microwave at 70% (Medium High) for 12 to 16 minutes, or until fish flakes easily with fork, stirring sauce 2 or 3 times. Stir in shrimp. Set aside.

In 1-quart casserole, place spinach and water. Cover. Microwave at High for 4 to 6 minutes, or until spinach is hot, stirring once to break apart. Drain. Arrange spinach on serving platter in an even layer. Top with fillets. Spoon sauce over fillets. Garnish with orange and lemon slices, if desired.

Lemon-Dijon Fillets

¾ lb. fish fillets, about ½ inch thick, cut into serving-size pieces
Lemon pepper seasoning (optional)
1 tablespoon plus 1 teaspoon butter or margarine
1 tablespoon plus 1 teaspoon all-purpose flour

1 teaspoon grated lemon peel
½ teaspoon dried parsley flakes
⅛ teaspoon salt
⅔ cup milk
1 to 2 teaspoons Dijon mustard
⅔ cup seeded finely chopped tomato (optional)

4 servings

In 9-inch square baking dish, arrange fish with thickest portions toward outside of dish. Sprinkle lightly with lemon pepper. Cover with plastic wrap. Microwave at High for 3½ to 5½ minutes, or until fish flakes easily with fork, rotating dish once. Set aside, covered.

In small bowl, microwave butter at High for 45 seconds to 1 minute, or until melted. Stir in flour, lemon peel, parsley and salt. Blend in milk. Microwave at High for 1½ to 3 minutes, or until mixture thickens and bubbles, stirring once or twice. Add mustard. Mix well. Arrange fish on serving platter. Top with sauce. Garnish with chopped tomato.

Fillets Florentine ▲ with Sesame Butter

¼ lb. fresh spinach, trimmed and torn, about 2 cups
1 teaspoon sesame seed
1 teaspoon sesame oil, divided
¼ cup butter or margarine
⅛ teaspoon cayenne
8 fish fillets (2 oz. each), about ¼ inch thick*
1 to 2 teaspoons grated orange peel

4 servings

In medium mixing bowl, combine spinach, sesame seed and ½ teaspoon sesame oil. Toss to coat. Set aside. In small bowl, combine butter, remaining ½ teaspoon sesame oil and the cayenne. Microwave at High for 1¼ to 1½ minutes, or until butter melts. Set aside.

Place 4 fish fillets on roasting rack. Brush with butter mixture. Top each fillet with one-fourth of spinach mixture. Top with remaining fillets. Brush with butter mixture. Sprinkle evenly with grated orange peel. Microwave at 70% (Medium High) for 7½ to 12½ minutes, or until fish flakes easily with fork, rotating rack once or twice. Drizzle fillets with any remaining butter mixture.

*Fillets should be of equal size and shape.

Mushroom-topped Fillets

8 oz. fresh mushrooms, finely chopped
½ cup chopped onion
2 tablespoons butter or margarine
1 teaspoon dried parsley flakes
¾ lb. fish fillets, about ½ inch thick, cut into serving-size pieces
1 tablespoon chopped pimiento
¼ teaspoon salt
Sour cream (optional)

4 servings

In 1½-quart casserole, combine mushrooms, onion, butter and parsley. Microwave, uncovered, at High for 5 to 7 minutes, or until onion is tender, stirring once. Cover. Set aside.

In 9-inch square baking dish, arrange fish fillets with thickest portions toward outside of dish. Cover with plastic wrap. Microwave at High for 3½ to 5½ minutes, or until fish flakes easily with fork, rotating dish once. Re-cover. Set aside. If necessary, microwave mushroom mixture at High for 1 to 2 minutes, or until hot. Drain. Stir in pimiento and salt. Arrange fish on serving platter. Top with mushroom mixture. Garnish with sour cream.

Mexican Salsa Fillets

2 medium tomatoes, seeded and chopped
½ cup chopped onion
2 tablespoons chopped green chilies
2 teaspoons olive oil
1 clove garlic, minced
¼ teaspoon ground cumin
¼ teaspoon salt
⅛ teaspoon dried oregano leaves
Dash crushed red pepper flakes
¾ lb. fish fillets, about ½ inch thick, cut into serving-size pieces

4 servings

In 1½-quart casserole, combine all ingredients, except fish fillets. Mix well. Microwave, uncovered, at High for 20 to 28 minutes, or until salsa is desired consistency, stirring once. Set aside.

In 9-inch square baking dish, arrange fish fillets with thickest portions toward outside of dish. Cover with plastic wrap. Microwave at High for 3½ to 5½ minutes, or until fish flakes easily with fork, rotating dish once. Let stand, covered, for 3 minutes. If necessary, microwave salsa at High for 1 to 2 minutes or until hot. Arrange fish on serving platter. Top with salsa.

Baked Stuffed Sole

¼ cup finely chopped celery
¼ cup finely chopped carrot
¼ cup butter or margarine, divided
½ teaspoon grated lemon peel
¼ teaspoon salt
⅛ teaspoon pepper
1 can (6¾ oz.) skinless, boneless salmon, drained
2 tablespoons mayonnaise
1 teaspoon prepared mustard
2 whole sole fillets (about 1 lb. each, ½ to ¾ inch thick)
1 pkg. (10 oz.) frozen peas and carrots
¼ teaspoon paprika
4 to 6 thin slices lemon

4 to 6 servings

How to Microwave Baked Stuffed Sole

Combine celery, carrot, 1 tablespoon butter, the lemon peel, salt and pepper in 1-quart casserole. Cover. Microwave at High for 2½ to 3½ minutes, or until vegetables are tender-crisp, stirring once during cooking time. Add salmon, mayonnaise and mustard. Mix well.

Place one sole fillet in center of 12-inch platter. Top with salmon mixture, spreading to within ½ inch of edge of fillet. Top with remaining fillet.

Cover with wax paper. Microwave at 70% (Medium High) for 13 to 20 minutes, or until fish flakes easily with fork, rotating platter 2 or 3 times. Set aside.

Place frozen vegetables in 1-quart casserole. Cover and microwave at High for 4 to 6 minutes, or until hot, stirring once. Spoon hot vegetables along one side of stuffed sole. Set aside.

Microwave remaining 3 tablespoons butter in small bowl, at High for 1 to 1¼ minutes, or until melted. Stir in paprika. Drizzle fish and vegetables with butter mixture. If desired, microwave platter at 70% (Medium High) for 1 to 2 minutes longer to reheat. Garnish with lemon slices.

Herb-seasoned Swordfish Steaks ▲

2 tablespoons vegetable oil
¼ teaspoon dried rosemary
   leaves
¼ teaspoon dried thyme leaves
¼ teaspoon paprika

⅛ teaspoon garlic powder
⅛ teaspoon salt
1 swordfish steak (1½ lbs.),
   about 1 inch thick, cut into
   4 serving-size pieces

4 servings

In small bowl, combine all ingredients, except swordfish. Mix well.
Microwave at High for 30 seconds, or just until warm. Set aside. Pre-
heat microwave browning dish at High as directed by manufacturer.
Brush one side of swordfish steaks with oil mixture.

Place steaks, oiled-side-down, on preheated dish. Brush with remaining oil. Microwave at 70% (Medium High) for 3 minutes. Turn steaks
over. Microwave at 70% (Medium High) for 4 to 5 minutes, or until fish
flakes easily with fork, rotating dish once or twice.

Easy Crab & Mushroom Dinner

1 cup sliced fresh mushrooms
¼ cup chopped celery
2 tablespoons butter or
   margarine
2 tablespoons all-purpose flour
½ teaspoon salt
   Dash cayenne

¾ cup milk
¼ cup sliced green onions
1 can (6 oz.) crab meat, rinsed,
   drained and cartilage
   removed
2 teaspoons sherry (optional)
   Toasted French bread slices

4 to 6 servings

In 1-quart casserole, combine mushrooms, celery and butter. Cover.
Microwave at High for 3½ to 5 minutes, or just until celery is tender-
crisp, stirring once. Stir in flour, salt and cayenne. Blend in milk. Stir in
onions. Microwave at High for 4 to 5½ minutes, or until mixture thickens
and bubbles, stirring every 2 minutes.

Stir in crab meat and sherry. Microwave at High for 1 to 2 minutes, or
until hot. Serve over French bread slices. Top with paprika or snipped
fresh parsley, if desired.

Salmon-stuffed Green Pepper Rings

¼ cup chopped green pepper
¼ cup chopped onion
2 tablespoons butter or
   margarine
1 can (6¾ oz.) skinless,
   boneless salmon, drained
1 cup crushed herb-seasoned
   stuffing
1 egg, beaten
½ teaspoon Worcestershire
   sauce
4 green pepper rings (1 inch
   thick)
½ cup shredded Cheddar
   cheese
   Dash cayenne

4 servings

In medium mixing bowl, combine
chopped green pepper, onion
and butter. Cover with plastic
wrap. Microwave at High for 2 to
4 minutes, or until vegetables are
tender, stirring once. Add salmon,
stuffing, egg and Worcestershire
sauce. Mix well.

Divide mixture into 4 equal portions. Press one-fourth of salmon
mixture into the center of each
pepper ring. Place rings in 9-
inch square baking dish. Cover
with plastic wrap. Microwave at
70% (Medium High) for 5 to 6 minutes, or until salmon mixture is
firm and pepper rings are tender-
crisp, rotating dish once or twice.

In small plastic food-storage
bag, shake cheese and cayenne.
Sprinkle one-fourth of cheese
mixture over each pepper ring.
Re-cover. Microwave at 70%
(Medium High) for 1 to 2 minutes, or until cheese melts.

Salmon Steaks with Peppers

¼ cup butter or margarine
2 tablespoons lemon juice
¼ teaspoon onion salt
¼ teaspoon Italian seasoning
1 medium green pepper, cut into ¼-inch strips
1 medium yellow pepper, cut into ¼-inch strips
1 medium red pepper, cut into ¼-inch strips
4 salmon steaks (6 to 8 oz. each) about 1 inch thick

4 servings

Place butter in 10-inch square casserole. Microwave at High for 1¼ to 1½ minutes, or until butter melts. Stir in lemon juice, onion salt and Italian seasoning. Toss green, yellow and red pepper strips in butter mixture. Cover with wax paper. Microwave at High for 4 to 6 minutes, or until peppers are tender-crisp, stirring once. Arrange salmon steaks in casserole with thickest portions toward outside of casserole. Spoon peppers and cooking liquid over salmon. Re-cover. Microwave at 70% (Medium High) for 14 to 18 minutes, or until fish flakes easily with fork, rotating casserole and basting with cooking liquid once or twice.

Saffron Shrimp & Tomatoes

1 cup uncooked long-grain
   white rice
1⅔ cups ready-to-serve chicken
   broth
⅓ cup milk
½ cup coarsely chopped
   green pepper
⅓ cup chopped onion

1 tablespoon olive oil
   (optional)
   Dash ground saffron
½ lb. medium shrimp, shelled
   and deveined
1 medium tomato, seeded
   and coarsely chopped

4 to 6 servings

In 2-quart casserole, combine all ingredients, except shrimp and tomato. Mix well. Cover. Microwave at High for 8 minutes. Microwave at 50% (Medium) for 12 to 20 minutes longer, or until rice is tender and liquid is absorbed. Stir in shrimp. Re-cover. Microwave at High for 3 to 5 minutes, or until shrimp is opaque. Stir in tomato. Let stand, covered, for 2 minutes.

130

Tuna-stuffed Shells

- ⅓ cup chopped celery
- ⅓ cup shredded carrot
- 2 tablespoons butter or margarine
- 1 teaspoon instant chicken bouillon granules
- ⅛ teaspoon garlic powder
- ½ cup instant rice
- ½ cup hot water
- 1 can (6½ oz.) water-pack tuna, drained
- 1 can (10¾ oz.) condensed cream of mushroom soup
- 1 cup milk
- 8 uncooked jumbo pasta shells
- 1 hard-cooked egg, chopped
- 1 tablespoon snipped fresh parsley

4 servings

In 1-quart casserole, combine celery, carrot, butter, chicken bouillon granules and garlic powder. Cover. Microwave at High for 2 to 4 minutes, or until vegetables are tender, stirring once. Add rice and water. Re-cover. Microwave at High for 2 to 4 minutes, or until rice is tender and water is absorbed. Mix in tuna. Set aside.

In 9-inch round baking dish, combine soup and milk. Prepare pasta shells as directed on package. Rinse and drain. Stuff shells evenly with tuna mixture. Arrange stuffed shells in baking dish. Sprinkle with egg and parsley. Cover with plastic wrap. Microwave at 70% (Medium High) for 8 to 12 minutes, or until hot, rotating dish once or twice.

Meatless Entrées

Fresh Vegetable Alfredo

Stuffed Cheese Potatoes ▲

  4 medium baking potatoes
      (8 to 10 oz. each)
1½ cups shredded Cheddar
      cheese, divided
  ¼ cup butter or margarine
  ½ cup milk
  ⅓ cup bacon-flavored bits
      (optional)
  ¼ cup sliced green onions
  ½ teaspoon salt
  ½ teaspoon dry mustard
  ¼ teaspoon pepper

4 servings

Pierce potatoes with fork. Arrange in circle on paper towel in microwave oven. Microwave at High for 10 to 16 minutes, or just until tender, turning over and rearranging once. Let stand for 5 minutes. Cut a thin slice from top of each potato. Scoop out pulp, leaving about ¼-inch shell. Set shells aside.

Place pulp in medium mixing bowl. Add 1 cup cheese, the butter, milk, bacon-flavored bits, onion, salt, dry mustard and pepper. Beat at medium speed of an electric mixer until blended. Spoon mixture evenly into potato shells. Arrange potatoes on platter. Sprinkle with remaining ½ cup cheese. Microwave at High for 5 to 10 minutes, or until potatoes are hot and cheese is melted, rotating platter once.

Zesty Stuffed Potatoes ▲

4 medium baking potatoes
   (8 to 10 oz. each)
½ cup cottage cheese
¼ cup butter or margarine
¼ cup grated Parmesan cheese
¼ cup milk
2 teaspoons prepared
   horseradish
2 teaspoons dried parsley
   flakes
½ cup sliced almonds (optional)

4 servings

Pierce potatoes with fork. Arrange in circle on paper towel in microwave oven. Microwave at High for 10 to 16 minutes, or just until tender, turning over and rearranging once. Let stand for 5 minutes. Cut a thin slice from top of each potato. Scoop out pulp, leaving about ¼-inch shell. Set shells aside.

Place pulp in medium mixing bowl. Add remaining ingredients, except almonds. Beat at medium speed of an electric mixer until blended. Gently stir in almonds. Spoon mixture evenly into potato shells. Arrange potatoes on platter. Microwave at High for 5 to 10 minutes, or until hot, rotating platter once.

Vegetable-topped Potatoes

4 medium baking potatoes (8 to 10 oz. each)
1 pkg. (.87 oz.) white sauce mix
1 cup milk
¼ cup grated Parmesan cheese
¼ teaspoon garlic salt
1 pkg. (10 oz.) frozen chopped broccoli
1 can (8 oz.) corn, drained
½ cup seeded chopped tomato
½ cup shredded Cheddar cheese

4 servings

Pierce potatoes with fork. Arrange in circle on paper towel in microwave oven. Microwave at High for 10 to 16 minutes, or just until tender, turning over and rearranging once. Set aside.

In 4-cup measure, blend white sauce mix and milk. Microwave at High for 2½ to 5 minutes, or until sauce thickens and bubbles, stirring 2 or 3 times. Add Parmesan cheese and garlic salt. Mix well. Set aside.

Unwrap broccoli and place on plate. Microwave at High for 4 to 6 minutes, or until defrosted, turning over and breaking apart once. Drain, pressing to remove excess moisture. In medium bowl, combine broccoli, corn and tomato. Pour white sauce over vegetables. Toss to coat.

Arrange potatoes on serving plate. Slash each potato lengthwise and then crosswise. Gently press both ends until center pops open. Top each potato with one-fourth of vegetable mixture. Sprinkle evenly with Cheddar cheese. Microwave at 50% (Medium) for 2 to 4 minutes, or until potatoes are hot and cheese is melted, rotating plate once.

4-Cheese Pie with Whole Wheat Crust

⅔ cup plus 1 tablespoon all-
    purpose flour, divided
⅓ cup whole wheat flour
½ teaspoon salt
⅓ cup shortening
2 to 3 tablespoons ice water
1 carton (15 oz.) ricotta cheese
3 eggs, beaten
⅓ cup sliced green onions
⅓ cup grated Parmesan cheese
¼ cup evaporated milk
½ teaspoon dried marjoram
    leaves
½ teaspoon salt
¼ teaspoon pepper
¾ cup shredded Cheddar
    cheese
½ cup shredded Swiss cheese

4 to 6 servings

In small mixing bowl, combine ⅔ cup all-purpose flour, the wheat flour and salt. Cut in shortening to form coarse crumbs. Sprinkle with water, 1 tablespoon at a time, mixing with fork until particles are moistened and cling together. Form dough into a ball. On lightly floured board, roll out dough at least 2 inches larger than inverted 9-inch pie plate. Ease dough into pie plate. Trim and flute edge. Prick thoroughly. Microwave at High for 5 to 8 minutes, or until crust appears dry and opaque, rotating once or twice. Set aside.

In medium mixing bowl, blend ricotta cheese, remaining 1 tablespoon flour and the eggs. Add remaining ingredients, except Cheddar and Swiss cheeses. Mix well. Stir in cheeses. Pour into prepared crust. Microwave at 70% (Medium High) for 13 to 23 minutes, or until center of filling is set, rotating pie plate 2 or 3 times. Let stand for 10 minutes.

Cheesy Chili Enchiladas ▶

1 cup shredded Monterey Jack
   cheese
1 cup shredded Cheddar
   cheese
¼ teaspoon chili powder
¼ teaspoon ground cumin
   Vegetable oil
6 corn tortillas (6-inch)
1 can (10 oz.) enchilada sauce
1 can (7 oz.) whole green
   chilies, drained
   Seeded chopped tomato
   Sliced green onion
   Sour cream

4 to 6 servings

How to Microwave Cheesy Chili Enchiladas

Combine cheeses, chili powder and cumin in large plastic food-storage bag. Shake to coat. Remove ½ cup cheese mixture for topping. Set aside.

Heat ⅛ inch vegetable oil conventionally in 8-inch skillet over medium-high heat. Dip both sides of each tortilla in hot oil. Place tortillas on paper-towel-lined plate. Set aside.

Pour enchilada sauce into shallow dish. Divide remaining cheese mixture into 6 equal portions. To assemble enchiladas, dip both sides of a tortilla in enchilada sauce. Sprinkle 1 portion cheese down the center of tortilla.

3-Bean Chili

½ cup chopped onion
½ cup chopped celery
⅓ cup chopped green pepper
1 tablespoon olive oil
1 can (28 oz.) whole tomatoes, cut up
1 can (15 oz.) tomato sauce
1 can (16 oz.) Great Northern beans, rinsed and drained
1 can (15½ oz.) kidney beans, rinsed and drained
1 can (15 oz.) garbanzo beans, rinsed and drained
2 teaspoons chili powder
1 teaspoon ground cumin
1 teaspoon sugar
½ teaspoon salt
¼ teaspoon garlic powder
⅛ teaspoon pepper
⅛ teaspoon cayenne

8 cups

In 3-quart casserole, combine onion, celery, green pepper and oil. Cover. Microwave at High for 5 to 8 minutes, or until vegetables are tender, stirring once or twice. Add remaining ingredients. Mix well. Re-cover. Microwave at High for 20 to 25 minutes, or until mixture is hot and flavors are blended, stirring 2 or 3 times.

Place 1 green chili in center of tortilla. Roll up tortilla to enclose cheese and chili. Place in 9-inch square baking dish. Repeat with remaining tortillas.

Pour any remaining enchilada sauce over enchiladas. Sprinkle with reserved cheese mixture. Cover with plastic wrap. Microwave at 70% (Medium High) for 8 to 10 minutes, or until enchiladas are hot and cheese is melted, rotating dish 2 or 3 times. Sprinkle with chopped tomato and onion slices. Top with sour cream before serving.

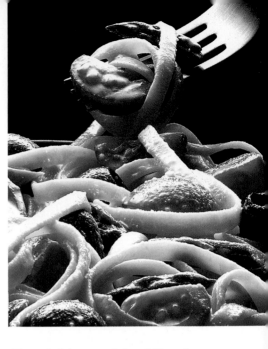

◄ Mediterranean Vegetable Sauté

1 medium green pepper, cut into ¾-inch chunks	1 small eggplant (about 1 lb.), cubed (½-inch cubes)
1 medium onion, thinly sliced	2 medium zucchini, cut into julienne strips (2 × ¼-inch)
1 cup thinly sliced carrot	1 medium tomato, seeded and cut into chunks
2 cloves garlic, minced	
⅓ cup olive oil	¾ teaspoon salt
¾ teaspoon dried marjoram leaves	Hot cooked couscous Grated Parmesan cheese
½ teaspoon dried oregano leaves	

6 servings

In 3-quart casserole, combine green pepper, onion, carrot, garlic, oil, marjoram and oregano. Mix well. Cover. Microwave at High for 2 to 3½ minutes, or until very hot. Add eggplant and zucchini. Mix well. Re-cover. Microwave at High for 13 to 20 minutes, or until eggplant is tender, stirring 2 or 3 times. Add tomato and salt. Mix well. Re-cover. Let stand for 5 to 10 minutes. Serve over couscous. Top with Parmesan cheese.

◄ Curried Potato & Garden Vegetable Sauce

2 cups cubed potatoes (½-inch cubes)	¾ cup milk
1 small onion, chopped	1 to 1½ teaspoons curry powder
2 tablespoons butter or margarine	¼ teaspoon salt Hot cooked rice
1 medium tomato, seeded and chopped	
1 small zucchini, cut in half lengthwise and thinly sliced	**Condiments:**
1 can (10¾ oz.) condensed cream of potato soup	Raisins
	Chopped hard-cooked eggs
	Chopped peanuts
	Sliced green onions

4 to 6 servings

In 2-quart casserole, combine potatoes, chopped onion and butter. Cover. Microwave at High for 7 to 10 minutes, or until potatoes are tender, stirring once or twice. Add remaining ingredients, except rice and condiments. Mix well. Re-cover. Microwave at High for 7 to 9 minutes, or until sauce is hot and flavors are blended, stirring once or twice. Serve over rice. Sprinkle each serving with desired condiments.

Fresh Vegetable Alfredo ▲

½ lb. fresh asparagus, cut into ¾-inch lengths
¼ cup butter or margarine
1 can (16 oz.) pitted black olives
½ cup whipping cream
2 eggs, beaten
½ cup grated Parmesan cheese
⅛ teaspoon garlic powder
⅛ teaspoon pepper
8 oz. uncooked fettuccini
1 cup quartered cherry tomatoes

4 servings

In 2-quart casserole, place asparagus and butter. Cover. Microwave at High for 3 to 4 minutes, or until butter is melted and asparagus is tender-crisp, stirring once. Add olives. Set aside. In small mixing bowl, blend whipping cream, eggs, Parmesan cheese, garlic powder and pepper. Add to asparagus mixture. Mix well. Set aside.

Prepare fettuccini as directed on package. Rinse and drain. Add to asparagus mixture. Toss to coat. Microwave at 50% (Medium) for 4 to 6 minutes, or until hot, stirring every 2 minutes. Add cherry tomatoes. Toss to combine. Before serving, sprinkle with additional grated Parmesan cheese if desired.

Scalloped Vegetable Bake

◄ **Scalloped Vegetable Bake**

1½ cups cubed zucchini
    (½-inch cubes)
  1 cup frozen corn
  ¼ cup chopped onion
  2 tablespoons butter or
    margarine
  1 tablespoon all-purpose flour
  ½ teaspoon salt
  2 cups onion and garlic-
    seasoned croutons
1½ cups shredded Swiss cheese
  1 cup milk
  2 eggs, beaten

4 servings

In 1½-quart casserole, combine zucchini, corn, onion and butter. Cover. Microwave at High for 5 to 9 minutes, or until vegetables are tender-crisp, stirring once. Add flour and salt. Mix well. Stir in croutons and cheese.

In 2-cup measure, blend milk and eggs. Pour over vegetable mixture. Let stand for 15 minutes. Microwave at High for 17½ to 22½ minutes, or until mixture is set, rotating 3 times. Let stand for 5 minutes. Before serving, garnish with fresh parsley sprigs and cherry tomatoes, if desired.

Crunchy Wild Rice Casserole

  1 cup uncooked wild rice
  2 tablespoons butter or
    margarine
  ⅓ cup chopped pecans
  1 cup sliced fresh mushrooms
  ⅓ cup chopped celery
  ½ teaspoon dried marjoram
    leaves
  ½ teaspoon salt
  ⅛ teaspoon pepper
  3 tablespoons all-purpose flour
  1 can (12 oz.) evaporated
    skimmed milk
  1 cup cubed smoked Cheddar
    cheese (½-inch cubes)

4 servings

Prepare wild rice as directed on package. Drain and set aside. In 2-quart casserole, microwave butter at High for 45 seconds to 1 minute, or until melted. Add pecans. Toss to coat. Microwave at High for 1½ to 2½ minutes, or until hot and bubbly.

Add mushrooms, celery and seasonings. Mix well. Cover. Microwave at High for 2 to 3 minutes, or until vegetables are tender, stirring once or twice. Stir in flour. Blend in evaporated milk. Re-cover. Microwave at High for 8 to 11 minutes, or until mixture is thick and creamy. Stir in cheese cubes. Re-cover. Let stand for 5 minutes.

Vegetable Chowder

1 pkg. (10 oz.) frozen chopped broccoli
1 medium potato, cut into ½-inch cubes
½ cup chopped carrot
⅓ cup chopped celery
½ teaspoon dried marjoram leaves
3 tablespoons butter or margarine
3 tablespoons all-purpose flour
½ teaspoon salt
1⅔ cups milk
1½ cups shredded Cheddar cheese
½ cup frozen corn
Cheddar cheese croutons (optional)

6 to 8 servings

Unwrap broccoli and place on plate. Microwave at High for 4 to 6 minutes, or until defrosted, turning over and breaking apart once. Drain. Set aside.

In 2-quart casserole, combine potato, carrot, celery, marjoram and butter. Cover. Microwave at High for 6 to 11 minutes, or until vegetables are tender, stirring once. Stir in flour and salt. Blend in milk. Microwave, uncovered, at High for 6½ to 9 minutes, or until chowder thickens and bubbles, stirring once or twice. Add cheese. Stir until cheese melts.

Add broccoli and corn to chowder. Stir. Cover. Microwave at High for 3 to 8 minutes, or until hot, stirring once. Top with croutons.

Italian Eggplant Bake

⅓ cup olive oil
1 large clove garlic, minced
¾ teaspoon dried basil leaves, divided
½ teaspoon dried oregano leaves, divided
8 eggplant slices (½ inch thick), peeled
2 cups shredded mozzarella or Provolone cheese
1 can (15 oz.) tomato purée
¼ teaspoon salt

4 servings

How to Microwave Italian Eggplant Bake

Combine oil, garlic, ½ teaspoon basil and ¼ teaspoon oregano in 1-cup measure. Cover with plastic wrap. Microwave at High for 45 seconds to 1 minute, or just until warm. Let stand for 5 minutes.

Brush both sides of each eggplant slice with oil mixture. Arrange slices in single layer on baking sheet. Add remaining oil mixture to cheese. Toss to coat. Set aside.

Place eggplant slices under conventional broiler, 3 to 4 inches from heat. Broil until lightly browned, 4 to 6 minutes. Turn slices over and broil until lightly browned, 4 to 6 minutes longer.

Combine tomato purée, salt, remaining ¼ teaspoon basil and oregano in small bowl. Spread ¼ cup tomato mixture in bottom of 9-inch round baking dish. Arrange 4 eggplant slices on top of tomato mixture.

Top each slice with a scant ¼ cup cheese mixture. Top with remaining eggplant slices and cheese.

Spoon remaining purée around eggplant. Cover with plastic wrap. Microwave at 70% (Medium High) for 7½ to 10 minutes, or until hot and bubbly around edges, rotating dish 2 or 3 times.

Linguine & Red-Peppered Broccoli

- ¼ cup pine nuts
- 8 oz. uncooked linguine
- 1 medium head broccoli (1 to 1½ lbs.)
- ½ teaspoon crushed red pepper flakes
- 2 tablespoons olive oil
- 3 tablespoons water
- ½ cup chopped onion
- 3 tablespoons butter or margarine, cut up
- 1 clove garlic, minced
- 3 tablespoons all-purpose flour
- 1 teaspoon dried parsley flakes
- ¾ teaspoon salt
- 2 cups half-and-half
- 4 to 6 drops red pepper sauce (optional)

4 to 6 servings

Place pine nuts in small skillet. Cook conventionally over medium heat just until golden, stirring constantly. Place in small bowl and set aside. Prepare linguine as directed on package. Rinse and drain. Set aside.

Cut broccoli into small flowerets, and thinly slice stalks. Place in 3-quart casserole. Add red pepper flakes and olive oil. Toss to coat. Sprinkle with water. Cover. Microwave at High for 6 to 8 minutes, or until tender-crisp, stirring once. Drain. Add linguine. Mix well. Set aside.

In 2-quart casserole, combine onion, butter and garlic. Cover. Microwave at High for 2½ to 4 minutes, or until butter is melted and onion is tender. Stir in flour, parsley and salt. Blend in half-and-half and red pepper sauce. Microwave at High for 6½ to 11 minutes or until mixture thickens and bubbles, stirring 2 or 3 times. Pour over broccoli mixture. Toss to coat. Sprinkle with pine nuts.

Florentine Mostaccioli Bake

- 1 pkg. (10 oz.) frozen chopped spinach
- 3 tablespoons butter or margarine
- ⅓ cup chopped onion
- 3 tablespoons all-purpose flour
- ¼ teaspoon salt
- ⅛ teaspoon ground nutmeg
- ⅛ teaspoon pepper
- 1½ cups half-and-half
- ½ cup grated Parmesan cheese
- 8 oz. uncooked mostaccioli

Topping:
- 2 tablespoons butter or margarine
- ½ cup seasoned dry bread crumbs
- 1 tablespoon grated Parmesan cheese

4 servings

Unwrap spinach and place on plate. Microwave at High for 4 to 6 minutes, or until defrosted, turning over and breaking apart once. Drain, pressing to remove excess moisture. Set aside.

In 2-quart casserole, combine 3 tablespoons butter and the onion. Cover. Microwave at High for 3 to 4½ minutes, or until butter is melted and onion is tender, stirring once. Stir in flour, salt, nutmeg and pepper. Blend in half-and-half. Microwave at High for 5 to 6 minutes, or until mixture thickens and bubbles, stirring 2 or 3 times. Add spinach and ½ cup Parmesan cheese. Mix well.

Prepare mostaccioli as directed on package. Rinse and drain. Add to sauce. Mix well. Cover. Microwave at High for 4 to 7½ minutes, or until hot, stirring once or twice. Set aside.

In small mixing bowl, microwave 2 tablespoons butter at High for 45 seconds to 1 minute, or until melted. Add remaining topping ingredients. Mix well. Sprinkle over casserole. Microwave at High for 2 to 3 minutes, or until topping is hot. Before serving, garnish casserole with snipped fresh parsley and whole black olives, if desired.

Vegetable Lasagna Spirals

8　uncooked spinach or egg
　　lasagna noodles

Vegetable Mixture:

1　pkg. (10 oz.) frozen chopped
　　broccoli
½　cup shredded carrot
¼　cup chopped onion
2　tablespoons butter or
　　margarine
¼　teaspoon dried thyme leaves

Cheese Filling:

1　carton (15 oz.) ricotta cheese
¼　cup grated Parmesan cheese
1　egg, beaten
¼　teaspoon dried thyme leaves
⅛　teaspoon garlic powder

Sauce:

1　package (.87 oz.) white
　　sauce mix
1　cup milk
1　teaspoon dried parsley flakes
1　cup shredded Monterey Jack
　　cheese

4 to 6 servings

Prepare lasagna noodles as directed on package. Drain. Cover with cool water. Set aside. In 2-quart casserole, combine all vegetable mixture ingredients. Cover. Microwave at High for 7½ to 12 minutes, or until vegetables are tender, stirring 2 or 3 times. Set aside. In medium mixing bowl, combine all cheese filling ingredients. Mix well. Set aside.

In 4-cup measure, blend white sauce mix, milk and parsley. Microwave at High for 2½ to 5 minutes, or until mixture thickens and bubbles, stirring 2 or 3 times. Stir in cheese. Set aside.

Remove lasagna noodles from water and place on damp paper towels. To assemble spirals, spread about ¼ cup cheese mixture onto each noodle. Sprinkle with about ¼ cup vegetable mixture. Roll up noodle to enclose filling. Arrange spirals on end in 9-inch round baking dish. Pour sauce evenly around spirals. Cover with plastic wrap. Microwave at 50% (Medium) for 14 to 20 minutes, or until spirals are hot, rotating dish 2 or 3 times.

Cheesy Chili-stuffed Tortillas ▲

- 1 can (7 oz.) whole green chilies, drained
- 2 oz. Monterey Jack cheese, thinly sliced
- 1½ cups shredded Cheddar cheese, divided
- 1 cup small curd cottage cheese
- ½ teaspoon ground cumin
- ¼ teaspoon garlic salt
- ¼ teaspoon dried oregano leaves
- 4 flour tortillas, 8-inch
- 1 envelope (.87 oz.) white sauce mix
- 1 cup milk

4 servings

How to Microwave Cheesy Chili-stuffed Tortillas

Place chilies on paper towels. Cut lengthwise slit in each chili. Remove seeds. Cut Monterey Jack cheese to fit inside each chili. Set aside.

Combine 1 cup Cheddar cheese, the cottage cheese, cumin, garlic salt and oregano in small mixing bowl. Mix well. Place one-fourth of cheese mixture down center of each flour tortilla.

Deluxe Macaroni & Cheese ▶

1 pkg. (7 oz.) elbow macaroni
2 cups small curd cottage
    cheese
2 cups shredded sharp
    Cheddar cheese

1 cup dairy sour cream
1 egg, slightly beaten
½ teaspoon salt
⅛ teaspoon pepper
    Paprika

6 to 8 servings

Prepare macaroni as directed on package. Rinse and drain. In 2-quart casserole, combine macaroni and remaining ingredients, except paprika. Mix well. Cover. Microwave at 70% (Medium High) for 9 to 12 minutes, or until heated through and cheese melts, stirring twice. Sprinkle with paprika.

To reheat: Place one serving on plate. Cover with wax paper. Microwave at High for 1½ to 2½ minutes, or until heated through, stirring once.

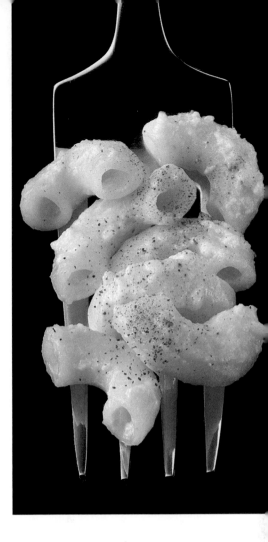

Arrange stuffed chili over cheese mixture. Roll up, enclosing cheese mixture and stuffed chili. Place stuffed tortillas seam-side down in 9-inch square baking dish. Set aside.

Place sauce mix in 2-cup measure. Blend in milk. Beat well with whisk. Microwave at High for 4 to 6 minutes, or until mixture thickens and bubbles, stirring with whisk 2 or 3 times.

Pour sauce evenly over tortillas. Sprinkle with remaining ½ cup Cheddar cheese. Microwave at 70% (Medium High) for 12 to 15 minutes, or until centers are heated through and cheese melts, rotating dish once or twice.

Chiles Rellenos José

Donald K. LaBerenz
Denver, Colorado

- 1 can (7 oz.) whole green chilies, drained
- 3 oz. Monterey Jack cheese, thinly sliced
- 1 cup shredded Cheddar cheese
- ½ teaspoon paprika
- 1¼ cups milk
- ¼ cup all-purpose flour
- 5 eggs
- ½ teaspoon salt
- ¼ teaspoon hot pepper sauce
- ⅛ teaspoon pepper

Salsa:

- 2 medium tomatoes, seeded and coarsely chopped
- 1 small onion, cut into 4 pieces
- 3 tablespoons canned diced green chilies, drained
- 4 teaspoons vinegar
- 1 tablespoon finely chopped fresh cilantro leaves
- 1 teaspoon salt

6 servings

How to Microwave Chiles Rellenos José

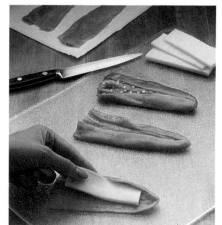

Place chilies on paper towels. Cut lengthwise slit in each chili. Remove seeds. Cut Monterey Jack cheese to fit inside each green chili.

Arrange stuffed chilies in 9-inch round baking dish. Top with Cheddar cheese. Sprinkle with paprika. Set aside. In 4-cup measure, blend milk and flour.

Mix in eggs, salt, hot pepper sauce and pepper. Beat well. Microwave at High for 3 to 5 minutes, or until mixture is hot and begins to set around edges, beating with whisk after every minute. Pour over stuffed chilies. Cover with plastic wrap.

Place dish on saucer in micro-wave oven. Microwave at 50% (Medium) for 15 to 22 minutes, or until no uncooked egg mixture remains on the bottom, rotating dish twice. Let stand, covered, for 6 to 8 minutes.

Combine all Salsa ingredients in food processor or blender bowl. Process until almost smooth.

Cut Chiles Rellenos into wedges. Top with Salsa. Refrigerate any extra Salsa and use as a dip for tortilla chips.

Sandwiches

◄ Tostadas

1 can (8 oz.) kidney beans
3 tablespoons chopped onion,
  divided
1 tablespoon water
¼ teaspoon ground cumin,
  divided
¼ teaspoon salt, divided
  Dash pepper
¼ lb. ground beef
½ teaspoon chili powder
  Dash garlic powder

Dash cayenne pepper
2 tostada shells

Toppings:
½ cup shredded Monterey Jack
  or Cheddar cheese
½ cup shredded lettuce
¼ cup chopped green pepper
1 medium tomato, chopped
2 tablespoons chopped black
  olives
  Dairy sour cream

Serves 2

In small bowl, mix beans, 1 tablespoon onion, the water, ⅛ teaspoon cumin, ⅛ teaspoon salt and the pepper; cover. Microwave at High 6 to 8 minutes, or until beans mash easily, stirring twice during cooking. Remove cover. Microwave at High 1 to 2 minutes, or until liquid is absorbed.

In small bowl mix ground beef, 2 tablespoons onion, the chili powder, ⅛ teaspoon cumin, ⅛ teaspoon salt, the garlic powder and cayenne. Microwave at High 1 to 3 minutes, or until meat is no longer pink, stirring to break apart 2 or 3 times. Drain.

Place tostada shells on paper towel. Microwave at High 30 to 45 seconds, or until hot to the touch. Spread half of the bean mixture on each shell. Top each with half of the meat mixture. Sprinkle with several or all of the suggested toppings.

Italian Meatball Sandwiches

¼ lb. ground beef
¼ lb. bulk Italian sausage
¼ teaspoon pepper, divided
1 can (8 oz.) tomato sauce
½ teaspoon sugar
¼ teaspoon Italian seasoning
⅛ teaspoon garlic powder
2 hot dog buns

Serves 2

Mix ground beef, sausage and ⅛ teaspoon pepper. Shape into six meatballs. Place in 2-qt. casserole; cover with wax paper. Microwave at High 2 to 3 minutes, or until no longer pink, stirring once or twice. Drain.

Stir in tomato sauce, sugar, Italian seasoning, garlic powder and ⅛ teaspoon pepper. Cover with wax paper. Reduce power to 50% (Medium). Microwave 3 to 5 minutes, or until flavors blend. Spoon into hot dog buns.

Italian Meatball Sandwich for One: Refrigerate half of the filling no longer than 2 days. To reheat, microwave at High 1 to 2½ minutes.

◄ Hot Barbecue Sandwiches

2½- lb. boneless pork loin roast	1 can (4 oz.) chopped green chilies
1½ teaspoons crushed red pepper flakes, divided	1 medium onion, thinly sliced
½ teaspoon dried oregano leaves	⅓ cup ready-to-serve chicken broth
¼ teaspoon dried thyme leaves	2 cups barbecue sauce Sandwich rolls

10 to 12 servings

Place pork roast in nylon cooking bag. Sprinkle evenly with 1 teaspoon red pepper flakes, the oregano and thyme. Top with chilies, onion and chicken broth. Secure bag loosely with nylon tie or string. Place in 9-inch square baking dish.

Microwave roast at High for 5 minutes. Rotate dish. Microwave at 70% (Medium High) for 35 to 40 minutes longer, or until internal temperature in center reaches 165°F, turning bag over once. Let bag stand, closed, for 10 minutes. Remove roast and set aside to cool slightly. Strain and discard cooking liquid, reserving onion mixture. Set aside.

Trim and discard fat and any gristle from roast. Shred roast, or shave on meat slicer. Set aside.

In medium mixing bowl, combine onion mixture, barbecue sauce and the remaining ½ teaspoon red pepper flakes. Microwave at High for 2 to 3 minutes, or until hot. Add shredded pork. Mix well. Microwave at High for 4 to 6 minutes, or until hot. Serve on sandwich rolls.

◄ Italian Sloppy Subs

½ lb. ground Italian sausage	½ teaspoon Italian seasoning
½ cup coarsely chopped onion	¼ cup butter or margarine
½ cup coarsely chopped green pepper	¼ teaspoon garlic powder
1 can (8 oz.) whole tomatoes, drained and cut up	4 French rolls (6 to 8-inch), split
¼ cup catsup	1 cup shredded mozzarella cheese

4 servings

In 1-quart casserole, combine sausage, onion and green pepper. Cover. Microwave at High for 4 to 5 minutes, or until meat is no longer pink, stirring several times to break apart. Drain. Add tomatoes, catsup and Italian seasoning. Microwave at High for 2 to 4 minutes, or until mixture is hot and flavors are blended, stirring once. Set aside.

In small bowl, microwave butter and garlic powder at High for 1¼ to 1½ minutes, or until butter melts. Brush on insides of rolls. Place rolls cut-side-up under conventional broiler, 2 to 3 inches from heat. Broil until golden brown.

Arrange bottom halves of rolls on paper-towel-lined plate. Top each with one-fourth of meat mixture. Sprinkle evenly with cheese. Microwave at 70% (Medium High) for 2 to 4 minutes, or until cheese melts. Add tops of rolls. Serve hot.

Chicken Cashew ▲ Sandwiches

Marinade:

¼ cup pineapple juice
½ teaspoon ground coriander
⅛ teaspoon ground ginger

1 boneless whole chicken breast (10 to 12 oz.), skin removed, cut into ¾-inch pieces
½ cup coarsely chopped cashews
½ cup sliced celery
⅓ cup finely chopped onion
¼ cup finely chopped red or green pepper
2 tablespoons mayonnaise
2 tablespoons sour cream
2 tablespoons drained crushed pineapple (optional)
¼ teaspoon salt
⅛ teaspoon ground coriander
Hard rolls or sliced bread

2 to 4 servings

In 1-quart casserole, mix all marinade ingredients. Add chicken pieces and stir to coat. Cover. Refrigerate for at least 1 hour, stirring once. Microwave at High for 3½ to 6 minutes, or until chicken is no longer pink, stirring once. Drain.

Add remaining ingredients, except rolls. Mix well. Chill, if desired. Spoon into hollowed-out rolls or use as sandwich filling with bread slices.

Vegie Bagels ▲

Bagel halves, toasted
Lemon-Basil Cream Cheese
(page 283)

Toppings:
Chopped fresh tomatoes
Chopped green pepper
Sliced green onions
Sliced olives (pimiento-stuffed
or pitted black)

Spread toasted bagel halves
with Lemon-Basil Cream Cheese.
Top with one or more toppings,
as desired. Store any remaining
Lemon-Basil Cream Cheese in refrigerator no longer than 2 weeks.

Mexican Pizza Muffins ▲

1 English muffin, split and
    toasted
    Taco sauce
2 slices salami
    Chopped green chilies

Sliced black olives
Sliced green onion
2 tablespoons shredded
    Monterey Jack cheese

1 serving

Spread toasted muffin halves lightly with sauce. Top each half with 1 slice
salami. Sprinkle muffin halves with chilies, olives and onion. Sprinkle
evenly with cheese. Place muffins on paper-towel-lined plate. Microwave at High for 30 seconds to 1 minute, or until cheese melts, rotating
plate once.

For two servings: Double all ingredients. Prepare 4 muffin halves as
directed above. Microwave at High for 1 to 2 minutes.

Quick Pizza Muffins ▲

1 English muffin, split and
  toasted
  Pizza sauce
2 slices Canadian bacon
  Chopped onion
  Chopped mushrooms
2 tablespoons shredded
  mozzarella cheese

1 serving

Spread toasted muffin halves lightly with sauce. Top each half with 1 slice Canadian bacon. Sprinkle muffin halves with onion and mushrooms. Sprinkle evenly with cheese. Place muffins on paper-towel-lined plate. Microwave at High for 30 seconds to 1 minute, or until cheese melts, rotating plate once.

Egg & Ham-topped Bagels ▲

1 pkg. (3 oz.) cream cheese
½ cup chopped fully cooked
  ham
2 hard-cooked eggs, chopped
2 tablespoons sliced green
  onion

2 tablespoons finely shredded
  Swiss cheese
1 tablespoon mustard-
  mayonnaise sandwich sauce
  Toasted bagel halves

1¼ cups filling

In small bowl, microwave cream cheese at High for 15 to 30 seconds, or until softened. Add remaining ingredients, except bagels. Blend well. Spread 3 to 4 tablespoons ham mixture on one toasted bagel half. Fold paper towel in quarters. Place bagel half on towel in microwave oven. Microwave at High for 20 to 40 seconds, or until heated through. Repeat with additional bagel halves, or refrigerate ham mixture for later use.

For two bagel halves: Microwave at High for 30 to 50 seconds.

Mexican Patty Melts ▼

1 lb. ground beef
2 tablespoons salsa
2 tablespoons sliced green
   onion
½ teaspoon chili powder
¼ teaspoon garlic salt
¼ teaspoon ground cumin
4 slices (¾ oz. each) Monterey
   Jack or Colby cheese
4 hamburger buns

4 sandwiches

In medium mixing bowl, combine ground beef, salsa, onion, chili powder, garlic salt and cumin. Mix well. Shape into 4 patties, about ½ inch thick. Arrange on roasting rack. Microwave at High for 4½ to 7½ minutes, or until meat is firm and no longer pink, rearranging and turning over once. Top each patty with cheese. Cover with wax paper and let stand for 2 to 3 minutes. Serve in buns. Garnish with leaf lettuce, if desired.

Mock Gyros

Sauce:

⅓ cup plain yogurt
2 tablespoons sour cream
2 tablespoons finely chopped
   cucumber
½ teaspoon grated lemon peel
¼ teaspoon dried mint flakes
¼ teaspoon sugar
⅛ teaspoon salt

Meat mixture:

½ lb. ground beef
½ lb. ground lamb
1 teaspoon dried oregano
   leaves
½ teaspoon salt
¼ teaspoon ground cinnamon
⅛ teaspoon dried thyme leaves
⅛ teaspoon garlic powder
4 pitas (6-inch)

4 sandwiches

Blend sauce ingredients in small mixing bowl. Cover. Chill for at least 30 minutes. In 1-quart casserole, combine beef, lamb, oregano, salt, cinnamon, thyme and garlic powder. Mix well. Microwave at High for 4 to 7 minutes, or until meat is no longer pink, stirring once. Drain. Spoon into pitas. Add shredded lettuce, if desired. Serve with sauce.

Variation: Prepare and chill sauce as directed. Combine meat and seasonings as directed. Mix well. Form into 4 patties, about ½ inch thick. Arrange on roasting rack. Microwave at High for 3½ to 5½ minutes, or until meat is firm and no longer pink, rearranging and turning patties over once. Serve in hamburger buns with sauce.

Philly Beef Sandwiches

1 medium green pepper, coarsely chopped
1 medium onion, sliced
2 tablespoons butter or margarine
4 frozen beef sandwich steaks (2 oz. each)
4 French rolls (6 to 8-inch), split
6 slices (¾ oz. each) pasteurized process American cheese, cut in half

4 sandwiches

How to Microwave Philly Beef Sandwiches

Combine green pepper, onion and butter in 1-quart casserole. Cover. Microwave at High for 3 to 4 minutes, or until vegetables are tender-crisp, stirring once. Set aside.

Cut frozen steaks in half. Place halves on roasting rack, overlapping if necessary. Microwave at High for 3 to 4½ minutes, or until meat is no longer pink, rearranging once.

Place 2 pieces of meat on each of 4 French roll halves. Top evenly with onion mixture and cheese.

Layer 2 paper towels on 12-inch round platter. Arrange open face sandwiches on platter. Microwave at High for 1¼ to 1¾ minutes, or until cheese melts. Add top halves of rolls to serve.

Sprouts & Beef Pitas ▶

1 small red onion, sliced
¼ cup Italian dressing
4 frozen beef sandwich steaks
  (2 oz. each)
2 pita breads, 6-inch
2 slices (1 oz. each) Provolone
  cheese, cut in half
2 cups alfalfa sprouts

4 servings

How to Microwave Sprouts & Beef Pitas

Line 9-inch square baking dish with 2 layers of paper towels. Set aside. In 1-quart casserole, combine onion and Italian dressing. Cover. Microwave at High for 2 to 3 minutes, or until onion is tender-crisp, stirring once. Set aside.

Cut frozen steaks in half. Place four halves on roasting rack. Microwave at High for 3 to 4 minutes, or until beef is no longer pink, turning steaks over once. Repeat with remaining four steak halves.

Cut each pita bread in half. Fill each half with cheese, 2 steak halves, one-fourth of onions and one-fourth of alfalfa sprouts, reserving dressing from onions.

Chorizo Sausage Tacos

½ lb. chorizo sausages,
   diagonally sliced ¼ inch
   thick
⅓ cup mild taco sauce
2 tablespoons sliced green
   onion
6 taco shells

Toppings:
  Shredded lettuce
  Chopped tomatoes
  Chopped avocados
  Shredded Cheddar cheese
  Sliced black olives
  Dairy sour cream

6 servings

In 1-quart casserole, combine sausage, taco sauce and onion. Cover. Microwave at High for 4 to 6 minutes, or until sausage is thoroughly cooked, stirring once. Spoon mixture evenly into taco shells. Serve with desired toppings.

Sprinkle 1 to 2 teaspoons reserved dressing over each pita filling. Place pita halves upright in paper towel-lined dish. Microwave at 70% (Medium High) for 2½ to 3½ minutes, or until sandwiches feel warm.

◄ Turkey Club Pitas

- 4 slices bacon
- 1 cup thin strips smoked turkey breast (3 to 4 oz.)
- ½ cup shredded Cheddar cheese
- ½ cup alfalfa sprouts
- 2 tablespoons finely chopped onion
- 2 pitas (6-inch), cut in half
  Mayonnaise
  Prepared mustard
- 4 thin slices tomato

4 sandwiches

Arrange bacon slices on roasting rack. Cover with paper towel. Microwave at High for 3 to 6 minutes, or until brown and crisp. Cool slightly. Crumble. In small mixing bowl, combine bacon, turkey, cheese, sprouts and onion. Mix well. Spread insides of pitas with mayonnaise and mustard. Place 1 tomato slice inside each pita. Place one-fourth of turkey mixture inside each pita.

Arrange pocket sandwiches on paper-towel-lined plate. Microwave at 70% (Medium High) for 2½ to 5 minutes, or just until cheese begins to melt, rotating plate once or twice.

Salmon Smokies ►

- 1 can (6¾ oz.) skinless, boneless salmon, drained
- 2 tablespoons mayonnaise
- 1 tablespoon sliced pimiento, drained
- 1 tablespoon sliced green onion
- ½ teaspoon lemon juice
  Dash pepper
- 2 English muffins, split and toasted
- 4 thin green pepper rings
- 4 slices (½ oz. each) smoked sharp Cheddar cheese

4 sandwiches

In small mixing bowl, combine salmon, mayonnaise, pimiento, onion, lemon juice and pepper. Mix well. Spread one-fourth of salmon mixture on each split English muffin. Top with green pepper ring and cheese slice. Place on paper-towel-lined plate. Microwave at 70% (Medium High) for 3 to 4½ minutes, or until cheese melts, rotating plate once.

Summer Vegie Melt ▶

¼ cup butter or margarine
1½ teaspoons lemon juice
1 teaspoon Dijon mustard
¼ teaspoon dried marjoram leaves
1 cup small fresh broccoli flowerets
8 small fresh asparagus spears, trimmed and cut in half
2 Kaiser rolls, split
½ cup torn fresh spinach leaves
½ cup thinly sliced fresh mushrooms
⅓ cup thinly sliced zucchini or summer squash
⅓ cup alfalfa sprouts
2 thin red or green pepper rings
2 slices (1 oz. each) Provolone cheese

2 sandwiches

In 1-cup measure, combine butter, lemon juice, mustard and marjoram. Microwave at High for 1¼ to 1¾ minutes, or until butter melts. Stir to blend. Place broccoli in small mixing bowl. Drizzle with 1 tablespoon butter mixture. Cover with plastic wrap. Microwave at High for 1 to 1¾ minutes, or until broccoli is very hot and color brightens. Uncover and set aside.

Place asparagus on small plate. Drizzle with 2 teaspoons butter mixture. Cover with plastic wrap. Microwave at High for 45 seconds to 1¼ minutes, or until asparagus is very hot and color brightens. Set aside.

Brush cut side of each roll half with remaining butter mixture. Arrange bottom halves of rolls on paper-towel-lined plate. Layer vegetables evenly on roll halves. Top each serving with slice of cheese. Microwave at 70% (Medium High) for 2¾ to 3½ minutes, or until cheese melts, rotating plate once. Top with remaining roll halves.

Triple-Cheese Sandwiches

1 pkg. (3 oz.) cream cheese
1 tablespoon mayonnaise
1 tablespoon sliced green onion
 Prepared mustard (optional)
8 slices rye bread, toasted

4 slices (¾ oz. each) Colby cheese
4 slices (¾ oz. each) Monterey Jack cheese
 Cherry tomatoes, cut in half (optional)

4 sandwiches

In small mixing bowl, microwave cream cheese at High for 15 to 30 seconds, or until softened. Add mayonnaise and onion. Mix well. Spread mustard on one side of each slice of bread. Spread cream cheese mixture evenly over mustard. Layer 4 slices of bread with 1 slice each of Colby and Monterey Jack cheeses. Top with remaining slices of bread.

On paper-towel-lined plate, microwave sandwiches at 70% (Medium High) for 2 to 3½ minutes, or until cheeses melt, rotating once or twice. Place cherry tomato halves on wooden picks and garnish sandwich tops.

Baby Burgers

For each burger: Shape 2 oz. ground beef into round 3½-inch patty, about ¼ inch thick. Place on roasting rack. Microwave at High as directed in chart (below), or until meat is firm and no longer pink, rotating rack once. Cover with wax paper and let stand for 2 minutes. If desired, cut 1 slice (¾ oz.) pasteurized process cheese food into 4 squares. Place 1 square on each burger. Place burger in small bun (2½ to 3-inch diameter). Heat from burger will melt cheese.

Amount	Microwave at High
2 patties	1 to 2½ minutes
4 patties	2 to 3 minutes

Quick Burgers

For each burger: Shape 4 oz. ground beef into round 4-inch patty, about ½ inch thick. Place on roasting rack. Microwave at High as directed in chart (below), or until meat is firm and no longer pink, turning patties over and rotating rack once. Cover burgers with wax paper and let stand for 2 minutes.

Amount	Microwave at High
2 patties	2½ to 4½ minutes
4 patties	4½ to 7½ minutes

Prepare choice of Toppings (right), and spoon over cooked hamburger patties.

Barbecue Onion Burger Topping

1 medium onion, sliced ¼ inch thick
1 tablespoon barbecue sauce

Place onion in 1-quart casserole. Drizzle with barbecue sauce. Cover. Microwave at High for 3 to 4½ minutes, or until onion is tender-crisp, stirring once.

Italian Pepper Burger Topping

1 small green pepper, cut into ¼-inch strips
1 small red pepper, cut into ¼-inch strips
2 tablespoons olive oil
¼ teaspoon Italian seasoning

In 1-quart casserole, place green and red pepper strips. Drizzle with oil. Sprinkle with Italian seasoning. Cover. Microwave at High for 4 to 5½ minutes, or until peppers are tender-crisp, stirring once.

Hot Pepper Deli Melt ▲

For each sandwich: Sprinkle small amount of Italian dressing on bottom half of 4-inch French roll or Kaiser roll. Top with 1 to 2 oz. thinly sliced fully cooked ham, turkey or beef. Add fresh onion ring slices and mushroom slices. Sprinkle with hot pickled pepper rings. Top with one slice (¾ oz.) mozzarella or Colby cheese. Fold paper towel in quarters. Place open-face sandwich on towel in microwave oven. Microwave at High for 30 seconds to 1 minute, or until cheese melts. Add top half of roll to serve. For 2 sandwiches, microwave at High for 1 to 1¾ minutes.

Pork Applesauce Sandwich

For each sandwich:
1 thin slice cooked pork roast
1 English muffin half, toasted
1 to 2 teaspoons applesauce
1 tablespoon shredded
  Cheddar cheese

Place pork slice on toasted muffin half. Spread with applesauce. Sprinkle with cheese. Fold paper towel in quarters. Place sandwich on towel in microwave oven. Microwave at High as directed (below), or until cheese melts.

Amount	Microwave at High
1 sandwich	30 to 45 seconds
2 sandwiches	¾ to 1½ minutes

Hot Stuffed Polish Sausages in Buns

Slit fully cooked Polish sausages lengthwise, starting ½ inch from ends, being careful not to cut all the way through. Fill sausages with 2 teaspoons pickle relish or chopped onion, or with thin strip of cheese. Place sausage in bun and wrap in paper towel. Microwave at High as directed in chart (right), or until heated through.

Amount	Microwave at High
1 sausage	¾ to 1¼ minutes
2 sausages	1¼ to 1¾ minutes

Pepper & Mushroom Melt Burgers ▶

1 lb. lean ground beef
1 teaspoon Worcestershire
   sauce
½ teaspoon salt
⅛ teaspoon pepper
¼ teaspoon garlic powder,
   divided
1 can (4 oz.) sliced
   mushrooms, drained
2 tablespoons butter or
   margarine
4 slices (¾ oz. each) hot
   pepper cheese

4 servings

How to Microwave Pepper & Mushroom Melt Burgers

Combine beef, Worcestershire sauce, salt, pepper and ⅛ teaspoon garlic powder in medium mixing bowl. Mix well. Shape into four patties, about ½ inch thick. Arrange patties on roasting rack.

Quick Mexican Pizzas ▲

4 tostada shells
½ cup refried beans
½ lb. lean ground beef
¼ cup chopped onion

3 tablespoons hot salsa
⅛ teaspoon salt
1 cup shredded Monterey
   Jack cheese

2 to 4 servings

Line 12-inch round platter with paper towel. Arrange tostada shells on paper towel-lined platter. Spread 2 tablespoons refried beans over each tostada shell. Set aside. Crumble beef into 1-quart casserole. Add onion. Cover. Microwave at High for 3 to 4½ minutes, or until beef is no longer pink, stirring once to break apart. Drain. Stir in salsa and salt. Spoon one-fourth of beef mixture over each tostada shell. Top each with ¼ cup cheese. Microwave at 50% (Medium) for 3½ to 4½ minutes, or until cheese melts, rotating platter once.

Microwave at High for 3 minutes. Turn patties over and rotate rack. Microwave at High for 2 to 4 minutes, or until patties are firm and no longer pink in center. Set aside.

Combine mushrooms, butter and remaining ⅛ teaspoon garlic powder in 1-quart casserole. Microwave at High for 1½ to 2½ minutes, or until butter melts, stirring once.

Top each patty with one-fourth of mushroom mixture and cheese slice. Microwave at High.for 1½ to 2½ minutes, or until cheese melts, rotating rack once.

Stuffed Pita Breads

For each sandwich:
⅓ cup prepared chicken or tuna
    salad
½ loaf pita bread (6-inch loaf)
2 teaspoons sweet pickle relish
    or sliced green onion
    Chopped hard-cooked egg
    (optional)
1 tablespoon shredded
    Cheddar cheese

Spoon salad into pita bread
half. Top with pickle relish and
chopped egg. Sprinkle with
Cheddar cheese. Line small,
shallow cereal bowl with paper
towel. Place sandwich upright in
bowl. Microwave at 50% (Medium)
as directed in chart (below), or until
sandwich is heated through and
cheese is melted.

Amount	Microwave at High
1 pita half	1½ to 3 minutes
2 pita halves	2 to 3 minutes

Chicken-Broccoli Tostadas ▲

½ cup frozen chopped broccoli
1 can (5 oz.) chunk chicken
⅓ cup shredded Monterey Jack
    cheese
¼ cup small-curd cottage
    cheese
8 to 10 drops red pepper sauce
4 tostada shells

4 servings

In small mixing bowl, microwave broccoli at High for 1 to 1½ minutes,
or until hot. Drain. Add remaining ingredients, except tostada shells.
Mix well. Spread chicken mixture evenly on tostada shells. Place tos-
tadas on paper-towel-lined platter. Microwave at 70% (Medium High)
for 2 to 3 minutes, or until cheese melts, rotating platter once.

Mexican Tostada ▶

For each tostada:
- ¼ cup refried beans
- 1 tostada shell
- 1 tablespoon finely chopped onion
- 1 tablespoon finely chopped green pepper
- 1 tablespoon chopped green chilies
- 2 tablespoons shredded taco-flavored Cheddar cheese
  Taco sauce

Spread refried beans on a tostada. Sprinkle with onion, green pepper and green chilies. Top with Cheddar cheese. Place tostada on paper-towel-lined plate. Microwave at High for 1 to 1¾ minutes, or until cheese melts. Top with taco sauce.

Chicken & Pepper Tacos

- ¼ cup chopped onion
- ¼ cup chopped green pepper
- ¼ cup chopped red pepper
- ½ teaspoon Mexican seasoning
- 1 teaspoon vegetable oil
- 1 cup cut-up cooked chicken
- ½ cup shredded Monterey Jack cheese
- ⅓ cup ricotta cheese
- ¼ teaspoon salt
- 4 taco shells

4 servings

In small mixing bowl, combine onion, green and red pepper, Mexican seasoning and oil. Microwave at High for 2 to 3 minutes, or until vegetables are tender, stirring once. Mix in chicken, cheeses and salt. Spoon chicken mixture evenly into taco shells. Place upright in paper-towel-lined 9-inch square baking dish. Microwave at High for 1½ to 2½ minutes, or until mixture is heated through and cheese is melted, rotating dish once. Top with taco sauce or guacamole, if desired.

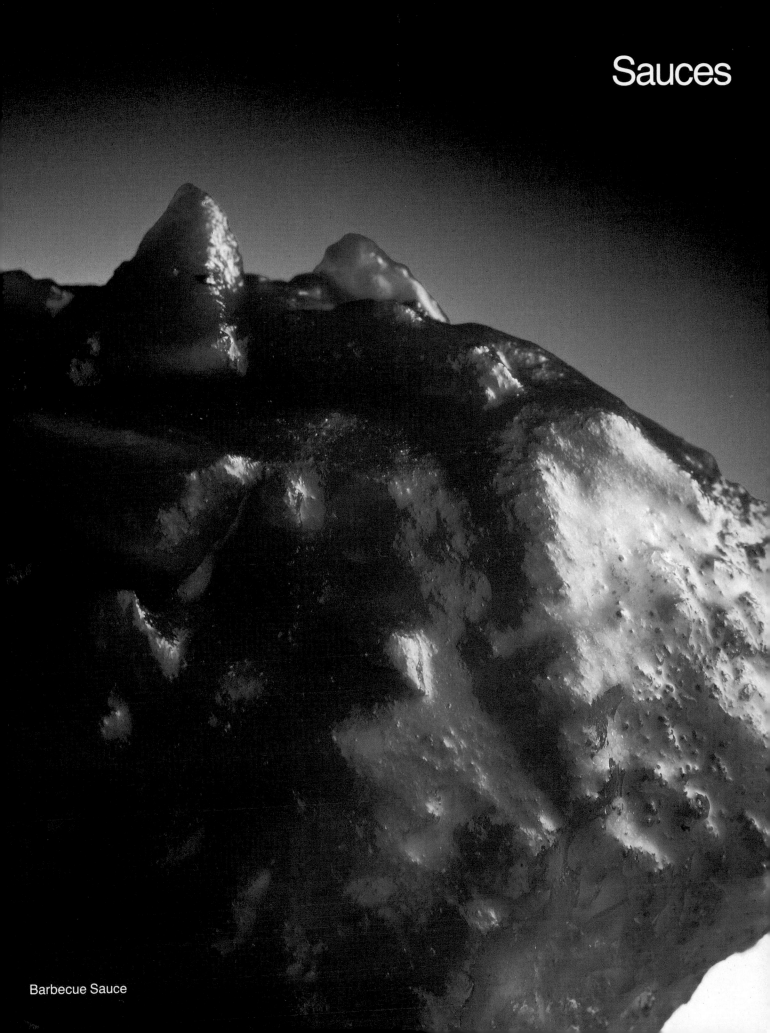

Sauces

Barbecue Sauce

Fresh Vegetable Sauce ▲

2 medium tomatoes, seeded
   and cut into wedges
½ cup shredded carrots
¼ cup chopped onion
2 tablespoons snipped fresh
   parsley
1 clove garlic, cut in half
3 tablespoons tomato paste
½ teaspoon salt
½ teaspoon sugar
¼ teaspoon dried crushed
   sage leaves
⅛ teaspoon pepper
   Dash ground nutmeg

About 1½ cups

In food processor or blender
container, combine tomatoes,
carrots, onion, parsley and
garlic. Process until smooth.
Pour into 1-quart casserole. Stir
in remaining ingredients. Microwave at High for 15 to 20 minutes, or until slightly thickened,
stirring 2 or 3 times. Serve hot
over fish fillets, chicken breasts
or turkey cutlets.

Cream Sauce

1½ cups half-and-half
⅛ teaspoon ground nutmeg
1 bay leaf
2 tablespoons butter or
   margarine
2 tablespoons all-purpose
   flour
¼ teaspoon salt
⅛ teaspoon pepper

1½ cups

In 2-cup measure, combine
half-and-half, nutmeg and bay
leaf. Microwave at 70% (Medium
High) for 3½ to 4½ minutes, or
until hot but not boiling, stirring
1 or 2 times. Remove bay leaf.
Set aside. Place butter in 4-cup
measure. Microwave at High for
45 seconds to 1 minute, or until
butter melts. Stir in flour, salt
and pepper. Blend in half-and-
half mixture. Reduce power to
70% (Medium High). Microwave
for 1½ to 2½ minutes, or until
mixture thickens and bubbles,
stirring after the first 30 seconds
and then after every minute.
Serve with fish, seafood
or chicken.

Tartar Sauce

2 tablespoons chopped onion
½ teaspoon freeze-dried
   chives
½ teaspoon vegetable oil
¼ teaspoon celery salt
   Dash pepper
½ cup mayonnaise
2 tablespoons dairy sour
   cream
2 tablespoons finely chopped
   dill or sweet pickle
1½ teaspoons lemon juice

¾ cup

In small mixing bowl, combine
onion, chives, oil, celery salt
and pepper. Cover. Microwave
at High for 1 to 1½ minutes, or
until onion is tender-crisp. Cool
slightly. Blend in remaining ingredients. Re-cover. Chill for at
least 30 minutes to blend flavors.
Serve with fish or seafood.

Creamy Orange Sauce ▲

- 2 tablespoons butter or margarine
- 2 tablespoons sliced green onion
- 2 teaspoons snipped fresh parsley
- 1 teaspoon grated orange peel
- 1 tablespoon all-purpose flour
- ¼ teaspoon salt
- ¼ teaspoon dry mustard
- ¾ cup milk
- 1 tablespoon fresh orange juice

About 1 cup

In 2-cup measure, combine butter, onion, parsley and orange peel. Microwave at High for 1 to 1¼ minutes, or until butter melts. Stir in flour, salt and mustard. Blend in milk. Microwave at High for 2½ to 4 minutes, or until mixture thickens and bubbles, stirring after every minute. Stir in orange juice. Serve over fish or chicken.

Clam Sauce

- ¼ cup butter or margarine
- ¼ cup snipped fresh parsley
- ¼ cup finely chopped onion
- 1 clove garlic, minced
- 2 tablespoons olive oil
- ¼ teaspoon salt
- ¼ teaspoon pepper
- 1 tablespoon all-purpose flour
- ¼ cup half-and-half
- 1 can (6½ oz.) minced clams, drained (reserve liquid)

About 1 cup

In small mixing bowl, combine butter, parsley, onion, garlic, olive oil, salt and pepper. Cover with plastic wrap. Microwave at High for 2 to 4 minutes, or until onion is tender. Stir in flour. Blend in half-and-half and reserved clam liquid. Microwave, uncovered, at High for 2 to 4 minutes, or until mixture thickens and bubbles, stirring after every minute. Stir in clams. Serve over hot cooked linguine.

Barbecue Sauce

- 4 slices bacon, cut-up
- 1 medium apple, peeled and chopped
- ½ cup chopped onion
- ½ teaspoon dried basil leaves
- ½ teaspoon dry mustard
- ¼ teaspoon garlic powder
- ¼ teaspoon pepper
- ¼ teaspoon dried crushed red pepper
- 1 can (15 oz.) tomato sauce
- ⅓ cup honey
- ¼ cup steak sauce

About 3 cups

Place bacon in 2-quart casserole. Microwave at High for 4 to 7 minutes, or until crisp, stirring after half the time. Drain. Reserve 1 tablespoon bacon fat. In same casserole, combine bacon, reserved fat, apple, onion, basil, mustard, garlic powder, pepper and red pepper. Cover. Microwave at High for 4 to 5 minutes, or until apple and onion are tender. Stir in remaining ingredients. Microwave, uncovered, at High for 6 to 9 minutes, or until mixture begins to boil, stirring 2 or 3 times. Serve with fish or poultry.

◀ Creamy Lemon-Tarragon Sauce

2 tablespoons butter or margarine
1 tablespoon finely chopped onion
½ teaspoon salt
½ teaspoon grated lemon peel
¼ teaspoon dried tarragon leaves
2 tablespoons all-purpose flour
1⅓ cups milk
4 to 6 drops hot pepper sauce
1 egg yolk, beaten

1⅓ cups

In 4-cup measure, combine butter, onion, salt, lemon peel and tarragon. Cover with plastic wrap. Microwave at High for 2 to 2½ minutes, or until butter melts. Stir in flour. Blend in milk and hot pepper sauce. Microwave, uncovered, at High for 3½ to 5½ minutes, or until mixture begins to boil, stirring after every minute. Blend small amount of hot mixture into egg yolk. Return egg yolk mixture to hot mixture, blending with whisk. Reduce power to 50% (Medium). Microwave for 1 to 1½ minutes, or just until thickened, stirring twice. Serve with fish or chicken.

Spicy Cocktail Sauce

½ cup chili sauce
¼ cup finely chopped celery
2 teaspoons frozen grapefruit juice concentrate
1 teaspoon grated onion
¾ teaspoon sugar
½ teaspoon prepared horseradish
¼ teaspoon Worcestershire sauce
Dash cayenne

¾ cup

In small mixing bowl, combine all ingredients. Mix well. Chill. Serve with fish or seafood.

Hollandaise Sauce

3 egg yolks
1 tablespoon plus 1½ tea-
    spoons fresh lemon juice
⅛ teaspoon salt
    Dash white pepper
½ cup butter or margarine

Makes ⅔ cup

Combine egg yolks, lemon juice, salt and white pepper in blender or food processor. Blend about 5 seconds, or until smooth. Place butter in 2-cup measure. Microwave at High 45 seconds to 1¼ minutes, or until melted and bubbly. Continue to blend egg yolk mixture at low speed, adding hot butter in slow and steady stream until sauce thickens. Serve immediately with vegetables or eggs.

Mornay Sauce

2 tablespoons butter or
    margarine
2 tablespoons all-purpose flour
1 teaspoon snipped fresh
    parsley
½ teaspoon instant chicken
    bouillon granules

    Dash white pepper
1 cup half-and-half
¼ cup shredded Swiss cheese
2 tablespoons grated
    Parmesan cheese

Makes 1¼ cups

Place butter in 2-cup measure. Microwave at High 30 to 45 seconds, or until melted. Stir in flour, parsley, bouillon granules and white pepper. Blend in half-and-half.

Reduce power to 50% (Medium). Microwave 4 to 6 minutes, or until thickened, stirring after each minute with fork or wire whip. Stir in cheeses until melted. Serve immediately with vegetables.

Mexican Seasoned Potatoes

Cheesy Bacon Asparagus

Mrs. Merrill Stateler
McComb, Ohio

2 pkgs. (10 oz. each) frozen
  asparagus cuts
2 slices bacon, cut up
2 cups Cheddar cheese
  crackers, finely crushed,
  divided
1 can (10¾ oz.) condensed
  cream of mushroom soup
2 tablespoons milk
1 tablespoon lemon juice
⅛ teaspoon pepper

6 to 8 servings

How to Microwave Cheesy Bacon Asparagus

Unwrap asparagus and place in 1½-quart casserole. Microwave at High for 5 to 6 minutes, or until defrosted, stirring once to break apart. Drain. Set aside.

Place bacon in small mixing bowl. Microwave at High for 2 to 3 minutes, or until brown and crisp, stirring once.

Stir ½ cup crushed crackers into bacon and fat. Set aside. Sprinkle remaining crushed crackers over asparagus.

Combine soup, milk, lemon juice and pepper in small mixing bowl until well blended.

Spoon evenly over asparagus. Cover. Microwave at High for 8 to 10 minutes, or until heated through, stirring once.

Sprinkle asparagus with bacon and crushed crackers. Microwave, uncovered, at High for 2 minutes.

◄ Spiced Oriental-style Carrots

Kaye Dunn
Van Buren, Arkansas

Can be served hot or cold.

- 3 cups sliced carrots, ¼ inch thick
- ½ cup chopped green pepper
- ¼ cup finely chopped onion
- 3 tablespoons water
- 1 can (8 oz.) sliced water chestnuts, drained
- 1 can (7¾ oz.) semi-condensed tomato soup
- ½ cup sugar
- 2 teaspoons vinegar
- 1 teaspoon soy sauce
- ½ teaspoon salt
- ½ teaspoon prepared mustard
- ⅛ teaspoon pepper

6 to 8 servings

In 1½-quart casserole, combine carrots, green pepper, onion and water. Cover. Microwave at High for 8 to 10 minutes, or until carrots are tender-crisp, stirring once. Stir in remaining ingredients. Re-cover. Microwave at High for 3 to 4 minutes, or until heated through.

Broccoli Casserole ▲

Joelle A. Faulks
Earlville, New York

- 1 pkg. (16 oz.) frozen broccoli cuts
- 1½ cups cheese and garlic croutons
- 1 can (10¾ oz.) condensed cream of mushroom soup
- ½ cup shredded Swiss cheese
- ½ cup shredded Cheddar cheese
- ¼ cup milk

6 to 8 servings

Place broccoli in 2-quart casserole. Cover. Microwave at High for 3 to 4 minutes, or until defrosted, stirring once to break apart. Drain. Stir in croutons, soup, cheeses and milk. Mix well. Re-cover. Microwave at High for 8 to 11 minutes, or until heated through, stirring twice. Let stand, covered, for 3 minutes before serving.

Mexican Seasoned Potatoes

Brenda Lee Moser
West Lawn, Pennsylvania

- 4 medium baking potatoes (8 oz. each)
- ¼ cup butter or margarine
- 1 tablespoon instant minced onion
- ½ teaspoon chili powder
- ½ teaspoon dried oregano leaves
- ¼ teaspoon ground cumin

6 to 8 servings

Cut each potato lengthwise into 4 equal wedges. Set aside. Place butter in 10-inch square casserole. Microwave at High for 1 to 1½ minutes, or until butter melts. Add potatoes, turning to coat with butter. In small bowl, combine remaining ingredients. Sprinkle over potatoes. Cover. Microwave at High for 14 to 18 minutes, or until potatoes are tender, re-arranging potatoes twice. Let stand, covered, for 5 minutes.

Cheesy Cauliflower ▲

Opal Schubert
Princeton, Illinois

1 medium head cauliflower, about 2 lbs., trimmed
1 cup shredded Cheddar cheese
½ cup mayonnaise
1 tablespoon prepared horseradish mustard

4 to 6 servings

Place cauliflower stem-side down on serving plate. Cover with plastic wrap. Microwave at High for 7 to 11 minutes, or until tender, rotating plate twice. Set aside. In small mixing bowl, combine cheese, mayonnaise and horseradish mustard. Mix well. Unwrap cauliflower. Spread cheese mixture evenly over cauliflower. Microwave at High for 1½ to 3 minutes, or just until cheese begins to melt. Let stand for 3 minutes.

Scalloped Corn

Cynthia R. Timmel
Vancouver, Washington

2 tablespoons butter or margarine
½ cup chopped celery
¼ cup chopped onion
¼ cup chopped green pepper
1 can (16 oz.) cream-style corn
1 cup shredded sharp Cheddar cheese
1 cup milk
½ cup saltine cracker crumbs
½ cup quick-cooking rolled oats
2 eggs, beaten
¾ teaspoon salt
Paprika

6 to 8 servings

In 1½-quart casserole, combine butter, celery, onion and green pepper. Cover. Microwave at High for 3 to 4 minutes, or until vegetables are tender-crisp, stirring once. Stir in corn, cheese, milk, cracker crumbs, oats, eggs and salt. Mix well. Reduce power to 70% (Medium High). Microwave, uncovered, for 15 to 20 minutes, or until mixture thickens and appears set, stirring after every 5 minutes. Sprinkle with paprika.

Horseradish Creamed ▲ Potatoes

Maurine Miller Welch
Spring Hill, Florida

2 tablespoons prepared
   horseradish
1 tablespoon instant chicken
   bouillon granules
2 teaspoons all-purpose flour
¼ teaspoon salt
⅛ teaspoon pepper
1 cup half-and-half
3½ cups peeled cubed
   potatoes, ¾-inch cubes
   Snipped fresh parsley or
   watercress (optional)

4 to 6 servings

In 1½-quart casserole, combine
horseradish, bouillon, flour, salt
and pepper. Mix well. Blend in
half-and-half. Stir in potatoes.
Cover. Microwave at 70%
(Medium High) for 20 to 26
minutes, or until potatoes are
tender, stirring twice. Let stand,
covered, for 5 minutes. Garnish
with parsley.

Eggplant Au Gratin

1 medium eggplant, about
   1½ lbs., peeled and
   cut into ½-inch cubes
1 medium tomato, seeded and
   chopped
1 medium onion, chopped
1 clove garlic, minced
¼ cup water
2 tablespoons butter or
   margarine

Eleonora E. Svelti
Bayomon, Puerto Rico

¼ cup milk
1 egg, slightly beaten
1 teaspoon salt
¼ cup grated Parmesan
   cheese
¼ cup seasoned dry bread
   crumbs
1 teaspoon dried parsley
   flakes

4 to 6 servings

In 2-quart casserole, combine eggplant, tomato, onion, garlic and
water. Cover. Microwave at High for 10 to 15 minutes, or until eggplant is tender, stirring twice. Let stand, covered, for 5 minutes.
Drain thoroughly. Set aside.

Place butter in 2-cup measure. Microwave at High for 45 seconds
to 1 minute, or until butter melts. Blend in milk, egg and salt. Stir
into eggplant mixture. In small mixing bowl, combine cheese, bread
crumbs and parsley. Mix well. Sprinkle over eggplant mixture.
Microwave, uncovered, at High for 5 to 6 minutes, or until set,
rotating casserole once.

Creamy Squash Casserole

Kathy Ferguson
Walnut Creek, California

- 1 lb. summer squash, cut into ¼-inch slices
- 1 lb. zucchini, cut into ¼-inch slices
- ¼ cup chopped onion
- ¼ cup butter or margarine
- 2 cups herb seasoned stuffing mix
- 1 can (10¾ oz.) condensed cream of chicken soup
- 1 cup shredded carrots
- 1 cup dairy sour cream
- ½ teaspoon salt
- ¼ teaspoon pepper

8 to 10 servings

In 10-inch square casserole, combine summer squash, zucchini and onion. Cover. Microwave at High for 7 to 8 minutes, or until vegetables are tender-crisp, stirring twice. Set aside. Place butter in small mixing bowl. Microwave at High for 1¼ to 1½ minutes, or until butter melts. Stir in stuffing mix until moistened. Set aside.

In small mixing bowl, blend soup, carrots, sour cream, salt and pepper. Stir into squash and onion mixture. Mix well. Sprinkle evenly with stuffing mixture. Reduce power to 70% (Medium High). Microwave, uncovered, for 12 to 18 minutes, or until hot and bubbly, rotating casserole once.

Zucchini Casserole

A tasty way to use excess zucchini from your garden.

Donna Champagne
Niagara, Wisconsin

2 slices bacon, cut up
2 cups chopped zucchini
1 can (16 oz.) stewed
   tomatoes
1 cup seasoned croutons
½ cup chopped green pepper
⅛ teaspoon garlic salt
2 tablespoons grated
   Parmesan cheese

4 to 6 servings

Place bacon in 1½-quart casserole. Microwave at High for 2 to 3 minutes, or until brown and crisp, stirring once. Drain. Stir in zucchini, tomatoes, croutons, green pepper and garlic salt. Mix well. Cover. Microwave at High for 10 to 15 minutes, or until zucchini is tender, stirring once. Sprinkle with Parmesan cheese. Microwave, uncovered, at High for 1 to 2 minutes, or until cheese melts.

Au Gratin Vegetables

Cheri A. Olson
Apple Valley, Minnesota

1 cup fresh broccoli flowerets
1 cup fresh cauliflowerets
1 cup sliced fresh mushrooms
⅓ cup sliced carrot, ⅛ inch thick
⅓ cup finely chopped onion
1 tablespoon water
2 tablespoons butter or margarine
2 tablespoons all-purpose flour
½ teaspoon salt
⅛ teaspoon pepper
⅔ cup milk
½ cup finely shredded sharp Cheddar cheese

4 servings

In 1-quart Pyroceram® casserole, combine broccoli, cauliflower, mushrooms, carrot, onion and water. Cover. Microwave at High for 5 to 7 minutes, or until vegetables are tender-crisp, stirring once. Set aside.

Place butter in 2-cup measure. Microwave at High for 45 seconds to 1 minute, or until butter melts. Stir in flour, salt and pepper. Blend in milk. Microwave at High for 2 to 3 minutes, or until mixture thickens and bubbles, stirring after every minute. Stir hot mixture into vegetables. Sprinkle with cheese. Place under broiler until cheese melts, if desired.

Szechwan Cauliflower

2 teaspoons vegetable oil
½ teaspoon dried parsley flakes
¼ teaspoon sesame oil (optional)
⅛ teaspoon dried crushed red pepper
1 cup small fresh cauliflowerets
¼ cup water

1 to 2 servings

In small mixing bowl, mix all ingredients, except cauliflower and water. Add cauliflower. Toss to coat. Following directions on page 194, place cauliflower on one of two connected paper towels. Close towels and moisten evenly with water. Microwave at High for 2½ to 4 minutes, or until cauliflower is tender-crisp. Let stand for 1 minute.

Lemony Asparagus ▲

1 lb. fresh asparagus
8 thin slices lemon, divided
4 medium fresh mushrooms, cut into halves
3 tablespoons chicken broth or water
3 tablespoons white wine or water

4 servings

To clean asparagus: Gently bend spears until tough ends snap off. Discard end pieces. If desired, trim away scales from each stalk using a sharp knife.

Following directions on page 194, place 4 lemon slices on one of two connected paper towels. Arrange asparagus spears in thin layer over lemon slices. Top with remaining 4 lemon slices. Arrange mushroom halves around edges of asparagus. Close paper towels.

In 1-cup measure, mix chicken broth and white wine. Moisten paper towel packet evenly with liquid. Microwave at High for 7 to 10 minutes, or until asparagus stalks in center are tender-crisp, rotating plate once or twice. Let asparagus stand for 2 minutes before serving.

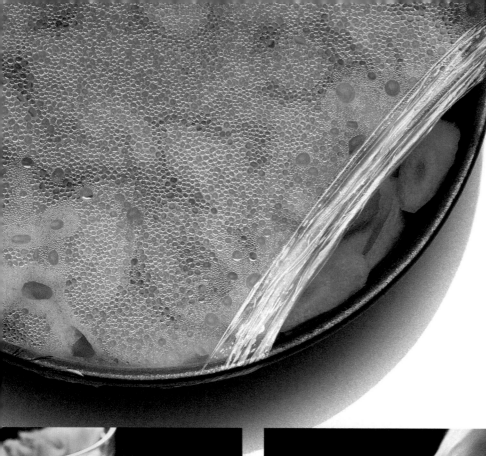

Microwaving Vegetables with Plastic Wrap

Plastic wrap is a versatile kitchen aid that performs a variety of microwave functions. Use plastic wrap when cooking vegetables to hold in steam and speed cooking. Leave a slight opening at one corner of dish to vent steam. To drain, hold plastic wrap down in place using oven mitts, and tilt dish to drain through vent opening. AVOID BURNS: Always be careful when removing plastic wrap after microwaving.

Easily Remove Cabbage Leaves

Remove and discard core from one medium head cabbage. Rinse cabbage and shake off excess water. Wrap loosely in one or two sheets plastic wrap. Place wrapped cabbage seam-side-down on plate. Microwave at High for 5 to 8 minutes, or until leaves are pliable. Let stand for 5 minutes. Unwrap and rinse cabbage under cold running water to loosen leaves. Carefully remove outer leaves. Use outer leaves for stuffed cabbage. Inner cabbage can be used in other recipes.

Removing Skins from Peppers

Cut ¼-inch slice off top of medium pepper. Remove and discard inside seeds and membrane. Wrap loosely in plastic wrap and place pepper seam-side-down on plate. Microwave at High for 4 to 6 minutes, or until soft. Let stand for 3 to 5 minutes. Carefully unwrap pepper and place in a bowl of ice water until cool, about 5 minutes. Peel off skin, working in sections from top to bottom. Use a thin-bladed knife to help peel, if necessary.

TIP: Removing skins from green or red peppers before slicing or chopping for use in salads or sauces makes them sweeter tasting.

Steaming Vegetables in Plastic Wrap

Wrapping vegetables in plastic wrap before microwaving helps retain nutrients and just-picked flavors. Use chart below for reference in following recipes. Prepare accompanying sauces while vegetables stand after microwaving.

Vegetables	Amount	Microwave at High
Artichokes, fresh	2 medium 4 medium	5½ to 8½ min. 9½ to 15 min.
Cauliflower, whole, fresh	1 medium	7½ to 14 min.
Corn-on-cob, fresh	2 ears 4 ears	5 to 10 min. 8 to 16 min.
Potatoes, whole, new	1 lb.	4 to 8 min.
Squash, Acorn, fresh	1 whole	8½ to 11 min.

Corn-on-the-Cob

Remove husks from ears of corn. Rinse. Wrap each ear in plastic wrap. Microwave as directed in chart (left). Let stand for 5 minutes. Carefully unwrap. Serve with plain or flavored softened butter (pages 280-281).

Artichokes

Trim stems from artichokes. Cut 1 inch off tops. Trim sharp ends from each leaf. Rinse artichokes and shake off excess water. Brush artichokes with lemon juice to prevent browning. Wrap each artichoke in plastic wrap. Microwave as directed in chart (above), re-arranging once. Carefully unwrap artichokes and serve with Caper Butter, if desired.

Caper Butter

¼ cup butter or margarine
1 tablespoon capers, drained
  Dash pepper

  ¼ cup

In small bowl, combine butter, capers, and pepper. Microwave at High for 1¼ to 1½ minutes, or until butter melts. Serve butter with artichokes.

Steamed Cauliflower with Cheese Sauce

Microwave cauliflower as directed in chart (above). Let stand. Remove lid from 1 jar (5 oz.) sharp pasteurized process cheese spread. Place jar in microwave oven. Microwave at 50% (Medium) for 1 to 2 minutes, or until cheese melts. Stir cheese and pour over cauliflower. Sprinkle with bacon bits or fresh snipped parsley.

Broccoli & Cauliflower Ring ▲

1 small tomato, cut into 6
   wedges and seeded
4 cups fresh broccoli flowerets
4 cups fresh cauliflowerets
¼ cup water
¼ cup butter or margarine
1 tablespoon fresh lemon juice
¼ teaspoon salt
⅛ teaspoon pepper

Serves 6 to 8

Arrange tomato wedges skin-side-down on bottom of 6-cup glass ring mold. Set aside. Place broccoli flowerets and cauliflowerets in 3-qt. casserole. Sprinkle water over vegetables; cover. Microwave at High 9 to 13 minutes, or until tender-crisp; stirring after half the time. Drain.

Arrange vegetables over tomatoes in mold, pressing to pack firmly. Set aside. Place butter in 1-cup measure. Microwave at High 45 to 60 seconds, or until melted. Blend in lemon juice, salt and pepper. Pour lemon butter over vegetables. Microwave molded vegetables at High 3 minutes. Invert onto serving plate.

Cauliflower With Carrots & New Potatoes

½ cup butter or margarine
2 lb. head fresh cauliflower
¾ lb. new potatoes
12 oz. fresh tiny carrots,
   scrubbed or peeled
1 medium onion, cut into
   8 wedges
2 tablespoons water

Serves 6 to 8

In medium mixing bowl, melt butter at High for 1½ to 1¾ minutes. Set aside. Trim cauliflower at base. Rinse. Place base-side-up at one end of 14-in. oval or 12-in. round microwave-safe platter.

Remove thin strip of peel from around middle of each potato. Toss potatoes, carrots and onions in melted butter. Reserve remaining melted butter. Arrange potatoes around edge of platter. Arrange carrots to fan around plate. Place onions in center. Sprinkle with water. Cover with plastic wrap.

Microwave at High 12 to 16 minutes, or until vegetables are fork tender, rotating platter 2 times and turning cauliflower right-side-up after half the time. Let stand 5 minutes. Serve with reserved butter.

Broccoli & Carrot Platter ▶

2 lbs. fresh broccoli
1 lb. fresh carrots, peeled
2 tablespoons water
   Mornay Sauce, page 175

Serves 6 to 8

Separate broccoli flowerets from stalks. Set aside. Trim 1 inch from ends of stalks and discard. Peel stalks. Shred stalk in food processor. Arrange shredded broccoli in center of 12- or 14-in. round microwave-safe platter. Surround with flowerets.

Roll-cut carrots by holding flat on cutting board. Make diagonal cut straight down. Roll carrot ¼ turn and cut again. Pieces should be about 1½ inches long. Arrange near edge of platter around flowerets. Sprinkle water over vegetables. Cover with plastic wrap.

Microwave at High 10 to 14 minutes, or until carrots are fork tender, rotating platter 2 times. Serve Mornay Sauce with vegetables.

Steamed Acorn Squash

1 whole squash
½ cup applesauce
1 tablespoon packed brown
   sugar
⅛ teaspoon apple pie spice
   Dash salt

2 servings

Cut squash in half crosswise.
Remove and discard seeds and
fiber. Set squash halves on a
large sheet of plastic wrap. (If
necessary, cut a small slice
from bottom of each half so
that squash will sit upright.) Mix
remaining ingredients in small
bowl. Spoon evenly into centers
of squash halves.

Bring corners of plastic wrap together above squash. Twist lightly
to seal. Place on plate. Microwave
at High as directed in chart (page
189), or until tender, rotating plate
once or twice. Let squash stand
for 3 minutes. Unwrap carefully.

Steamed New Potatoes

1 lb. new potatoes
¼ teaspoon dried rosemary
   leaves
⅓ cup butter or margarine
1 teaspoon lemon juice

6 to 8 servings

Trim ½-inch strip from around
center of each potato. Place
potatoes on a large sheet of plastic wrap. Sprinkle with rosemary.
Bring long ends of plastic wrap
together and fold over potatoes.
Fold in sides to form loose packet. Place packet seam-side-up
on plate. Microwave at High as directed in chart (page 189), or until
potatoes are tender, rotating plate
once. Let stand for 2 minutes.

Combine remaining ingredients
in 1-cup measure. Microwave at
High for 1½ to 1¾ minutes, or
until butter melts. Serve lemon
butter over potatoes.

Elegant Stuffed Baked Potatoes

Mrs. Tally Orange
Paw Paw, Michigan

4 medium baking potatoes (8 oz. each)
¾ cup small curd cottage cheese
¼ cup butter or margarine, cut up
2 tablespoons milk
1 tablespoon freeze-dried chives
1 teaspoon seasoned salt
¼ teaspoon pepper
¼ cup shredded Cheddar cheese
¼ cup canned French fried onions

4 servings

Pierce potatoes with fork. Arrange in circular pattern on paper towel in microwave oven. Microwave at High for 10 to 14 minutes, or until tender, turning potatoes over and rearranging after half the time. Wrap each potato in foil. Let stand for 10 minutes. Cut thin slice from top of each potato. Scoop out pulp, leaving about ¼-inch shell. Place pulp in medium mixing bowl. Arrange shells on paper towel-lined plate. Set aside. Add cottage cheese, butter, milk, chives, seasoned salt and pepper to potato pulp. Beat with electric mixer until smooth and fluffy. Spoon mixture into potato shells. Microwave at High for 2 to 3 minutes, or until hot. Sprinkle each potato with cheese and onions. Microwave at High for 1½ to 2½ minutes, or until cheese melts, rotating plate once.

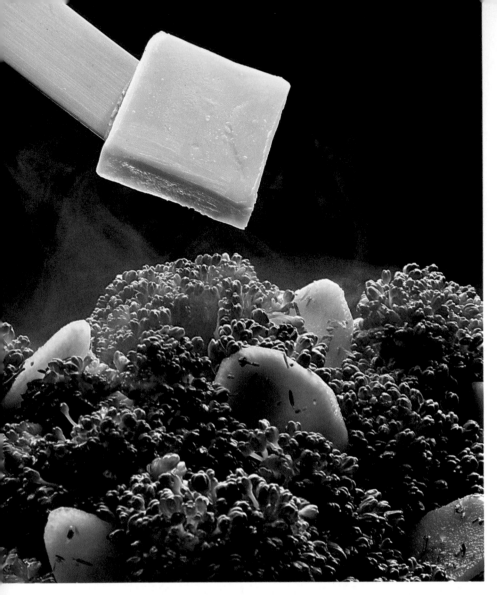

Steamed Garden Vegetables

1 cup fresh broccoli flowerets
½ cup thinly sliced carrot
  Dash dried thyme leaves
¼ cup water
1 to 1½ teaspoons butter or
  margarine

1 to 2 servings

Following directions (below), combine broccoli and carrots on one of two connected paper towels. Sprinkle vegetables with thyme. Close towels and moisten evenly with water. Microwave at High for 3 to 4½ minutes, or until vegetables are tender-crisp. Let stand for 2 minutes. Top with butter.

How to Microwave Food in Paper Towels

Leave two paper towels connected. Place one paper towel on plate. Place food in center of towel, then fold second towel at perforation, enclosing food.

Moisten paper towels evenly as directed in recipe. Fold in the unconnected sides to within 1 to 2 inches from food.

Microwave as directed. Let stand to complete cooking. Open carefully at perforation.

Quick Steamed Vegetable Packets

Combine vegetables for any of the following recipes in center of a 15 × 12-inch sheet of plastic wrap. Sprinkle vegetables with water, as directed. Bring long ends of plastic wrap together over vegetables. Fold sides in to form loose packet. Place packet seam-side-up on plate. Microwave at High as directed, or until vegetables are tender-crisp. Let packet stand for 2 to 3 minutes. Unwrap carefully.

Fresh Peapod Medley ▲

On sheet of plastic wrap, combine 1 cup fresh peapods, ⅓ cup diagonally sliced celery (⅛ inch thick), and 1 tablespoon sliced pimiento. Sprinkle with 1 tablespoon water. Fold as directed. Microwave at High for 2 to 3 minutes.

Cauliflower & Carrots

On sheet of plastic wrap, combine 1 cup frozen cauliflowerets and ⅓ cup thinly sliced carrots. Sprinkle with 2 tablespoons water. Fold as directed. Microwave at High for 3 to 4½ minutes.

Green Beans & Shallots

On sheet of plastic wrap, combine 1 cup frozen green beans and 1 thinly sliced shallot. Sprinkle with 2 tablespoons water. Fold as directed. Microwave at High for 5 to 6 minutes.

Twice-baked Yams

2 yams or sweet potatoes
   (8 to 10 oz. each)
⅓ cup chopped pecans
2 tablespoons butter or
   margarine
½ cup marshmallow cream
1 teaspoon grated orange peel
½ teaspoon salt

4 servings

Wash yams and pierce with fork. Place directly in oven on paper towel. Microwave at High for 8 to 10 minutes, or just until yams feel soft. Let cool slightly.

Cut baked yams in half lengthwise and scoop out pulp, leaving about ¼-inch shells. Set shells and pulp aside.

In medium mixing bowl, combine pecans and butter. Microwave at High for 45 seconds to 1 minute, or until butter melts. Add yam pulp and remaining ingredients. Beat at medium speed of electric mixer until mixture is smooth. Pipe or spoon mixture evenly into shells. Arrange stuffed yams on plate. Microwave at High for 2 to 4 minutes, or until yams are hot, rotating plate once.

Stuffed Orange Cups

3 large oranges (9 to 10 oz. each)
1 can (18 oz.) sweet potatoes
¼ teaspoon ground coriander
⅛ teaspoon ground nutmeg
1 tablespoon butter or margarine
2 tablespoons sour cream
1 tablespoon packed brown sugar
⅛ teaspoon salt
  Dash pepper
¼ cup raisins, divided

6 servings

How to Microwave Stuffed Orange Cups

Cut each orange in half crosswise, angling knife in sawtooth fashion to form decorative edge. Squeeze and reserve 2 tablespoons juice from one orange half. Spoon out pulp of each half, leaving shells. Set shells aside. In a medium mixing bowl, combine sweet potatoes and reserved 2 tablespoons orange juice.

Sprinkle with coriander and nutmeg. Add butter. Cover with plastic wrap. Microwave at High for 4 to 5 minutes, or until mixture is hot, stirring once. Add sour cream, brown sugar, salt and pepper. Beat at medium speed of electric mixer until mixture is smooth. Stir in 2 tablespoons raisins.

Spoon sweet potato mixture evenly into orange shells. Arrange stuffed oranges around outside of plate. Microwave at High for 3 to 5 minutes, or until hot, rotating plate once. Sprinkle with remaining 2 tablespoons raisins.

Herbed Stuffed Onions

 4 large red or yellow onions
(10 to 12 oz. each)
 ¼ cup chopped celery
 1 teaspoon dried parsley
flakes
 ¼ teaspoon poultry seasoning
 3 tablespoons butter or
margarine
1¼ cups herb-seasoned stuffing
mix
 ¼ cup plus 3 tablespoons
water, divided

4 servings

Cut ¾-inch slice from top of each onion. Cut small slice from root ends to allow onions to stand upright. Peel onions. With a thin, flexible knife, loosen center of each onion. Scoop out center portions, leaving ¼-inch shells. (Onion centers may be chopped and frozen for later use.) Place onion shells cut-sides-up in pie plate. Set aside.

In small mixing bowl, combine celery, parsley, poultry seasoning and butter. Cover with plastic wrap. Microwave at High for 2 to 3 minutes, or until celery is tender. Stir in stuffing mix. Sprinkle with 3 tablespoons water, stirring to moisten. Spoon stuffing mixture evenly into onion shells. Pour remaining ¼ cup water around onions in pie plate. Cover with plastic wrap. Microwave at High for 9 to 12 minutes, or until onions are tender, rotating and rearranging onions once. Let stuffed onions stand, covered, for 3 to 5 minutes before serving.

Stuffed Fennel Stalks

1 fennel bulb
3 tablespoons finely chopped onion
3 tablespoons butter or margarine
1⅓ cups cornbread stuffing mix
1 teaspoon dried parsley flakes
  Dash salt
1 egg, beaten
½ cup tomato purée
1 teaspoon dried basil leaves
1 teaspoon olive oil

4 servings

Cut green upper stems and feathery leaves from fennel bulb. Cut thin slice from base of bulb to release stalks. Separate stalks. Remove coarse fibers on outside surface of largest stalks, as directed (right). Cut very large stalks lengthwise into 2 or 3 shells. Set aside.

In small mixing bowl, combine onion and butter. Microwave at High for 1½ to 2½ minutes, or until onion is tender. Stir in stuffing mix, parsley flakes and salt. Mix in egg. Spoon mixture evenly onto fennel shells, pressing lightly. Place shells in 10-inch square casserole. Add water. Set aside.

In 1-cup measure, mix tomato purée, basil and olive oil. Microwave at High for 1 to 2 minutes, or until hot. Spoon mixture over stuffing. Cover. Microwave at 70% (Medium High) for 7 to 10 minutes, or until fennel is tender, rotating casserole once.

How to Remove Coarse Fibers

Use a small knife to cut into, but not through, the top of largest fennel stalks.

Hold fibers against knife blade with finger and pull downward to remove coarse fibers.

Fluffy
French Bread Stuffing

Garda Slorp
Hayden Lake, Idaho

6 tablespoons butter or
  margarine
¾ cup sliced celery, ⅛ inch
  thick
1 medium onion, finely
  chopped
⅓ cup snipped fresh parsley
1 teaspoon dried crushed
  sage leaves
½ lb. cubed French bread,
  ¾-inch cubes, about
  8 cups
¼ cup chopped walnuts
1 can (10¾ oz.) condensed
  cream of chicken soup
2 eggs, beaten
¼ cup milk

6 to 8 servings

In large mixing bowl, combine
butter, celery, onion, parsley
and sage. Cover with plastic
wrap. Microwave at High for 5
to 7 minutes, or until celery is
tender, stirring once. Mix in
bread cubes and walnuts. In
small mixing bowl, blend soup,
eggs and milk. Pour over bread
mixture. Stir to moisten. Spoon
into 1½-quart casserole. Microwave at 70% (Medium High) for
10 to 16 minutes, or until heated
through and mixture is set,
stirring twice.

Sausage & Apple Stuffing

Susanne Adams
Livingston, Montana

½ lb. pork sausage
¼ cup butter or margarine
1⅓ cups sliced fresh
    mushrooms
1 medium apple, chopped
½ cup chopped celery
½ cup chopped onion
½ teaspoon salt
½ teaspoon poultry seasoning
½ teaspoon dried crushed
    sage leaves
¼ teaspoon pepper
5 cups unseasoned whole
    wheat and white croutons
¾ cup ready-to-serve chicken
    broth

6 to 8 servings

How to Microwave Sausage & Apple Stuffing

Crumble sausage into 1-quart casserole. Cover. Microwave at High for 3 to 6 minutes, or until sausage is no longer pink, stirring once to break apart. Drain. Set aside.

Combine butter, mushrooms, apple, celery and onion in 2-quart casserole. Cover. Microwave at High for 7 to 9 minutes, or until celery is tender, stirring once. Stir in sausage and remaining ingredients, except chicken broth.

Pour broth evenly over croutons and vegetables. Stir to moisten. Re-cover. Microwave at High for 3 to 5 minutes, or until heated through, stirring once.

Salads

Tossed Garden Salad with Sirloin

Apple-Ginger Fruit Salad

3 tablespoons sugar
2 teaspoons cornstarch
    Dash salt
½ cup apple juice
½ teaspoon lemon juice
¼ teaspoon grated fresh
    gingerroot
1 medium cantaloupe or
    honeydew melon (about
    3¾ lbs.)*
8 to 10 cups cut-up mixed fruit
    (fresh, canned or frozen)

10 to 12 servings

In 2-cup measure, mix sugar, cornstarch and salt. Blend in apple juice. Stir in lemon juice and gingerroot. Microwave at High for 2½ to 3½ minutes, or until mixture is thickened and translucent, stirring once or twice. Cool.

Cut melon in half. Cut edge of each half with decorative zigzagged or scalloped pattern, if desired. Using small spoon or melon baller, scoop out centers of melon halves to form shells. Reserve melon balls to include in salad, as desired. Set shells aside. Combine fruit in large mixing bowl. Add dressing, stirring gently to coat. Spoon fruit salad into melon shells to serve. Refill with additional fruit salad as needed.

*For variety, use one cantaloupe half and one honeydew melon half for salad shells. Reserve remaining melon halves for future use.

7-Layer Beef Salad ▶

- 1 lb. boneless beef sirloin steak, about 1 inch thick
- 1 tablespoon Worcestershire sauce
- ¼ teaspoon onion powder
- ⅛ teaspoon garlic powder
- ½ teaspoon coarsely ground pepper
- 4 oz. fresh pea pods
- 2 tablespoons water
- 4 cups torn fresh spinach leaves or leaf lettuce
- 1 cup cherry tomato halves
- ¾ cup fresh sliced mushrooms
- ½ cup sliced red onion
- ½ cup sour cream
- ¼ cup mayonnaise
- 2 teaspoons white wine vinegar
- ¼ teaspoon salt
- ¼ cup crumbled blue cheese
- 1 tablespoon snipped fresh parsley

6 to 8 servings

Pierce sirloin thoroughly with fork. Place on roasting rack. Set aside. In small bowl, combine Worcestershire sauce and onion and garlic powders. Mix well. Brush on all surfaces of sirloin. Sprinkle top of sirloin with pepper. Microwave at 70% (Medium High) for 6 to 11 minutes, or until medium rare, rotating rack once. Cool slightly. Cut into ½-inch cubes. Place in large mixing bowl. Set aside.

In 1-quart casserole, combine pea pods and water. Cover. Microwave at High for 1 to 2 minutes, or until pea pods are very hot and color brightens. Rinse with cold water. Drain. Set aside. To assemble salad, layer spinach leaves over beef. Continue layering tomato halves, mushrooms, onion, and pea pods. Set aside.

In 2-cup measure, combine sour cream, mayonnaise, vinegar and salt. Mix well. Stir in blue cheese. Pour over salad. Spread evenly. Sprinkle with parsley. Cover and chill for at least 3 hours. Toss salad before serving.

Tossed Garden Salad with Sirloin

- 1 lb. boneless beef sirloin steak, about 1 inch thick
- 1 small onion, thinly sliced
- 1 clove garlic, cut into quarters
- 2 tablespoons red wine vinegar
- 1 tablespoon vegetable oil
- 2 teaspoons Worcestershire sauce
- ¼ teaspoon dried marjoram leaves
- 1 cup fresh cauliflowerets
- ⅓ cup sliced carrot (¼-inch slices)
- 2 tablespoons water
- 4 cups torn romaine lettuce
- ⅓ cup julienne zucchini (1½ × ¼-inch strips)
- ½ small red pepper, cut into ¼-inch strips

Dressing:
- ¼ cup vegetable oil
- 1 tablespoon plus 1 teaspoon red wine vinegar
- ¼ teaspoon garlic salt
- ⅛ teaspoon pepper

6 to 8 servings

In large plastic food-storage bag, combine steak, onion and garlic. Set aside. In 1-cup measure, blend vinegar, oil, Worcestershire sauce and marjoram. Add to steak mixture. Secure bag. Refrigerate for at least 2 hours.

Remove steak from marinade, discarding marinade. On roasting rack, microwave steak at 70% (Medium High) for 6 to 11 minutes, or just until medium rare, rotating rack once. Chill for at least 1 hour. Slice into thin strips and place in large mixing bowl. Set aside.

In 1-quart casserole, combine cauliflower, carrot and water. Cover. Microwave at High for 2 to 3 minutes, or just until vegetables are tender-crisp, stirring once. Rinse under cold water. Drain. Add cauliflower, carrot, lettuce, zucchini and red pepper to sirloin strips. Set aside. Blend all dressing ingredients in 1-cup measure. Pour over salad and toss to coat. Sprinkle with croutons, if desired. Serve immediately.

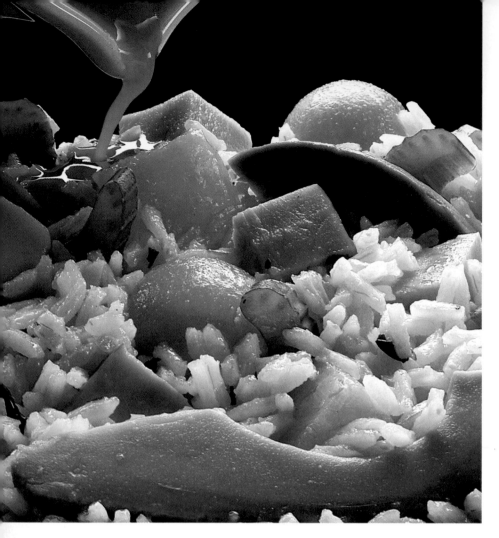

Chicken Taco Salad

2½ to 3-lb. broiler-fryer chicken,
      cut into quarters, skin
      removed
  ¾ teaspoon dried oregano
      leaves
  ½ teaspoon ground cumin
  ⅛ teaspoon ground cinnamon
  1 can (16 oz.) pinto beans,
      drained
  1 small onion, chopped
  ½ cup chopped green pepper
  ½ cup taco sauce
  5 cups shredded lettuce
  1 medium tomato, cut into
      wedges
      Black olives (optional)
      Sour cream or guacamole

6 to 8 servings

In 10-inch square casserole,
arrange chicken with thickest
portions toward outside. Set
aside. In small bowl, combine
oregano, cumin and cinnamon.
Mix well and sprinkle evenly over
chicken. Cover. Microwave at
High for 13 to 19 minutes, or until
chicken near bone is no longer
pink and juices run clear, rearranging once. Cool slightly. Remove
meat from bones and cut into bite-
size pieces.

In medium mixing bowl, combine
chicken, beans, onion and green
pepper. Add taco sauce. Mix well.
Spread shredded lettuce on serving platter. Mound chicken mixture
on lettuce. Garnish with tomato
wedges and black olives. Top
chicken mixture with sour cream.

Festive Turkey Rice Salad ▲

  2 cups hot water
  1 cup uncooked long-grain
      white rice
  1 teaspoon dried parsley flakes
  1 teaspoon grated orange peel
  1 teaspoon grated lemon peel
  1 teaspoon instant chicken
      bouillon granules
  ½ teaspoon salt
  1 cup cubed cooked turkey
      (½-inch cubes)
  1 cup small cantaloupe chunks
      or balls
  1 can (8 oz.) pineapple chunks,
      drained
  ½ cup sliced celery
  1 avocado, peeled and sliced

Dressing:
  ¼ cup vegetable oil
  2 tablespoons orange juice
  1 tablespoon vinegar
  ½ teaspoon sugar
  ¼ teaspoon dry mustard
  ¼ teaspoon paprika

6 to 8 servings

In 2-quart casserole, combine water, rice, parsley, grated orange and
lemon peels, chicken bouillon granules and salt. Cover. Microwave at
High for 5 minutes. Microwave at 50% (Medium) for 12 to 15 minutes
longer, or until liquid is absorbed. Let stand, covered, for 5 minutes.
Stir. Re-cover. Chill for at least 3 hours.

Place rice in large mixing bowl. Add turkey, cantaloupe, pineapple,
celery and avocado. Set aside. In 1-cup measure, blend all dressing
ingredients. Pour over salad and mix well. Serve immediately, or cover
and chill before serving.

Chicken Platter with Orange-Basil Dressing

Dressing:

½ cup ricotta cheese
¼ cup mayonnaise
¼ cup snipped fresh basil
3 tablespoons olive oil
1 teaspoon grated orange peel
⅛ teaspoon salt
  Dash dry mustard

2 boneless whole chicken
    breasts (10 to 12 oz. each),
    split in half, skin removed
1 tablespoon Dijon mustard
2 teaspoons water
1 head Bibb lettuce, torn into
    bite-size pieces
1 cup sliced fresh mushrooms
½ cup salted cashews
  Orange slices (optional)

4 to 6 servings

How to Microwave Chicken Platter with Orange-Basil Dressing

Combine all dressing ingredients in blender or food processor. Process until smooth. Place in bowl. Cover and chill. In 9-inch square baking dish, arrange chicken with thickest portions toward outside.

Blend mustard and water in small bowl. Spoon evenly over chicken. Cover with plastic wrap. Microwave at 70% (Medium High) for 9 to 12 minutes, or until chicken is no longer pink and juices run clear, rotating once.

Cut chicken into thin julienne strips. Line large serving platter with lettuce. Arrange chicken, mushrooms and cashews on lettuce. Garnish with orange slices. Serve with dressing.

◀ Oriental Shrimp & Pasta Salad

½ lb. medium shrimp, shelled and deveined
8 oz. uncooked rotini pasta
1 cup diagonally sliced carrots (⅛-inch thick)
4 oz. fresh pea pods
2 tablespoons water
1 can (8 oz.) sliced water chestnuts, rinsed and drained
¼ cup sliced green onions

Dressing:
2 tablespoons vegetable oil
2 tablespoons soy sauce
2 tablespoons rice wine vinegar
2 teaspoons sesame seed
1 teaspoon sesame oil
1 teaspoon sugar
¼ teaspoon crushed red pepper flakes

4 servings

Place shrimp in 1½-quart casserole. Cover. Microwave at 70% (Medium High) for 2½ to 4 minutes, or until shrimp are firm, stirring once or twice. Rinse with cold water. Drain and set aside. Prepare pasta as directed on package. Rinse with cold water. Drain and set aside.

In 2-quart casserole, combine carrots, pea pods and water. Cover. Microwave at High for 3 to 4 minutes, or until vegetables are very hot and colors brighten, stirring once or twice. Rinse with cold water. Drain. In same 2-quart casserole, combine carrots, pea pods, cooked pasta, shrimp, water chestnuts and onions. Set aside.

In 2-cup measure, combine dressing ingredients. Microwave at High for 30 seconds to 1 minute, or until dressing is warm and sugar is dissolved, stirring once. Pour dressing over pasta mixture. Toss to coat. Cover and chill for 3 to 4 hours.

Creamy Tortellini & Salmon Salad ▲

Dressing:
½ cup mayonnaise
⅓ cup half-and-half
⅓ cup grated Parmesan cheese
1 teaspoon dried parsley flakes
¼ teaspoon dried thyme leaves
⅛ teaspoon garlic powder
⅛ teaspoon pepper

1 pkg. (6 oz.) uncooked spinach tortellini

¼ lb. fresh asparagus, cut into ½-inch pieces
1 tablespoon water
1 jar (6 oz.) marinated artichoke hearts, drained and cut up
½ cup quartered cherry tomatoes
½ cup pitted black olives, cut in half
1 can (6¾ oz.) skinless, boneless salmon, drained

4 to 6 servings

In small mixing bowl, combine all dressing ingredients. Mix well. Set aside. Prepare tortellini as directed on package. Rinse with cold water. Drain. Place in large mixing bowl. Set aside.

In 1-quart casserole, combine asparagus and water. Cover. Microwave at High for 1 to 2 minutes, or until asparagus is very hot and color brightens. Rinse with cold water. Drain. Add to cooked tortellini with dressing and remaining ingredients. Toss gently to coat. Cover and chill for 2 to 3 hours before serving.

Creamy Tortellini & Ham Salad: Follow recipe above, except substitute ⅔ cup fully cooked cubed ham (½-inch cubes) for salmon.

Hot Potato
& Endive Salad

Mrs. Cindy Hoelscher
Little Canada, Minnesota

2 cups peeled cubed red
　　potatoes, ½-inch cubes
2 tablespoons water
3 slices bacon, cut up
2 tablespoons chopped onion
2 teaspoons all-purpose flour
½ cup water
3 tablespoons vinegar
1 tablespoon sugar
¾ teaspoon salt
2 cups trimmed and torn curly
　　endive (chicory)
2 hard-cooked eggs, sliced

4 to 6 servings

How to Microwave Hot Potato & Endive Salad

Combine potatoes and 2 table-spoons water in 1-quart casse-role. Cover. Microwave at High for 4 to 6 minutes, or until tender, stirring once or twice. Drain. Set aside.

Place bacon in same casserole. Cover. Microwave at High for 3 to 4 minutes, or until crisp, stir-ring once. Remove bacon with slotted spoon onto paper towel. Set aside. Reserve bacon fat.

Stir onion into bacon fat. Re-cover. Microwave at High for 1 minute. Stir in flour.

Blend in ½ cup water, vinegar, sugar and salt. Microwave, uncovered, at High for 2 to 3 minutes, or until mixture thickens and bubbles, stirring once.

Stir in potatoes and bacon. Set aside. Place endive in medium salad bowl.

Pour potato mixture over endive. Toss to coat. Top with egg slices. Serve immediately.

Zucchini Salad

Deborah D. Lathum
Highland, Indiana

6 cups sliced zucchini, ¼ inch thick, about 2 lbs.
¼ cup water
¼ cup olive oil
2 tablespoons white wine vinegar
1 teaspoon salt
½ to 1 teaspoon white pepper
½ teaspoon sugar
Salad greens
¼ cup grated Parmesan cheese

6 servings

In 2-quart casserole, combine zucchini and water. Cover. Microwave at High for 6 to 8 minutes, or until zucchini is tender-crisp, stirring twice. Drain. Set aside. In 1-cup measure, blend olive oil, vinegar, salt, white pepper and sugar.

Pour oil and vinegar mixture over zucchini. Re-cover. Chill for 4 to 5 hours, stirring occasionally. Serve on salad greens. Sprinkle with Parmesan cheese.

Asparagus Vinaigrette

Marilyn Mancewicz
Grand Rapids, Michigan

2 lbs. fresh asparagus spears, trimmed and large scales removed
¼ cup water
½ cup vegetable oil
2 tablespoons vinegar
2 tablespoons lemon juice
½ teaspoon salt
½ teaspoon Worcestershire sauce
½ cup chopped fresh mushrooms
2 hard-cooked egg yolks, mashed
2 tablespoons sliced pimiento-stuffed olives
1 tablespoon snipped fresh parsley

4 servings

Arrange asparagus with tender tips toward center of 10-inch square casserole. Add water. Cover. Microwave at High for 8 to 12 minutes, or until asparagus is tender-crisp, rearranging spears once. Drain. Set aside.

In 2-cup measure, blend oil, vinegar, lemon juice, salt and Worcestershire sauce. Microwave at High for 1½ to 2 minutes, or until mixture boils. Stir in mushrooms, egg yolks, olives and parsley. Arrange asparagus on serving platter. Pour oil and vinegar mixture over asparagus. Cover with plastic wrap. Chill for at least 4 hours before serving.

Marinated Vegetables ▲

Margaret Houghtaling
Seattle, Washington

1 cup diagonally sliced carrots, ¼ inch thick
1 cup fresh broccoli flowerets
1 cup fresh cauliflowerets
½ cup green pepper pieces, 1-inch pieces
1 small onion, thinly sliced
1 clove garlic, minced
¼ cup water
1 pkg. (8 oz.) fresh mushrooms, halved
⅔ cup white vinegar
½ cup vegetable oil
2 teaspoons salt
2 teaspoons dried basil leaves
1½ teaspoons sugar
¼ teaspoon pepper

6 to 8 servings

In 2-quart casserole, combine carrots, broccoli, cauliflower, green pepper, onion, garlic and water. Cover. Microwave at High for 4 to 5 minutes, or just until colors brighten, stirring once. Stir in mushrooms. Set aside. In small mixing bowl, blend remaining ingredients. Pour vinegar and oil mixture over vegetables. Mix gently. Chill for at least 8 hours or overnight, stirring occasionally.

Chinese Orange Salad

Nancy D. Halferty
Broken Bow, Nebraska

A colorful accompaniment to an Oriental stir-fry.

6 cups trimmed and torn mixed salad greens (romaine, leaf or iceberg lettuce, spinach)
3 small navel oranges, peeled, white membrane removed, cut into thin crosswise slices
½ cup sliced celery, ¼ inch thick
2 tablespoons sliced green onion
⅓ cup whole blanched almonds
¼ cup vegetable oil, divided
2 tablespoons sugar
2 tablespoons white rice vinegar
⅛ teaspoon almond extract

6 to 8 servings

In large salad bowl, combine salad greens, oranges, celery and green onion. Set aside. In 9-inch round baking dish or pie plate, combine almonds and 1 tablespoon oil. Microwave at High for 3½ to 5½ minutes, or just until almonds begin to brown, stirring after every minute. Set aside. In 2-cup measure, mix remaining 3 tablespoons oil, sugar, rice vinegar and almond extract. Microwave at High for 1 to 1½ minutes, or until mixture boils. Pour hot mixture over salad. Toss to coat. Mix in toasted almonds.

Zesty Potato Salad ▲

Barbara Bronken
Bozeman, Montana

4 cups peeled cubed red potatoes, ¾-inch cubes
2 tablespoons water
¼ cup finely chopped green pepper
¼ cup chopped onion
2 hard-cooked eggs, chopped
1 tablespoon diced pimiento, drained
1 tablespoon chopped black olives

Dressing:
½ cup mayonnaise
¼ cup salad dressing
1 tablespoon prepared horseradish
1 teaspoon prepared mustard
¾ teaspoon salt
⅛ teaspoon pepper

4 to 6 servings

In 1½-quart casserole, combine potatoes and water. Cover. Microwave at High for 7 to 10 minutes, or until tender, stirring once or twice. Chill for at least 2 hours. Stir in green pepper, onion, eggs, pimiento and olives. In small mixing bowl, blend all dressing ingredients. Pour dressing over salad. Mix well. Re-cover. Chill for at least 3 hours.

Shrimp Salad
with Remoulade Sauce

Myra C. Brooks
Port Allen, Louisiana

1 lb. large shrimp, shelled and
   deveined

Remoulade Sauce:
⅔ cup olive oil
⅓ cup Dijon mustard
¼ cup catsup
¼ cup vinegar
2 tablespoons prepared
   horseradish
2 cloves garlic, minced
½ teaspoon hot pepper sauce
¼ teaspoon salt
2 teaspoons sugar

4 cups shredded lettuce
½ cup sliced celery, ¼ inch
   thick

4 servings

How to Microwave Shrimp Salad with Remoulade Sauce

Place shrimp in 1½-quart casserole. Set aside. In 2-cup measure, blend all Remoulade Sauce ingredients, except sugar. Pour ¾ cup Remoulade Sauce over shrimp. Stir to coat. Cover. Chill for 1 hour.

Stir sugar into remaining sauce. Cover. Chill. For shrimp, microwave covered at 70% (Medium High) for 5½ to 8 minutes, or until shrimp are opaque, stirring twice. Drain. Place on serving platter. Cover with plastic wrap. Chill for at least 3 hours.

Place lettuce on salad plates. Arrange shrimp and celery on lettuce. Serve with reserved Remoulade Sauce.

Pasta & Grains

◄ Hot Pasta Salad

1 medium green pepper, cut
  into ¼-inch strips
½ medium red onion, cut in half
  lengthwise and thinly sliced
2 tablespoons reconstituted
  natural butter-flavored mix
2 teaspoons poppy seed
⅛ teaspoon salt
¾ cup cooked spaghetti
1 medium tomato, cut into thin
  wedges

4 servings

In 1-quart casserole, combine
all ingredients, except spaghetti
and tomato. Cover. Microwave
at High for 3 to 5 minutes, or
just until pepper and onion
are tender, stirring once. Add
remaining ingredients. Toss
lightly. Re-cover. Microwave at
High for 2 to 3 minutes longer,
or until hot. Let stand, covered,
for 1 minute.

Garlic Rice & Pasta

2 tablespoons reduced-calorie
  margarine
1 cup uncooked brown rice
½ cup uncooked broken
  spaghetti
3 cups hot water
2 tablespoons sliced green
  onion
1 clove garlic, minced
½ teaspoon salt
⅛ teaspoon pepper
2 tablespoons snipped fresh
  parsley

8 servings

In 3-quart casserole, combine
margarine, rice and spaghetti.
Microwave at High for 4 to 7
minutes, or until spaghetti is
golden brown, stirring after first
2 minutes, then after every
minute. Stir in remaining ingredients, except parsley. Cover.
Microwave at High for 5
minutes. Reduce power to 50%
(Medium). Microwave for 35 to
40 minutes longer, or until liquid
is absorbed and rice is tender.
Add parsley. Let stand, covered,
for 5 minutes. Toss lightly.

Rice Medley

½ cup uncooked brown rice
¼ cup uncooked wild rice,
  rinsed and drained
¼ cup chopped green or red
  pepper
2 tablespoons snipped fresh
  parsley
1 tablespoon finely chopped
  celery
2¼ cups hot water
2 tablespoons white wine
1 teaspoon low-sodium instant
  beef bouillon granules
¼ teaspoon salt
¼ teaspoon bouquet garni
  seasoning
1 bay leaf

6 servings

In 2-quart casserole, combine
all ingredients. Mix well. Cover.
Microwave at High for 5
minutes. Reduce power to 50%
(Medium). Microwave for 45 to
55 minutes longer, or until liquid
is absorbed and rice is tender.
Let stand, covered, for 5
minutes. Remove bay leaf.
Toss lightly.

◄ Double Cheese Linguine

1 pkg. (7 oz.) linguine
1 cup chopped zucchini
1 cup frozen peas
3 tablespoons butter or
   margarine
3 eggs
¼ cup half-and-half
¼ teaspoon salt
1 cup finely shredded
   mozzarella cheese
½ cup grated Parmesan
   cheese

4 servings

Prepare linguine as directed on package. Rinse and drain. Set aside. In 2-quart casserole, combine zucchini, peas and butter. Cover. Microwave at High for 4 to 6 minutes, or until vegetables are tender-crisp, stirring once. Set aside.

In small mixing bowl, blend eggs, half-and-half and salt. Add egg mixture, linguine, mozzarella and Parmesan cheeses to vegetable mixture. Toss to coat. Microwave, uncovered, at High for 6 to 8 minutes, or until mixture is set, tossing after every 2 minutes. Sprinkle with freshly ground pepper, if desired.

To reheat: Place one serving on plate. Cover with wax paper. Microwave at High for 2 to 3 minutes, or until heated through.

Cheese Grits

1½ cups hot water
½ cup uncooked
   quick-cooking grits
¼ teaspoon salt
⅓ cup half-and-half
2 eggs

2 cups shredded Cheddar
   cheese
½ cup seeded chopped
   tomato
2 tablespoons sliced
   green onion

4 to 6 servings

In 2-quart casserole, combine water, grits and salt. Microwave at High for 3½ to 5 minutes, or until desired consistency. In 2-cup measure, blend half-and-half and eggs. Add egg mixture and remaining ingredients to grits. Mix well. Microwave at 70% (Medium High) for 10 to 14 minutes, or until heated through and mixture thickens, stirring twice.

To reheat: Place one serving on plate. Cover with wax paper. Microwave at 70% (Medium High) for 1½ to 2½ minutes, or until heated through, stirring once.

Easy Beans & Rice

⅔ cup hot water
½ cup uncooked quick-cooking
   brown rice
½ cup chopped onion
 1 clove garlic, minced
 2 tablespoons butter or
   margarine
¼ teaspoon salt
 1 can (16 oz.) Great Northern
   beans, drained
 1 can (15 oz.) garbanzo
   beans, drained
 1 can (8 oz.) whole tomatoes,
   drained and cut up
½ cup tomato juice
 2 tablespoons molasses
½ teaspoon dry mustard
⅛ teaspoon pepper

4 to 6 servings

In 1½-quart casserole, combine water, rice, onion, garlic, butter and salt. Cover. Microwave at High for 5 minutes. Microwave at 50% (Medium) for 10 to 15 minutes, or until liquid is absorbed and rice is tender. Mix in remaining ingredients. Re-cover. Microwave at High for 10 to 15 minutes, or until flavors are blended, stirring once.

To reheat: Place one serving on plate. Cover with wax paper. Microwave at High for 2 to 3 minutes, or until heated through, stirring once.

Red Beans with Rice ▲

1 cup chopped onion
1 clove garlic, minced
1 tablespoon vegetable oil
1 can (15½ oz.) kidney beans,
   drained
1 can (15½ oz.) kidney beans,
   undrained

¼ cup chili sauce
¼ teaspoon cayenne
¼ teaspoon dried thyme leaves
⅛ teaspoon pepper
1 bay leaf
  Hot cooked rice

4 to 6 servings

In 1½-quart casserole, combine onion, garlic and oil. Cover. Microwave at High for 3 to 4 minutes, or until onion is tender-crisp. Stir in kidney beans, chili sauce, cayenne, thyme, pepper and bay leaf. Microwave, uncovered, at High for 12 to 15 minutes, or until mixture thickens slightly and flavors are blended, stirring twice. Remove bay leaf. Serve over hot cooked rice.

To reheat: Place one serving on plate. Microwave at High for 1½ to 2½ minutes, or until heated through, stirring once.

Rice Oregano

Sharon Allen
Wichita, Kansas

2 cups hot water
1 cup uncooked long grain white rice
¼ cup finely chopped onion
2 tablespoons butter or margarine

4 teaspoons instant chicken bouillon granules
½ teaspoon dried oregano leaves
⅛ teaspoon pepper

6 servings

In 2-quart casserole, combine all ingredients. Mix well. Cover. Microwave at High for 5 minutes. Reduce power to 50% (Medium). Microwave for 13 to 19 minutes, or until liquid is absorbed and rice is tender. Let stand, covered, for 5 minutes. Stir with fork.

Spanish Rice with Shrimp

Debra Kay Hampton
Aiea, Hawaii

1 can (16 oz.) stewed
   tomatoes
1½ cups water
 ⅔ cup uncooked long grain
   white rice
 ⅓ cup finely chopped onion
 ¼ cup chopped celery
 3 tablespoons tomato paste
 1 teaspoon salt

1 teaspoon sugar
1 teaspoon instant chicken
   bouillon granules
½ teaspoon dried oregano
   leaves
¼ to ½ teaspoon garlic
   powder
1 can (4¼ oz.) small shrimp,
   rinsed and drained

6 to 8 servings

In 2-quart casserole, combine all ingredients, except shrimp. Mix well. Cover. Microwave at High for 10 minutes. Reduce power to 50% (Medium). Microwave for 28 to 35 minutes, or until liquid is absorbed and rice is tender. Stir in shrimp. Let stand, covered, for 5 minutes.

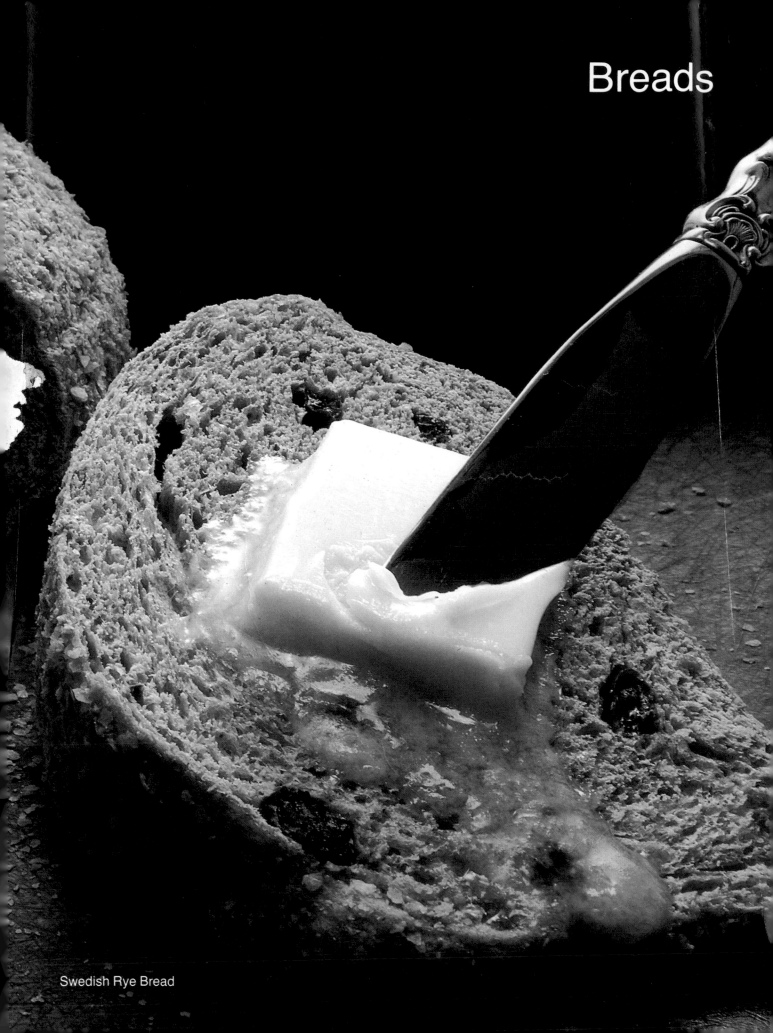

Breads

Swedish Rye Bread

Swedish Rye Bread

1 cup rye flour
⅓ cup dark or black strap molasses
¼ cup shortening
1 teaspoon salt
¾ cup boiling water
1 packet active dry yeast
¼ cup warm water
½ cup raisins, optional
2 to 2½ cups all-purpose flour
   Wheat germ or cornmeal
   Milk

Makes 1 loaf

Variation:

Swedish Rye Bread Loaf:
Punch down dough; let rest 10 minutes. Shape into loaf. Brush with milk, then coat with wheat germ. Place in well-greased 8 × 4-in. loaf dish. Let rise as directed. Place loaf dish on inverted saucer in microwave oven; microwave as directed.

To shape loaf: Roll out on lightly floured surface to 15 × 6-in. rectangle. Roll up tightly starting with 6-in. end. Seal ends and bottom.

How to Microwave Swedish Rye Bread

Combine rye flour, molasses, shortening, salt and boiling water in large mixing bowl. Cool to warm. Combine yeast and warm water. Stir yeast and raisins into rye flour mixture. Stir in all-purpose flour gradually to form a very stiff dough.

Knead on well-floured surface about 8 minutes, or until smooth. Place in greased bowl; cover. Let rise in warm place until light and doubled in size, 1 to 1½ hours. Punch down; shape into ball. Cover with bowl; let rest 10 minutes.

Sprinkle well-greased 10-in. pie plate or microwave-proof baking sheet with wheat germ. Shape dough into 15-in. strip. Brush with milk; coat well with additional wheat germ. Shape into ring in pie plate. Pinch ends together.

◀ Butter Crumb Rye Rolls

1 recipe Swedish Rye Bread
   Dough, opposite
½ cup dry bread crumbs
½ teaspoon each oregano, basil
   and marjoram
¼ cup butter or margarine,
   melted

Makes 24 rolls

Combine crumbs and herbs. Divide dough into 24 pieces. Shape into balls. Coat with butter, then crumbs. Place 9 rolls around edge and 3 rolls in center of each of 2 well-greased 10-in. pie plates or baking dishes. Cover; let rise in warm place until light and doubled in size, 1 to 1½ hours.

Microwave 1 plate at a time at 50% (Medium) 6 to 8 minutes, or until tops spring back when touched lightly, rotating ¼ turn every 1½ to 2 minutes. Let stand 5 minutes. Remove rolls; cool on wire rack.

Place greased glass, open-end-up, in center. Cover; let rise in warm place until light and doubled in size, 1 to 1½ hours.

Microwave at 50% (Medium) 6 minutes, rotating ¼ turn every 3 minutes. Increase power to High. Microwave 2½ to 6 minutes, rotating ¼ turn every 2 minutes.

Test by touching lightly in several places, top will spring back when done. Let stand 10 minutes. Remove bread; cool on wire rack.

◄ Chocolate-Banana Nut Bread

Linda Kay Jerew
Richwood, Ohio

¼ cup granola cereal
3 tablespoons milk
¼ cup butter or margarine
3 squares (1 oz. each)
    semisweet chocolate
½ cup dairy sour cream
½ cup mashed ripe banana
1 egg
1¼ cups all-purpose flour
½ cup sugar
⅓ cup chopped nuts
½ teaspoon baking powder
½ teaspoon baking soda
½ teaspoon salt

               1 loaf

Line bottom of 9 × 5-inch loaf dish with wax paper. Set aside. In small bowl, combine granola and milk. Set aside. In medium mixing bowl, combine butter and chocolate. Microwave at 50% (Medium) for 3 to 4 minutes, or until chocolate melts and can be stirred smooth, stirring once. Cool slightly. Add remaining ingredients and granola and milk mixture. Beat at high speed of electric mixer for 1 minute, scraping bowl occasionally. Spread batter evenly into prepared dish. Shield ends with 2-inch strips of foil, covering 1 inch of batter and molding remainder around handles of dish.

Place dish on saucer in microwave oven. Microwave at 50% (Medium) for 9 minutes, rotating dish after every 4½ minutes. Remove foil. Increase power to High. Microwave for 3 to 7 minutes, or until top appears dry and loaf starts to pull away from sides, rotating dish once. Let stand on counter for 5 to 10 minutes. Invert onto wire rack. Cool.

◄ Whole Grain Muffins

Kandace A. Beale
Kersey, Pennsylvania

A smaller recipe for a family of two.

1 large shredded wheat
    biscuit, crumbled
½ cup quick-cooking
    rolled oats
⅓ cup 100% bran cereal
⅔ cup milk
1 egg, slightly beaten
2 tablespoons vegetable oil
2 tablespoons honey
1 tablespoon packed brown
    sugar
⅓ cup all-purpose flour
½ teaspoon baking soda
⅛ teaspoon salt

Topping:
1 tablespoon granulated sugar
¼ teaspoon ground cinnamon

              6 muffins

Line six muffin cups with two paper baking cups in each. Set aside. In medium mixing bowl, combine shredded wheat, rolled oats and bran cereal. Pour milk over mixture. Mix well. Stir in egg, oil, honey and brown sugar. Mix well. In small bowl, combine flour, baking soda and salt. Add flour mixture to cereal mixture, stirring just until dry ingredients are moistened. Fill each paper-lined muffin cup half full. Microwave at High for 3½ to 5½ minutes, or until tops spring back when touched lightly, rotating cups twice. (Some moist spots will remain.) Remove from muffin cups to wire rack. In small bowl, mix topping ingredients. Sprinkle topping on warm muffins.

Cornbread Ring

Victoria E. Inscho
Etters, Pennsylvania

Based on grandmother's recipe.

Vegetable cooking spray
¼ cup cornflake crumbs
1 cup all-purpose flour
1 cup yellow cornmeal
½ cup sugar
1 teaspoon baking soda
¼ cup butter or margarine
1 egg, slightly beaten
1 cup buttermilk

8 servings

Spray 9-inch ring dish with vegetable cooking spray. Sprinkle with cornflake crumbs. Tilt dish to coat. Set aside. In medium mixing bowl, combine flour, cornmeal, sugar and baking soda. Set aside. Place butter in small bowl. Microwave at High for 1¼ to 1½ minutes, or until butter melts. Add butter, egg and buttermilk to cornmeal mixture. Stir just until dry ingredients are moistened. Pour batter evenly into prepared dish. Microwave at 50% (Medium) for 5 minutes, rotating dish after half the time. Increase power to High. Microwave for 4 to 7 minutes, or until top springs back when touched lightly, rotating dish after every 2 minutes. Let stand on counter for 5 minutes. Invert onto serving plate. Serve warm.

Apple-Wheat Coffee Cake

Carol A. Bodenhorn
Monongahela, Pennsylvania

1 cup whole wheat flour
¾ cup packed brown sugar
½ cup all-purpose flour
½ cup butter or margarine
¾ teaspoon baking powder
½ teaspoon salt
⅔ cup milk
1 egg, slightly beaten
1 medium apple, peeled, cored and thinly sliced
¼ cup chopped walnuts
1 teaspoon ground cinnamon

9 servings

In large mixing bowl, combine whole wheat flour, brown sugar and all-purpose flour. Set aside. Place butter on small plate. Microwave at 30% (Medium Low) for 15 seconds to 1 minute, or until softened, checking after every 15 seconds. Cut butter into flour mixture until coarse crumbs form. Reserve 1 cup flour and butter mixture. Set aside. Add baking powder, salt, milk and egg to remaining mixture. Stir just until dry ingredients are moistened. Spread batter evenly into 9-inch square baking dish. Arrange apple slices on batter. Add walnuts and cinnamon to reserved flour and butter mixture. Mix well. Sprinkle over apple slices. Shield corners of dish with foil.

Place dish on saucer in microwave oven. Microwave at 50% (Medium) for 9 minutes, rotating dish after every 3 minutes. Remove foil. Increase power to High. Microwave for 3 to 6 minutes, or until center springs back when touched lightly and no uncooked batter remains on the bottom, rotating once. Let stand on counter for 5 minutes. Serve warm.

Whole Wheat Beer Bread

William R. Buziak
Miami, Florida

2 tablespoons cornflake
   crumbs
1¾ cups whole wheat flour
1 cup all-purpose flour
¼ cup 100% bran cereal
¼ cup grated Parmesan
   cheese
2 teaspoons baking powder
1 teaspoon garlic salt
1 teaspoon dried oregano
   leaves
1 teaspoon dried parsley
   flakes
1 can (12 oz.) beer, room
   temperature
⅓ cup vegetable oil
1 egg, beaten
2 tablespoons honey

1 loaf

Grease 9 × 5-inch loaf dish. Sprinkle with cornflake crumbs. Tilt dish to coat. Set aside. In medium mixing bowl, combine whole wheat and all-purpose flours, cereal, cheese, baking powder, garlic salt, oregano and parsley. Set aside. In small mixing bowl, blend remaining ingredients. Pour into flour mixture. Beat well. Spread batter evenly into prepared dish. Shield ends with 2-inch strips of foil, covering 1 inch of batter and molding remainder around handles of dish.

Place dish on saucer in microwave oven. Microwave at 50% (Medium) for 8 minutes, rotating dish after every 4 minutes. Remove foil. Increase power to High. Microwave for 5 to 7 minutes, or until center springs back when touched lightly and top appears dry, rotating dish once. Let stand on counter for 5 minutes. Invert onto wire rack. Serve warm with butter and honey.

Raisin-Spice Loaf

This loaf has no eggs, milk or butter.

Mrs. Constance H. Reagor
Bella Vista, Arkansas

2 tablespoons graham cracker crumbs
1 cup raisins
1 cup packed brown sugar
1 cup hot strong coffee
⅓ cup vegetable shortening
1 teaspoon ground cinnamon
½ teaspoon ground cloves
¼ teaspoon ground nutmeg
¼ teaspoon vanilla
2 cups all-purpose flour
1 teaspoon baking soda
1 teaspoon baking powder
½ teaspoon salt

1 loaf

Grease 9 × 5-inch loaf dish. Sprinkle with graham cracker crumbs. Tilt dish to coat. Set aside. Grind raisins in meat grinder or place in food processor bowl. Process until raisins form a ball and clean sides of bowl. In 4-cup measure, combine raisins, brown sugar, coffee, shortening, cinnamon, cloves, nutmeg and vanilla. Mix well. Microwave at High for 3 to 4 minutes, or until shortening melts, stirring after every minute. Set aside. In medium mixing bowl, combine flour, baking soda, baking powder and salt. Add raisin mixture. Beat at medium speed of electric mixer for 1 minute, scraping bowl occasionally. Spread batter evenly into prepared dish. Shield ends with 2-inch strips of foil, covering 1 inch of batter and molding remainder around handles of dish.

Place dish on saucer in microwave oven. Microwave at 70% (Medium High) for 8 minutes, rotating dish after half the time. Remove foil. Microwave at 70% (Medium High) for 4 to 7 minutes, or until top appears dry and no uncooked batter remains on the bottom, rotating dish once. Let stand on counter for 5 to 10 minutes. Invert onto wire rack. Cool.

Baking & Desserts

Fresh Fruit-topped Cheesecake

◄ Triple Delicious Strawberry Pie

An award-winning recipe in a local contest combines several types of strawberry pies.

Theta Nicholson
Bardwell, Kentucky

1 baked and cooled 9-inch pastry shell, below
⅓ cup chopped pecans
1 pkg. (8 oz.) cream cheese
2 cups prepared whipped topping
1 cup powdered sugar
¾ cup granulated sugar
2 tablespoons cornstarch
⅛ teaspoon salt
¾ cup water

2 tablespoons dry strawberry-flavored gelatin
1 teaspoon vanilla
2 drops red food coloring, optional
1 pint strawberries, hulled and sliced
Whole strawberries (optional)
Whipped topping (optional)

One 9-inch pie

Prepare pastry shell as directed. Sprinkle pecans over bottom of cooled pastry shell. Set aside. Place cream cheese in small mixing bowl. Microwave at 50% (Medium) for 1 to 1½ minutes, or until softened. Blend in whipped topping and powdered sugar. Spread over pecans in pastry shell. Chill for 1 hour.

In 4-cup measure, combine granulated sugar, cornstarch and salt. Blend in water. Microwave at High for 3½ to 4½ minutes, or until mixture is thickened and translucent, stirring after every minute. Stir in gelatin, vanilla and food coloring. Cover with plastic wrap. Chill for 2 hours. Stir in sliced strawberries. Spread over cream cheese mixture. Chill for 2 hours, or until set. Garnish with whole strawberries and whipped topping.

Harvest Gold Pie

Rev. Margaret Strodtz
Maynard, Iowa

1 baked and cooled 9-inch pastry shell, below
1 pkg. (3 oz.) egg custard mix
2 cups half-and-half
1 cup canned pumpkin
1 teaspoon pumpkin pie spice
Whipped topping (optional)

One 9-inch pie

Prepare pastry shell as directed. Set aside. Place custard mix in 2-quart measure. Blend in half-and-half. Microwave at High for 6½ to 10 minutes, or until mixture boils, stirring after every 2 minutes. Cool for 15 minutes, stirring occasionally. In small mixing bowl, combine pumpkin and pumpkin pie spice. Mix well. Blend pumpkin mixture into custard mixture. Pour filling into prepared pastry shell. Chill for at least 3 hours, or until set. Garnish with whipped topping.

One-Crust Pastry Shell

1 cup all-purpose flour
½ teaspoon salt
⅓ cup shortening
2 tablespoons butter or margarine, cut up
2 to 4 tablespoons cold water

One 9-inch pastry shell

In medium mixing bowl, combine flour and salt. Cut in shortening and butter to form coarse crumbs. Sprinkle with water, 1 tablespoon at a time, mixing with fork until particles are moistened and cling together. Form dough into a ball. Roll out on lightly floured board at least 2 inches larger than inverted 9-inch pie plate. Ease into plate. Trim and flute edge. Prick thoroughly. Microwave at High for 5 to 7 minutes, or until pastry appears dry and opaque, rotating plate after every 2 minutes. Cool.

Or, preheat conventional oven to 400°F. Bake until light golden brown, 10 to 12 minutes.

Company Coconut Cream Pie

Mrs. Alyce D. Peiffer
York, Pennsylvania

An elegant pie for dinner guests.

Pastry:
1½ cups all-purpose flour
½ teaspoon salt
½ cup shortening
4 to 5 tablespoons cold water

Filling:
¾ cup sugar
6 tablespoons cornstarch
½ teaspoon salt
3½ cups milk
4 egg yolks, beaten
4½ teaspoons butter or
    margarine
1½ teaspoons vanilla
2 cups flaked coconut

Meringue:
4 egg whites
½ teaspoon cream of tartar
5 tablespoons sugar
¾ teaspoon vanilla

One 10-inch pie

In medium mixing bowl, combine flour and salt. Cut in shortening to form coarse crumbs. Sprinkle with water, 1 tablespoon at a time, mixing with fork until particles are moistened and cling together. Form dough into a ball. Roll out on lightly floured board at least 2 inches larger than inverted 10-inch deep dish pie plate. Ease into plate. Trim and flute edge. Prick thoroughly. Microwave at High for 5 to 8 minutes, or until pastry appears dry and opaque, rotating plate after every 2 minutes. Cool. Set aside.

In 2-quart measure, combine sugar, cornstarch and salt. Blend in milk. Microwave at High for 9 to 14 minutes, or until mixture comes to a rolling boil, stirring 3 times with whisk. Microwave at High for 1 minute. Blend small amount of hot mixture into egg yolks. Add back to hot mixture, stirring constantly. Reduce power to 70% (Medium High). Microwave for 1½ to 2 minutes, or until mixture thickens, stirring once or twice with whisk. Blend in butter and vanilla. Stir in coconut. Pour filling into cooled pastry shell.

Preheat conventional oven to 400°F. In large mixing bowl, combine egg whites and cream of tartar. Beat until foamy. Gradually add sugar, beating until stiff peaks form. Blend in vanilla. Spread meringue over hot filling, sealing to edge of pastry. Bake until lightly browned, 8 to 10 minutes. Cool. Chill for at least 6 hours before serving.

Red Apple Crisp Pie ▶

Linda L. Ilg
Worland, Wyoming

1 baked and cooled 9-inch
   pastry shell, page 235

Filling:
4 cups unpeeled grated red
   cooking apples
¾ cup granulated sugar
2 tablespoons all-purpose flour
¼ teaspoon ground cinnamon
⅛ teaspoon salt
1 tablespoon lemon juice

Topping:
⅓ cup packed brown sugar
⅓ cup all-purpose flour
⅛ teaspoon salt
3 tablespoons butter or
   margarine, cut up

One 9-inch pie

Prepare pastry shell as directed. Set aside. In medium mixing bowl, combine all filling ingredients. Mix well. Spoon filling into prepared pastry shell. Smooth top of filling.

Place pie plate on saucer in microwave oven. Microwave at 70% (Medium High) for 20 to 25 minutes, or until center is hot, rotating plate twice. In small mixing bowl, combine brown sugar, flour and salt. Cut in butter to form fine crumbs. Sprinkle topping evenly over hot pie. Place under preheated broiler 2 to 3 inches from heat, until golden brown, about 2 minutes. Serve with ice cream.

Chocolate S'more Pie

Susanne Adams
Livingston, Montana

Graham Cracker Crust:
5 tablespoons butter or
   margarine
1⅓ cups graham cracker
   crumbs
2 tablespoons sugar

Filling:
1 bar (8 oz.) milk chocolate
   with almonds, broken into
   small pieces

16 large marshmallows
¼ cup milk
2½ cups prepared whipped
   topping
   Whipped topping (optional)
   Chocolate curls (optional)

One 9-inch pie

Place butter in 9-inch pie plate. Microwave at High for 1¼ to 1½ minutes, or until butter melts. Stir in graham cracker crumbs and sugar. Mix well. Press mixture firmly against bottom and sides of pie plate. Microwave at High for 1½ to 2 minutes, or until set, rotating plate after 1 minute. Cool. Set aside.

Place chocolate pieces in 2-quart measure. Add marshmallows and milk. Microwave at High for 2 to 3½ minutes, or until chocolate and marshmallows melt, stirring after every minute. Cover. Chill for 45 minutes. Fold whipped topping into chocolate mixture. Pour filling into prepared crust. Chill for at least 4 hours, or until set. Garnish with whipped topping and chocolate curls.

Creamy Orange Chiffon Pie

Crust:

- ¼ cup plus 1 tablespoon butter or margarine
- 2 teaspoons grated orange peel
- 1⅓ cups finely crushed crisp rice cereal crumbs
- 2 tablespoons sugar

Filling:

- 4 eggs, separated
- ⅔ cup orange juice
- ¾ cup plus 2 tablespoons sugar, divided
- 1 envelope (.25 oz.) unflavored gelatin
- 2 teaspoons grated orange peel
- ⅓ cup half-and-half

6 to 8 servings

Place butter and 2 teaspoons orange peel in 9-inch pie plate. Microwave at High for 1½ to 1¾ minutes, or until butter melts. Stir in remaining crust ingredients. Press mixture firmly against sides and bottom of pie plate. (Pressing with a custard cup works well.) Microwave at High for 1½ to 2 minutes, or until crust is set, rotating plate once. Set aside.

Place 4 egg yolks in medium mixing bowl. Reserve egg whites in large mixing bowl. To egg yolks, add orange juice, ½ cup sugar, the gelatin and orange peel. Mix well. Blend in half-and-half. Microwave at 50% (Medium) for 8 to 14 minutes, or until mixture thickens slightly, stirring with whisk 3 or 4 times. Place bowl in larger bowl containing 1 to 2 inches ice water. Chill both bowls for about 20 minutes, or until mixture is very cold, but not set.

Using electric mixer, beat reserved egg whites until foamy. Gradually add remaining ¼ cup plus 2 tablespoons sugar while continuing to beat until mixture forms stiff peaks. Fold orange mixture into egg white mixture. Pour evenly into crust. Chill for at least 3 hours, or until set. Garnish pie with orange slices or orange zest, if desired.

Quick & Easy Ice Cream Pie

1 quart ice cream (cardboard container)
½ cup chopped nuts
¼ cup liqueur (any complementary flavor)
1 6 oz. (8-inch) ready-to-use graham cracker pie crust

One pie

Open ice cream carton and place directly in microwave oven. Microwave at 50% (Medium) for 30 seconds to 1 minute, or until ice cream softens. Place ice cream in medium mixing bowl. Stir in nuts and liqueur. Spoon filling into graham cracker crust. Freeze for at least 2 hours, or until pie is firm. Garnish with ice cream topping, fresh fruit or whipped topping, if desired.

Pink Piña Colada Pie ▲

2 cups flaked coconut
¼ cup butter or margarine
2 pkgs. (8 oz. each) cream cheese
½ cup cream of coconut
2 egg yolks
1 can (8 oz.) crushed pineapple, drained
3 or 4 drops red food coloring

6 to 8 servings

Spread coconut evenly in bottom of 9-inch pie plate. Microwave at High for 4½ to 6 minutes, or until golden brown, tossing with fork after every minute. Set aside.

In 1-cup measure, microwave butter at High for 1¼ to 1½ minutes, or until melted. Drizzle butter over coconut. Toss to coat. Press coconut mixture against sides and bottom of pie plate. Microwave crust at High for 1 minute. Set aside.

In medium mixing bowl, microwave cream cheese at 50% (Medium) for 3½ to 4½ minutes, or until softened, stirring once. Add remaining ingredients. Beat at medium speed of electric mixer until mixture is smooth. Pour mixture into prepared crust. Microwave at 50% (Medium) for 10 to 12 minutes, or until pie is almost set in center, rotating plate 3 or 4 times. Refrigerate pie for 8 hours or overnight before serving. Garnish with maraschino cherries, if desired.

Fluffy Butter Pecan Cooler ▶

Chris Anderson
Negaunee, Michigan

Crust:

 1 cup all-purpose flour
 ⅓ cup chopped pecans
 3 tablespoons granulated
    sugar
 ½ cup butter or margarine,
    cut into ½-inch cubes

Filling:

 1 pkg. (3 oz.) cream cheese
2½ cups prepared whipped
    topping, divided
 ½ cup powdered sugar
 1 pkg. (3½ oz.) instant butter
    pecan pudding and pie
    filling
1½ cups milk
 ⅓ cup chopped pecans

9 servings

How to Microwave Fluffy Butter Pecan Cooler

Combine flour, pecans and sugar in medium mixing bowl. Add butter. Cut in butter at low speed of electric mixer to form coarse crumbs.

Press mixture firmly against bottom of 9-inch square baking dish. Place dish on saucer in microwave oven. Microwave at 70% (Medium High) for 6 to 8 minutes, or until crust appears dry and firm, rotating dish once. Cool. Set aside.

Place cream cheese in small mixing bowl. Microwave at 50% (Medium) for 30 to 45 seconds, or until softened. Blend in ½ cup whipped topping and powdered sugar. Mix well. Spread over cooled crust.

Fresh Fruit-topped Cheesecake

Penny Dunbar
Green Bay, Wisconsin

Crust:
- 5 tablespoons butter or margarine
- 1⅓ cups graham cracker crumbs
- 2 tablespoons sugar

Filling:
- 1 pkg. (8 oz.) cream cheese
- ½ cup sugar
- 1 egg, slightly beaten
- 1 tablespoon milk
- 1 teaspoon vanilla

Topping:
- 2 cups fresh fruit (sliced kiwi fruit, strawberries, peaches, dark sweet cherries or blueberries)

6 to 8 servings

Place butter in 9-inch pie plate. Microwave at High for 1¼ to 1½ minutes, or until butter melts. Stir in graham cracker crumbs and sugar. Mix well. Press mixture firmly against bottom and sides of pie plate. Microwave at High for 1½ to 2 minutes, or until set, rotating plate after 1 minute. Cool. Set aside.

Place cream cheese in 2-quart measure. Microwave at 50% (Medium) for 1½ to 3 minutes, or until softened. Add remaining filling ingredients. Beat at medium speed of electric mixer until well blended. Microwave at High for 2 to 3 minutes, or until mixture is very hot and starts to set, beating once with whisk. Pour filling into prepared crust.

Place pie plate on saucer in microwave oven. Microwave at 50% (Medium) for 4 to 9 minutes, or until center is almost set. Filling will become firm as it cools. Cool for 1 hour. Chill for at least 6 hours. Arrange or spoon topping over cheesecake.

Combine pudding mix and milk in medium mixing bowl. Beat at low speed for 1 to 2 minutes until blended. Pour over cream cheese layer.

Spread remaining 2 cups whipped topping over pudding. Sprinkle with pecans. Cover with plastic wrap. Chill for at least 3 hours.

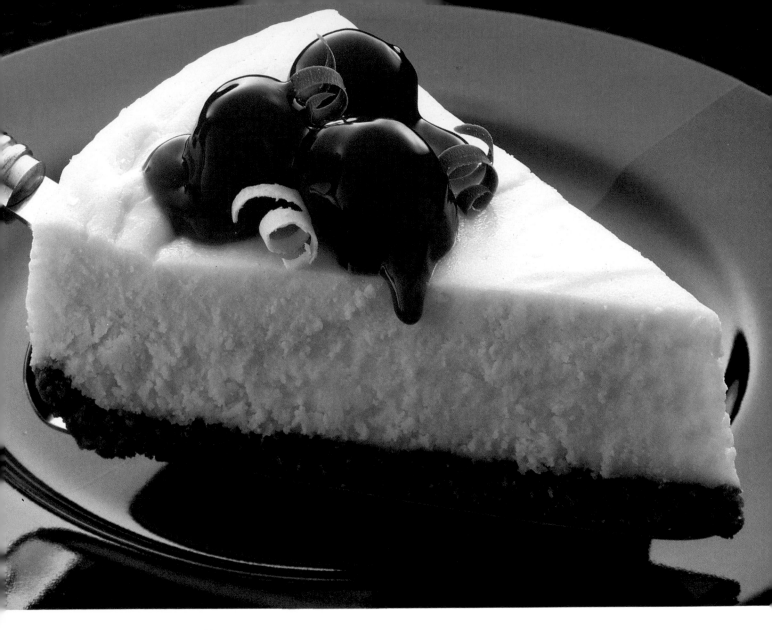

Chocolate Cheese Tarts

1 tablespoon butter or
    margarine
1 tablespoon sugar
½ cup graham cracker crumbs
2 squares (1 oz. each)
    semisweet chocolate
1 pkg. (3 oz.) cream cheese,
    softened (page 282)
2 eggs
2 tablespoons lemon juice
1 can (14 oz.) sweetened
    condensed milk

Toppings:
    Cherry pie filling
    Whipped cream
    Chocolate curls

8 servings

Place 2 paper liners in each of eight 6-oz. custard cups. Set aside. In small bowl, microwave butter at High for 45 seconds to 1 minute, or until melted. Stir in sugar and cracker crumbs. Mix well. Place 1 tablespoon crumb mixture in bottom of each lined custard cup, pressing lightly. Set aside.

In small bowl, microwave chocolate at 50% (Medium) for 2½ to 3½ minutes, or until chocolate is glossy and can be stirred smooth, stirring once or twice. In medium mixing bowl, combine chocolate and softened cream cheese. Mix well. Add eggs, lemon juice and condensed milk. Beat at medium speed of electric mixer until mixture is smooth, scraping bowl frequently.

Spoon chocolate mixture evenly into paper liners. Arrange 4 tarts in microwave oven. Microwave at 50% (Medium) for 4 to 6 minutes, or until tarts are firm and just begin to puff. Repeat with remaining tarts. Chill for 3 to 4 hours. Top tarts with one or more toppings before serving.

How to Microwave White Chocolate Cheesecake

White Chocolate Cheesecake

Crust:

⅓ cup butter or margarine
1⅓ cups finely crushed chocolate-covered graham cookie crumbs (about 20 cookies)

Filling:

1 pkg. (8 oz.) cream cheese, softened (page 282)
1⅓ cups ricotta cheese
3 eggs
2 tablespoons cornstarch
2 tablespoons cherry liqueur
½ lb. white chocolate or white candy coating, melted (page 262)

8 to 10 servings

Line 9-inch round cake dish with two 4 × 15-inch strips of parchment paper, crisscrossing strips at bottom. (Ends of paper should hang over edge of dish.)

Place butter in small mixing bowl. Microwave at High for 1½ to 1¾ minutes, or until butter melts. Add cookie crumbs, stirring until moistened. Press crumb mixture onto bottom of prepared cake dish. Set aside.

Combine cream cheese, ricotta, eggs, cornstarch and liqueur in large mixing bowl. With electric mixer, beat until mixture is well blended. Mix in white chocolate.

Pour batter into prepared dish. Microwave at 50% (Medium) for 15 to 20 minutes, or until cheesecake is almost set in center, rotating dish 2 or 3 times. (Mixture firms as it cools.) Let stand for 15 minutes. Refrigerate for at least 8 hours, or overnight.

Lift cheesecake from pan using ends of parchment paper. Peel away parchment and place cheesecake on serving plate. Decorate top with chocolate curls, cherry pie filling or fresh cherries, if desired.

243

Chocolate-Amaretto Cheesecake

Shirley J. Portouw
Steamboat Springs, Colorado

Crust:
- ¼ cup butter or margarine
- 1 cup graham cracker crumbs
- 2 tablespoons granulated sugar

Filling:
- 2 squares (1 oz. each) semisweet chocolate
- 2 pkgs. (8 oz. each) cream cheese
- ⅔ cup granulated sugar
- 4 eggs, slightly beaten
- 3 tablespoons amaretto liqueur
- 1 teaspoon vanilla
- ½ teaspoon almond extract

Topping:
- 2 tablespoons powdered sugar
- 1 tablespoon cocoa
- ½ cup dairy sour cream
- 1 teaspoon amaretto liqueur

8 to 10 servings

How to Microwave Chocolate-Amaretto Cheesecake

Place butter in 9-inch round baking dish. Microwave at High for 1¼ to 1½ minutes, or until butter melts. Stir in graham cracker crumbs and sugar. Mix well.

Press mixture firmly against bottom of dish. Microwave at High for 1½ to 2 minutes, or until set, rotating dish once. Set aside.

Place chocolate in custard cup. Microwave at 50% (Medium) for 3½ to 5 minutes, or until chocolate melts and can be stirred smooth, stirring once. Set aside. Place cream cheese in 2-quart measure. Microwave at 50% (Medium) for 2¼ to 4 minutes, or until softened. Blend in chocolate.

Add remaining filling ingredients. Beat at medium speed of electric mixer until well blended. Microwave at High for 4 to 5 minutes, or until mixture is very hot and starts to set, beating with whisk after every 2 minutes. Pour filling into prepared crust.

Place dish on saucer in microwave oven. Microwave at 50% (Medium) for 7 to 15 minutes, or until center is almost set, rotating dish twice. Filling will become firm as it cools. Cool for 1 hour.

Combine powdered sugar and cocoa in small mixing bowl. Blend in sour cream and amaretto until smooth. Spread topping over cheesecake. Chill for at least 8 hours, or overnight. Garnish with chocolate curls, if desired.

Carrot Almond Torte ▲

Cake:

½ cup granulated sugar
¼ cup packed brown sugar
3 tablespoons vegetable oil
3 eggs, separated
1 cup finely shredded carrot
2 tablespoons lemon juice
1 teaspoon grated lemon peel
1 cup ground almonds
½ cup all-purpose flour
⅓ cup unseasoned dry
   bread crumbs
¾ teaspoon baking powder
¾ teaspoon pumpkin pie spice
¼ teaspoon salt

Glaze:

½ cup peach preserves
1 teaspoon lemon juice

Topping:

½ cup whipping cream
1 tablespoon powdered sugar
Sliced almonds (optional)

8 servings

How to Microwave Carrot Almond Torte

Line bottom of 9-inch round cake dish with wax paper and set aside. In medium mixing bowl, combine sugars, oil and egg yolks. Reserve egg whites. With electric mixer, beat until mixture is light and fluffy. Add remaining cake ingredients. Beat until well mixed. Set aside.

Beat egg whites until stiff peaks form using clean beaters. Fold egg whites into torte mixture. Pour batter into prepared dish. Place on saucer in microwave oven. Microwave at 50% (Medium) for 6 minutes. Rotate dish half turn.

Chocolate Rum Cake

1 pkg. (9 oz.) devil's food cake mix

Glaze:
½ cup sugar
¼ cup butter or margarine
⅓ cup dark rum

Frosting:
1⅓ cups whipping cream
2 tablespoons sugar
2 tablespoons dark rum (optional)

8 servings

Line bottom of 9-inch square baking dish with wax paper and set aside. Prepare cake mix as directed on package. Pour batter into prepared baking dish. Place dish on saucer in microwave oven. Microwave at 50% (Medium) for 6 minutes. Rotate dish half turn. Microwave at High for 2 to 5 minutes longer, or until top appears dry and center springs back when touched lightly, rotating dish once or twice. Let cake stand on counter for 10 minutes. Pierce cake thoroughly with thin knife and set aside.

In 2-cup measure, combine all glaze ingredients. Microwave at 50% (Medium) for 3 to 4 minutes, or until mixture boils, stirring once or twice. Pour glaze slowly over hot cake. Chill cake for at least 3 hours, or overnight.

Loosen edges and invert cake onto wire rack. Peel off wax paper. Set cake aside. In medium mixing bowl, beat whipping cream until thickened. Gradually add sugar while continuing to beat until mixture is stiff. Fold in rum. Set frosting aside.

Cut cake in half. Place one half on serving plate and top evenly with about 1 cup frosting. Top with remaining cake half. Spread remaining frosting evenly over top and sides. Decorate cake with chocolate shavings and maraschino cherries, if desired. Serve immediately.

Microwave at High for 3 to 6 minutes longer, or until top appears dry and no uncooked batter remains on bottom, rotating dish twice. Let cake stand on counter for 5 minutes. Invert cake onto wire rack. Cool slightly. Place on serving plate.

Combine all glaze ingredients in 1-cup measure. Microwave at High for 1 to 2 minutes, or until mixture is hot and bubbly, stirring once. Spread glaze on top and sides of cake. Cool cake completely.

Beat whipping cream in small mixing bowl until thickened. Gradually add powdered sugar, while continuing to beat until mixture is stiff. Pipe frosting around edge of cake. Decorate top of cake with almonds.

Chocolate Chip Zucchini Cake

Cindy Hosfelt
Shippensburg, Pennsylvania

Try peanut butter chips instead of chocolate chips for a new taste.

¼ cup butter or margarine
1 cup sugar
¼ cup vegetable oil
1 cup all-purpose flour
2 tablespoons cocoa
½ teaspoon baking soda
¼ teaspoon baking powder
¼ teaspoon ground cinnamon
1 cup shredded zucchini
¼ cup buttermilk
1 egg
½ teaspoon vanilla
6 tablespoons semisweet
   chocolate chips

Frosting:
2 tablespoons all-purpose flour
½ cup milk
2 tablespoons butter or
   margarine
½ cup sugar
Dash salt
¼ cup vegetable shortening
½ teaspoon vanilla

9 to 12 servings

Place butter in medium mixing bowl. Microwave at 30% (Medium Low) for 15 to 45 seconds, or until softened, checking after every 15 seconds. Add sugar and oil. Beat at medium speed of electric mixer until light and fluffy. Add remaining cake ingredients, except chocolate chips. Beat at low speed until moistened. Beat at medium speed for 1 minute, scraping bowl occasionally. Stir in chocolate chips. Spread batter into 9-inch square baking dish. Shield corners of dish with triangles of foil.

Place dish on saucer in microwave oven. Microwave at 50% (Medium) for 6 minutes. Rotate dish half turn. Remove foil. Increase power to High. Microwave for 5 to 10 minutes, or until top appears dry and center springs back when touched lightly, rotating dish twice. Let stand on counter. Cool completely.

Place flour in medium mixing bowl. Blend in milk. Microwave at High for 2 to 2½ minutes, or until mixture becomes very thick and paste-like, stirring with whisk after every minute. Chill for 45 minutes. Place butter in small bowl. Microwave at 30% (Medium Low) for 15 to 30 seconds, or until softened. Add butter and remaining frosting ingredients to flour mixture. Beat at high speed for 3 minutes, or until light and fluffy. Spread frosting over top of cooled cake.

Chocolate Brownie Cake

Mrs. Patricia M. Birdsall
Kenosha, Wisconsin

2 tablespoons cocoa
½ cup water
¼ cup vegetable oil
1 cup all-purpose flour
1 cup granulated sugar
½ teaspoon salt
½ teaspoon baking soda
½ teaspoon ground cinnamon
¼ cup buttermilk
1 egg
½ teaspoon vanilla

Frosting:
¼ cup butter or margarine
3 tablespoons milk
2 tablespoons cocoa
⅛ teaspoon salt
1⅔ cups powdered sugar
½ cup chopped nuts

9 to 12 servings

Place cocoa in 2-cup measure. Gradually blend in water. Stir in oil. Microwave at High for 2½ to 3 minutes, or until mixture boils. Set aside. In medium mixing bowl, combine flour, sugar, salt, baking soda and cinnamon. Add hot cocoa mixture. Beat at low speed of electric mixer until moistened. Add buttermilk, egg and vanilla. Beat at medium speed for 2 minutes, scraping bowl occasionally. Pour batter into 9-inch square baking dish. Shield corners of dish with triangles of foil.

Place dish on saucer in microwave oven. Microwave at 70% (Medium High) for 7 minutes, rotating dish once. Remove foil. Microwave at 70% (Medium High) for 3 to 9 minutes, or until top appears dry and center springs back when touched lightly, rotating dish once or twice. Let stand on counter for 10 minutes.

In 4-cup measure, combine butter, milk, cocoa and salt. Microwave at High for 2½ to 3 minutes, or until mixture boils, stirring after every minute. Beat in powdered sugar until smooth. Stir in nuts. Spread frosting over top of hot cake. Serve warm or cool.

Caramel Apple Torte ▶

  2 cups all-purpose flour
  2 tablespoons sugar
1½ teaspoons ground cinnamon
 ½ teaspoon salt
 ½ cup shortening
 ¼ cup butter or margarine,
      cut up
  3 to 6 tablespoons cold water
20 caramels
  1 tablespoon milk
  1 can (20 oz.) apple pie filling

6 servings

TIP: For Pastry Circle: Roll dough into circle slightly larger than 7 inches. Use a 7-inch plate as a guide to cut perfect pastry circle.

How to Microwave Caramel Apple Torte

Combine flour, sugar, cinnamon and salt in large mixing bowl. Cut in shortening and butter until particles are size of small peas. Sprinkle water over mixture one tablespoon at a time, mixing with fork, just until particles are moistened enough to cling together. Form mixture into ball. Flatten slightly. Wrap ball in plastic wrap and chill for 15 minutes.

Caribbean Cobbler ▲

 ½ pkg. (17¼ oz.) frozen puff
      pastry sheets
  3 lbs. papayas (about 3 large)
 ½ cup packed brown sugar
  2 tablespoons all-purpose flour

 ½ teaspoon ground cinnamon
  2 tablespoons butter or
      margarine, cut up
  2 tablespoons lime juice
 ½ teaspoon grated lime peel

4 to 6 servings

Heat conventional oven to 400°F. Unfold one pastry sheet on a lightly floured surface. Using cover from 2-quart round casserole as guide, cut circle from pastry sheet. Place circle on baking sheet. Score pastry sheet with decorative designs, if desired. Bake for 10 to 15 minutes, or until puffed and golden brown. Remove pastry from oven and set aside.

Peel each papaya and cut in half lengthwise. Remove seeds. Cut papaya into 1-inch chunks. Set aside. In a 2-quart casserole, combine brown sugar, flour and cinnamon. Mix well. Add papaya, butter, lime juice and lime peel. Stir gently to combine. Cover, and microwave at High for 10 to 16 minutes, or until papaya is very tender, stirring once or twice. Top hot papaya mixture with baked pastry. Serve immediately.

Divide dough into 3 equal portions. On lightly floured surface, roll each portion and cut into 7-inch circle. Transfer each pastry circle to sheet of wax paper. Prick circles generously with fork. Microwave one at a time on wax paper at High for 3 to 4 minutes, or until firm and dry, rotating after every minute.

Cool pastry on wire rack. Remove wax paper. Set pastry aside. Repeat with remaining pastry circles. In medium mixing bowl, combine caramels and milk. Microwave at High for 2 to 2½ minutes, or until caramels are melted and can be stirred smooth, stirring twice.

Place one pastry circle on plate. Top with 2 tablespoons melted caramel, spreading to within ½ inch of edge. Top with one-third of apple pie filling and another pastry circle. Repeat sequence twice. Cut torte into wedges to serve.

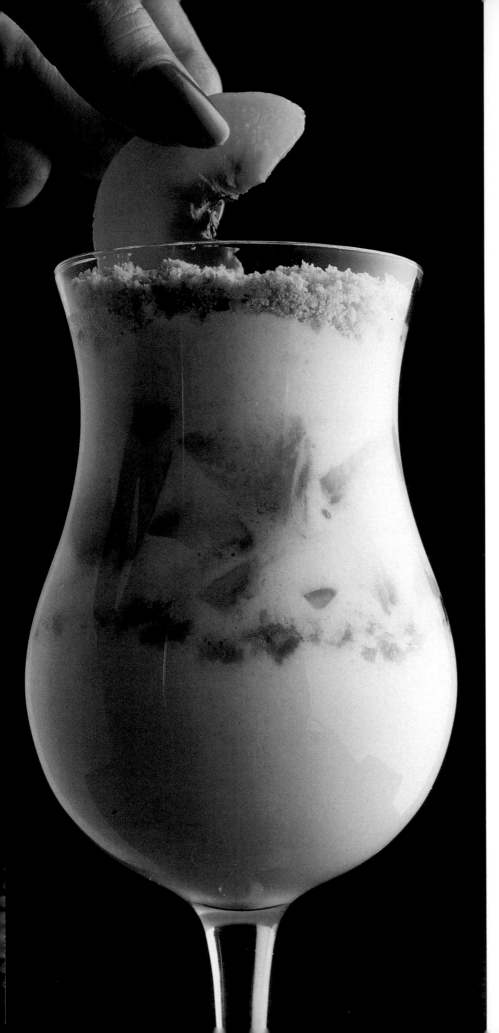

Peachy Orange Parfait

½ cup milk
⅓ cup sugar
2 egg yolks
½ teaspoon cornstarch
1 cup orange juice
1 teaspoon unflavored gelatin
1 cup prepared whipped topping
2 cups frozen sliced peaches
1 cup coarsely crushed vanilla
  wafer crumbs

4 servings

In 1-cup measure, microwave milk at High for 1¼ to 1½ minutes, or until scalded. Set aside. In medium mixing bowl, combine sugar, egg yolks and cornstarch. Mix well. Gradually blend hot milk into sugar mixture. Microwave at 50% (Medium) for 4 to 6 minutes, or until custard thickens enough to coat back of metal spoon, stirring after every minute. Chill.

Place orange juice in 2-cup measure. Sprinkle gelatin over orange juice. Let stand for 5 minutes to soften. Microwave at High for 1 to 1½ minutes, or until mixture is hot and gelatin is dissolved, stirring once. Chill for about 1½ hours, or until soft-set. Blend gelatin into custard. Fold in whipped topping.

In small mixing bowl, microwave frozen peaches at 50% (Medium) for 3 to 5 minutes, or until defrosted, stirring once. Chop peaches and set aside. In each of 4 individual parfait glasses or sherbet dishes, layer ingredients in the following order: orange juice mixture, wafer crumbs, peaches, orange juice mixture and wafer crumbs. Chill parfaits for about 2 hours, or until orange layers are firm.

Lemon Custard Pudding ▶

½ cup sugar
2 tablespoons cornstarch
1 tablespoon all-purpose flour
1 teaspoon grated lemon peel
¼ teaspoon salt
1 cup milk
1 cup half-and-half
2 egg yolks, beaten
3 tablespoons lemon juice

4 servings

In medium mixing bowl, combine sugar, cornstarch, flour, lemon peel and salt. Mix well. Blend in milk and half-and-half. Microwave at 70% (Medium High) for 11 to 14 minutes, or until mixture thickens, stirring with whisk 3 or 4 times. Gradually stir small amount of hot milk mixture into egg yolks. Blend egg yolks back into hot mixture. Microwave at 50% (Medium) for 1 to 2 minutes longer, or until custard thickens. Blend in lemon juice.

Place sheet of plastic wrap directly on surface of custard to prevent skin from forming. Chill for at least 3 hours. Garnish with whipped cream or fresh, sliced fruit, if desired.

TIP: Serve pudding over individual shortcakes or a split ladyfinger.

Bourbon Pecan Cream

1 cup sugar, divided
1 tablespoon plus 1½ teaspoons cornstarch
⅛ teaspoon salt
1½ cups half-and-half
4 egg yolks, beaten
3 tablespoons bourbon

2 pkgs. (3 oz. each) cream cheese
¼ cup butter or margarine, softened (page 280)
2 cups finely chopped pecans
Whipped cream
Finely chopped pecans

4 to 6 servings

In medium mixing bowl, mix ½ cup sugar, the cornstarch and salt. Blend in half-and-half. Microwave at High for 5 to 10 minutes, or until mixture is very thick, stirring 2 or 3 times. Gradually stir small amount of hot mixture into egg yolks. Blend egg yolks back into hot mixture. Microwave at High for 1 to 2 minutes longer, or until mixture thickens, stirring with whisk every 30 seconds. Blend in bourbon. Place sheet of plastic wrap directly on surface to prevent skin from forming. Chill for 2 to 3 hours, or until mixture is cool.*

In medium mixing bowl, microwave cream cheese at 50% (Medium) for 1 to 1½ minutes, or until softened. Set aside. Add softened butter and remaining sugar to cream cheese. Using electric mixer, beat until blended. Stir in pecans. Fold in custard mixture. Spoon into dessert dishes. Top with whipped cream, and sprinkle with pecans.

*For faster cooling, place mixing bowl in larger dish containing 1 to 2 inches ice water. Chill both bowls until custard cools.

Caramel Fruit Platter

1 can (8 oz.) pineapple chunks
1 medium apple, cut into chunks
1 banana, cut into chunks
1 pear, cut into chunks
1 dozen strawberries
1 pkg. (14 oz.) caramels
¼ cup half-and-half

6 servings

Combine fruit in medium bowl. Toss to coat with pineapple juice. Drain. Set aside. Arrange caramels in even layer in center of 12-inch round platter. Pour half-and-half over caramels. Microwave at High for 3½ to 5 minutes, or until caramels melt and mixture can be stirred smooth, stirring 3 or 4 times using a fork.

Arrange fruit around outside edges of platter. Serve fruit platter warm with wooden picks for dipping fruit in caramel.

Cherry Cheese Roll

1 cup ricotta cheese
1 egg
2 tablespoons powdered sugar
¼ teaspoon almond extract
¼ cup sliced almonds
1 round sheet lefse (about
   12-inch)
1 cup cherry pie filling
   Sliced almonds (optional)

4 servings

In small mixing bowl, blend ricotta cheese, egg, powdered sugar and almond extract. Stir in almonds. Spread mixture evenly down center of lefse.

Fold in opposite sides of lefse to enclose filling. Place roll on 12-inch platter.

Microwave at 50% (Medium) for 7 to 11 minutes, or until center of roll is hot, rotating platter once or twice. Top with pie filling. Microwave at High for 1 to 2½ minutes, or until pie filling is hot. Top cheese roll with sliced almonds.

Strawberry-Rhubarb Crisp

Barbara F. Aslakson
St. Louis Park, Minnesota

Topping:

1 cup quick-cooking rolled
  oats
½ cup all-purpose flour
½ cup packed brown sugar
⅓ cup granulated sugar
1 teaspoon ground cinnamon
½ teaspoon ground nutmeg
6 tablespoons butter or
  margarine, cut into ½-inch
  cubes

4 cups cut-up fresh rhubarb,
  ¾-inch pieces
3 tablespoons all-purpose flour
2 pkgs. (10 oz. each) frozen
  strawberries in syrup,
  thawed

6 to 8 servings

In medium mixing bowl, combine rolled oats, ½ cup flour, brown and granulated sugars, cinnamon and nutmeg. Mix well. Cut in butter to form fine crumbs. Set aside.

Place rhubarb in 2-quart casserole. Sprinkle with 3 tablespoons flour. Stir to coat. Cover. Microwave at High for 7 to 10 minutes, or until rhubarb is tender, stirring once. Stir in strawberries. Sprinkle topping evenly over rhubarb mixture. Reduce power to 70% (Medium High). Microwave, uncovered, for 10 to 13 minutes, or until bubbly in center, rotating casserole once. Serve warm with ice cream, if desired.

Blackberry Cobbler

Helen May
Salem, Oregon

¾ cup sugar
2 tablespoons cornstarch
½ teaspoon ground cinnamon
1 bag (16 oz.) frozen
   blackberries
1 teaspoon lemon juice

Topping:
1 tablespoon graham cracker
   crumbs
⅛ teaspoon ground nutmeg
¼ cup butter or margarine
2 cups buttermilk baking mix
1 tablespoon sugar
⅔ cup milk

6 servings

In 2-quart casserole, combine ¾ cup sugar, cornstarch and cinnamon. Stir in frozen blackberries and lemon juice. Microwave at High for 8 to 12 minutes, or until mixture is thickened and translucent, stirring twice. Set aside.

In custard cup, combine graham cracker crumbs and nutmeg. Set aside. Place butter in small mixing bowl. Microwave at High for 1¼ to 1½ minutes, or until butter melts. Add baking mix, sugar and milk. Stir until soft dough forms. Spoon six equal portions of dough onto hot blackberry mixture. Sprinkle tops of biscuits with graham cracker mixture. Microwave at High for 4 to 6 minutes, or until biscuits appear dry and are cooked through, rotating casserole once. Serve warm with cream.

Light Yogurt Freeze Pops ▲

1⅔ cups cold water, divided
1 pkg. (0.3 oz.) low-calorie
   strawberry gelatin
1 pkg. (16 oz.) frozen
   unsweetened strawberries
1⅓ cups plain low-fat yogurt
2 tablespoons honey

6 pops

In 2-cup measure, microwave 1 cup water at High for 2 to 3 minutes, or until boiling. Add gelatin, stirring thoroughly to dissolve. Stir in remaining ⅔ cup cold water. Set aside.

In large mixing bowl, microwave strawberries at 50% (Medium) for 5 to 7 minutes, or until defrosted but still very cold, stirring once. Stir in yogurt and honey. Blend in gelatin mixture. Freeze for about 1½ hours, or until mixture is slushy. With electric mixer, beat yogurt mixture until smooth.

Spoon mixture evenly into six 7-oz. wax-coated paper cups. Insert flat sticks in center of each filled cup. Freeze for about 5 hours, or until pops are firm.

TIP: To serve pudding and gelatin pops, run bottoms of cups under warm water to loosen pops.

◄ Frozen Pudding Treats

1 pkg. (3 oz.) vanilla pudding and pie filling
2 cups milk
½ cup semisweet or milk chocolate chips
½ cup butterscotch chips
2 cups non-dairy whipped topping

6 pops

Place pudding mix in 1-quart measure. Blend in milk. Microwave at High for 6 to 9 minutes, or until mixture boils, stirring with whisk after every 2 minutes.

Pour one-half of the pudding into small mixing bowl. Add chocolate chips to one portion. Add butterscotch chips to second portion. Stir each mixture smooth. Place plastic wrap directly on pudding surface of each portion and chill for 1 hour.

Blend 1 cup whipped topping into each pudding. Alternate layers of chocolate and butterscotch mixtures evenly filling six 7-oz. wax-coated paper cups.

Insert flat wooden stick in center of each filled pudding cup. Freeze for about 6 hours, or until firm.

▲ Orange-Pineapple Freezer Pops

1 cup cold water, divided
1 teaspoon unflavored gelatin
1 can (8 oz.) crushed pineapple in heavy syrup (undrained)
1 can (6 oz.) frozen orange juice concentrate

6 pops

Place ½ cup water in 1-quart measure. Sprinkle with gelatin. Let stand for 5 minutes to soften. Microwave at High for 30 seconds to 1 minute, or until gelatin dissolves. Set aside.

In food processor or blender, purée pineapple. Add pineapple and remaining ½ cup water to gelatin mixture. Set aside. Remove lid from frozen juice concentrate. Microwave at High for 30 seconds to 1½ minutes, or until juice defrosts. Mix juice into pineapple mixture. Pour mixture evenly into six 5-oz. wax-coated paper cups. Freeze for 1½ hours. Insert flat stick in center of each cup. Freeze for about 4 hours, or until firm.

Apple Freezer Pops: Follow recipe above, except substitute 1 cup applesauce for the puréed pineapple and 1 can (6 oz.) frozen apple juice concentrate for the orange juice.

Sweet Shop

Deluxe Truffles

Melting Chocolate

The secret of successfully melting chocolate is to microwave chocolate at 50% (Medium) and stir often. Without stirring, fully melted chocolate holds its shape and may not look melted. To avoid overheating, microwave just until the last small pieces can be stirred smooth.

The chart below is for candy coating. Some recipes call for other forms of chocolate. Be sure you use the type specified.

For dipping candies, melt chocolate in a measuring cup. Melt it in a mixing bowl when additional ingredients are to be stirred in.

Cool chocolate-dipped candies on a baking sheet lined with wax paper, or on a rack set over wax paper to catch the drips.

Stir cereal, nuts or pretzels into leftover melted candy coating to make quick crunches. Spread mixture on wax paper, cool and break into pieces.

Make truffles on a cool day and work quickly so heat from your hands doesn't melt the rich mixture.

Candy Coating Melting Chart

Amount	Container	Method	Microwave at 50% (Medium)
¼ lb., broken into squares	Small mixing bowl, or 2-cup measure	Place candy coating and 1 teaspoon to 2 tablespoons shortening in container. Microwave until coating can be stirred smooth, stirring once or twice.	2 to 4 min.
½ lb., broken into squares			2½ to 5 min.
¾ lb., broken into squares	Medium mixing bowl, or 1-quart measure	Place candy coating and 1 to 2 tablespoons shortening in container. Microwave until coating can be stirred smooth, stirring once or twice.	2½ to 5½ min.
1 lb., broken into squares			4 to 8 min.

Chocolate Wafer Creams

Line a baking sheet with wax paper and set aside. In 1-quart measure, combine ½ lb. white or chocolate-flavored candy coating and 1 tablespoon shortening. Microwave as directed in chart (opposite), or until mixture is melted. Using a fork, dip 2 dozen cream-filled wafers to coat. Place cookies on prepared baking sheet, and let cool until set. Store wafer creams in airtight container or plastic food-storage bag. Yields 2 dozen wafers.

Chocolate-covered Pudding or Gelatin Pops

Line a baking sheet with wax paper and set aside. In 1-quart measure, place ½ lb. white or chocolate-flavored candy coating and 1 to 2 tablespoons shortening. Microwave as directed in chart (opposite), or until melted. Dip a frozen pudding or gelatin bar (1.75 to 1.8 oz. each) in coating. If desired, quickly coat with colored or chocolate shot. Hold bar a few seconds to allow coating to set. Place bar on prepared baking sheet in freezer. Wrap coated bars in plastic wrap to store in freezer. Yields 12 coated bars.

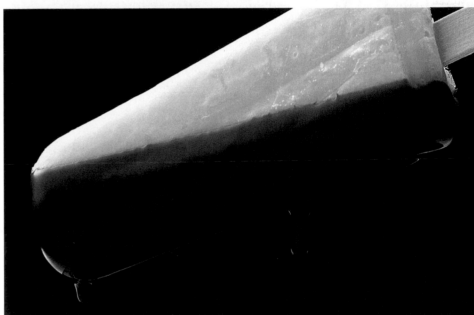

All-American Kids' Treats

Count out forty 100% whole wheat wafers from 9½-oz. box. Spread 20 of the crackers with peanut butter. Spread the rest of the crackers with your favorite jam, jelly or preserves. Sandwich the peanut butter and jam sides together. Line a baking sheet with wax paper and set aside.

In 2-cup measure, place ½ lb. chocolate-flavored candy coating and 1 tablespoon shortening. Microwave as directed in chart (opposite), or until melted. Using 2 forks, dip each sandwich into melted chocolate to coat. Place treats on prepared baking sheet, and chill until set. Store treats in airtight container or plastic food-storage bag. Yields 20 treats.

How to Microwave Chocolate-covered Cherries

Chocolate-covered ▲ Cherries

¼ cup butter or margarine
2 cups powdered sugar
¼ cup sweetened condensed
    milk
36 maraschino cherries
1 lb. chocolate-flavored candy
    coating, broken into squares
1 tablespoon shortening

                3 dozen cherries

Place butter in medium mixing bowl. Microwave at 30% (Medium Low) for 15 to 45 seconds, or until softened, checking after every 15 seconds. Add powdered sugar. Mix well. Blend in condensed milk. (Mixture will be stiff.)

Cover each cherry with about 1 teaspoon sugar mixture. (For easy handling, coat hands with powdered sugar.) Place cherries on wax-paper-lined baking sheet. Chill cherries for 30 minutes.

Combine chocolate and shortening in 1-quart casserole. Microwave at 50% (Medium) for 5 to 8 minutes, or until the mixture can be stirred smooth, stirring once or twice.

Dip coated cherries in chocolate using two forks. Place on prepared baking sheet and chill until set. (If necessary, microwave chocolate at 50% (Medium) for 1 to 3 minutes, or until remelted.)

Redip cherries in chocolate. Let cherries cool until chocolate sets. Cover loosely with wax paper. Set aside in cool place for 2 to 3 days to allow centers to soften.

Chocolate Apricot Chews ▲

1 pkg. (3 oz.) cream cheese
1 tablespoon powdered sugar
¼ teaspoon vanilla
1 pkg. (6 oz.) dried apricot
   halves

1 pkg. (6 oz.) semisweet
   chocolate chips
1 tablespoon shortening

About 15 candies

In small bowl, microwave cream cheese at High for 15 to 30 seconds, or until softened. Add powdered sugar and vanilla. Mix well. Place small amount of cream cheese mixture between two apricot halves. Press halves together lightly. Repeat with remaining apricot halves and cream cheese mixture. Arrange stuffed apricots on plate. Chill for 15 minutes, or until cream cheese filling is firm. Line a baking sheet with wax paper and set aside.

In small mixing bowl, combine chocolate chips and shortening. Microwave at 50% (Medium) for 3½ to 4½ minutes, or until chocolate is glossy and mixture can be stirred smooth, stirring once or twice. Using two forks, dip stuffed apricots into chocolate mixture, turning to coat completely. Or dip one half only. Arrange apricots on prepared baking sheet. Chill for 15 to 20 minutes, or until chocolate is set. Serve chilled.

Caramel Pecan Clusters ▲

Remove wrappers from 12 caramels. Set aside. Line a baking sheet with wax paper and set aside. In small mixing bowl, combine ¼ lb. chocolate-flavored candy coating and 1 teaspoon shortening. Microwave as directed in chart (page 262), or until mixture melts. Stir in 2 tablespoons finely chopped pecans. With spoon, dip each caramel into chocolate mixture to coat. Drop dipped caramels onto prepared baking sheet. Let clusters cool until set. Store in airtight container or plastic food-storage bag.

Yields 12 clusters

Chocolate Chews

2 squares (1 oz. each)
   unsweetened chocolate
2 tablespoons butter or
   margarine
⅓ cup light corn syrup
½ teaspoon vanilla
2 cups powdered sugar,
   divided
½ cup non-fat dry milk powder

1¼ lbs.

In medium mixing bowl, combine chocolate and butter. Microwave at 50% (Medium) for 3 to 4½ minutes, or until chocolate is glossy and mixture can be stirred smooth, stirring once or twice. Blend in corn syrup and vanilla. Microwave at High for 1 minute.

Mix in 1¾ cups powdered sugar and the dry milk powder. Spread remaining ¼ cup powdered sugar on wooden board. Turn chocolate out onto sugared board and knead until extra sugar is absorbed. Divide dough into 8 equal portions. Roll each portion into ½-inch diameter rope. Cut each piece into 1½-inch lengths. Let chocolate chews cool. Wrap each in wax paper.

Basic Truffles

2 bars (4 oz. each) sweet baking
  chocolate, cut up
⅓ cup whipping cream
3 tablespoons butter or
  margarine
½ teaspoon vanilla

Coatings:
  Powdered sugar
  Cocoa
  Finely chopped nuts
  Shredded coconut

24 truffles

Line an 8 × 4-inch loaf dish with plastic wrap. Set aside. In 1-quart measure, combine chocolate, whipping cream and butter. Microwave at 50% (Medium) for 4 to 6 minutes, or until chocolate melts and mixture can be stirred smooth, stirring once. Beat mixture until smooth and shiny. Blend in vanilla. Pour mixture into prepared loaf dish. Refrigerate for 4 hours. Lift chocolate mixture from dish and cut into 24 equal portions. Let stand for 10 minutes.

Coat hands lightly with powdered sugar and roll each portion into ¾-inch ball. Place desired coating in small bowl and roll each ball to coat. Place each truffle in paper candy cup and chill for at least 1 hour before serving. Store truffles in refrigerator for no longer than 2 weeks.

Variation: Follow recipe above, except omit vanilla and substitute another complementary flavored extract (maple, almond, cherry, orange, peppermint, etc.).

TIP: Work quickly when rolling mixture into balls. Chocolate mixture is rich, and melts easily.

266

◄ Deluxe Truffles

2 bars (4 oz. each) sweet
    baking chocolate, cut up
⅓ cup whipping cream
3 tablespoons butter or
    margarine
1 tablespoon liqueur (almond,
    cherry, orange, etc.)

Coating:
½ lb. white or chocolate-
    flavored candy coating,
    divided
¼ cup shortening, divided

Decoration:
1 square (1 oz.) semisweet
    chocolate
1 teaspoon shortening

10 truffles

TIP: For pastel-colored truffles, or decorative toppings, tint Coating
(above) with 1 or 2 drops food coloring.

How to Microwave Deluxe Truffles

Line an 8 × 4-inch loaf dish with plastic wrap. Set aside. In 1-quart measure, combine chocolate, whipping cream and butter. Microwave at 50% (Medium) for 4 to 6 minutes, or until chocolate melts and mixture can be stirred smooth, stirring once. Beat until smooth and shiny. Blend in liqueur. Pour into prepared loaf dish. Refrigerate for 4 hours.

Lift chocolate mixture from dish and cut into 10 equal portions. Let stand for 10 minutes. Line a baking sheet with wax paper and set aside. Coat hands lightly with powdered sugar and roll each portion into 1¼-inch ball. Place on prepared baking sheet. Chill for 15 minutes.

Combine ¼ lb. candy coating and 2 tablespoons shortening in 2-cup measure. Microwave as directed in chart (page 262), or until mixture melts. Using fork, dip each chocolate ball in candy coating. Place on prepared baking sheet. Chill until set.

Combine remaining candy coating and shortening in clean 2-cup measure. Microwave as directed in chart (page 262), or until melted. Redip truffles and chill until coating is set.

Place semisweet chocolate square and 1 teaspoon shortening in small bowl. Microwave at 50% (Medium) for 2½ to 4½ minutes, or until chocolate is glossy and mixture can be stirred smooth, stirring once. Drizzle melted chocolate in decorative design over tops of coated truffles. Chill before serving. Store truffles in refrigerator for no longer than 2 weeks.

Candy Pizza

1 recipe pizza base (right)
2 cups stir-ins (right)
½ to ¾ cup toppings (right)
1 recipe frosting (right)

1½ lbs.

How to Make
Candy Pizza

Line baking sheet with wax or parchment paper. Set aside. Microwave candy pizza base. Add combined choice of stir-ins. Mix well to coat.

Spread base mixture evenly on prepared baking sheet to 10-inch diameter. Sprinkle with combined choice of toppings. Set aside.

Microwave frosting. Drizzle frosting over candy pizza. Chill for at least 1½ hours, or until set. Peel off wax paper. Break candy apart, or serve in wedges.

Candy Pizza Base

Light Chocolate:
In medium mixing bowl, combine 1½ cups milk chocolate chips and 3 squares (1 oz. each) semisweet chocolate. Microwave at 50% (Medium) for 4 to 6 minutes, or until chocolate can be stirred smooth, stirring twice.

White Chocolate:
In medium mixing bowl, combine ¾ lb. white candy coating (broken into squares) and 1 tablespoon shortening. Microwave at 50% (Medium) for 2½ to 5½ minutes, or until mixture can be stirred smooth, stirring twice.

Peanut Butter:
In medium mixing bowl, combine 1½ cups peanut butter chips and 3 oz. white candy coating. Microwave at 50% (Medium) for 4 to 6 minutes, or until mixture can be stirred smooth, stirring twice.

Dark Chocolate:
In medium mixing bowl, combine 1½ cups semisweet chocolate chips and 3 squares (1 oz. each) unsweetened chocolate. Microwave at 50% (Medium) for 4 to 6 minutes, or until chocolate can be stirred smooth, stirring twice.

Mint Chocolate:
In medium mixing bowl, combine 1½ cups mint-flavored semisweet chocolate chips and 3 squares (1 oz. each) semisweet chocolate. Microwave at 50% (Medium) for 4 to 6 minutes, or until chocolate can be stirred smooth, stirring once or twice.

Butterscotch:
In medium mixing bowl, combine 1½ cups butterscotch chips and 3 oz. white candy coating. Microwave at 50% (Medium) for 4 to 6 minutes, or until mixture can be stirred smooth, stirring twice.

Candy Pizza Stir-ins

Use one or more of the following, to equal 2 cups:

Crisp rice cereal
Toasted round oat cereal
Corn flakes cereal
Crisp square rice, wheat or
  corn cereal
Coarsely crushed pretzel sticks
Coarsely crushed shoestring
  potatoes
Salted mixed nuts
Chopped nuts
Salted dry-roasted peanuts
Whole or slivered almonds
Miniature marshmallows

Candy Pizza Toppings

Use one or more of the following toppings, to equal ½ to ¾ cup:

Miniature jelly beans
Jellied orange slices, cut up
Candied fruit
Candied cherries, cut up
Maraschino cherries, drained
Red or black licorice pieces
Shredded coconut
Candy-coated plain or peanut
  chocolate pieces
Candy-coated peanut butter
  pieces
Chocolate-covered raisins
Candy corn

Candy Pizza Frosting

¼ lb. white or chocolate-flavored
  candy coating

1 teaspoon shortening

Frosts one candy pizza

In 2-cup measure, combine candy coating and shortening. Microwave as directed in chart (page 262), or until melted. Drizzle frosting over candy pizza.

Mock Toffee ▲

1 lb. butterscotch confectioners'
   candy coating
2 cups butter brickle chips
1 cup chocolate chips
½ cup chopped pecans

              Makes about 3 lbs.

Place confectioners' candy
coating and butter brickle chips
in large bowl or 2-qt. casserole.
Microwave at 50% (Medium) 5
to 6 minutes, or until softened.
Stir until smooth and completely
melted. Spread to ¼-in.
thickness on wax paper. Cool
until hard.

Microwave chocolate chips at
50% (Medium) 3 to 5 minutes,
or until chips are shiny and
softened. Stir until melted.
Spread chocolate on set brickle;
sprinkle with chopped nuts.
Chill until set. Break into pieces.

Chocolate Marshmallow ▲ Squares

1 pkg. (12 oz.) semi-sweet
   chocolate chips or 1 pkg.
   (11½ oz.) milk chocolate
   chips
1 pkg. (6 oz.) butterscotch
   chips
½ cup peanut butter
1 pkg. (10 to 10½ oz.) miniature marshmallows
1 cup salted peanuts

             Makes 20 pieces

In 3-qt. casserole combine
chocolate chips, butterscotch
chips and peanut butter.
Microwave at 50% (Medium)
3½ to 4½ minutes, or until chips
are softened, stirring after half
the time. Stir until smooth and
melted. Mix in marshmallows
and peanuts. Spread in lightly
greased 8 × 8-in. baking dish.
Cool completely before cutting.

Confetti Candy ▲

1 lb. white confectioners' candy
   coating
2 tablespoons vegetable
   shortening
1 pkg. (16 oz.) sugared gum
   drops

             Makes 2 lbs.

Line 8 × 8-in. baking dish with
wax paper. Place confectioners'
candy and shortening in large
bowl or 2-qt. casserole.
Microwave at 50% (Medium) 3
to 5 minutes, or until pieces are
soft, stirring after first 3 minutes.
Stir in gum drops. Spread
mixture evenly in prepared dish.
Refrigerate until set. Cut into
1-in. pieces.

Variation:
Chocolate Coconut Candy:
Use 1 lb. chocolate
confectioners' candy coating,
1 cup dry roasted, salted peanuts and 1 cup flaked coconut.
Spread on wax paper-lined
baking sheet. Refrigerate until
set; break into pieces.

Peanut Butter Fudge ▶

2 cups peanut butter chips
1 cup chocolate chips
⅓ cup chopped peanuts
¼ cup butter or margarine
1 can (14 oz.) condensed milk

Makes 8 × 8-in. dish

Place all ingredients in 2-qt. mixing bowl. Microwave at 50% (Medium) 3 to 4 minutes, or until chips are melted, stirring once. Stir to blend. Pour into 8 × 8-in. baking dish. Chill until set. Cut into squares.

Chocolate Crunch Cups ▶

1 pkg. (11½ oz.) butterscotch chips
1 pkg. (6 oz.) milk chocolate chips
1½ cups dry roasted salted peanuts
1 cup crushed ripple potato chips

Makes 1½ lbs.

In medium bowl combine butterscotch and milk chocolate chips. Microwave at 50% (Medium) 2 to 4 minutes, or until softened, stirring each minute. Stir in peanuts and potato chips. Drop by spoonfuls onto wax paper or into paper candy cups. Chill until set.

Raisin Bran Chewies ▶

½ bag (14 oz.) caramels, about 24
1 can (5 oz.) evaporated milk
3½ cups raisin bran cereal

Makes 2½ dozen

In large bowl combine the caramels and evaporated milk. Microwave at High 5 to 9 minutes, or until boiling, stirring after each minute. Stir in cereal. Drop by teaspoonfuls onto wax paper. Chill until firm.

How to Microwave Monster Cookies

Monster Cookies

¾ cup shortening
1 cup packed brown sugar
1 egg
¼ cup water
1 teaspoon vanilla
3 cups rolled oats
1 cup all-purpose flour
¾ teaspoon salt
½ teaspoon baking soda
1 cup butterscotch chips or
   candy-coated plain
   chocolate pieces
½ cup chopped nuts

5 cookies

Combine shortening, brown sugar, egg, water and vanilla in large mixing bowl. Beat at medium speed of electric mixer until mixture is light and fluffy.

Add oats, flour, salt and baking soda. Mix well. Stir in butterscotch chips and nuts.

Divide dough into 5 equal portions (about 1 cup dough for each). On wax-paper-lined plate, pat one portion into ½-inch thickness (diameter will be 5½ to 6 inches).

Microwave cookie at 70% (Medium High) for 3 to 5 minutes, or just until dry on surface, rotating plate once.

Press extra chips or candies into top of cookie, if desired. Let cookie stand on counter until cool. Repeat with remaining dough.

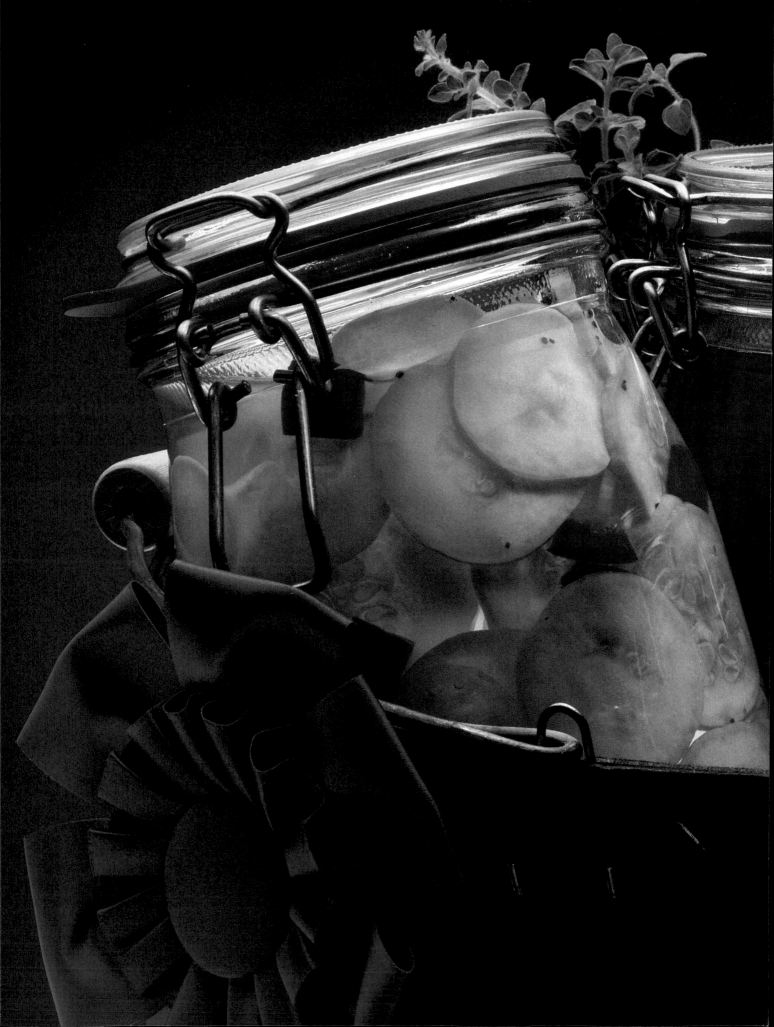

Blue Ribbon Extras

Yellow Summer Squash Pickles
Pickled Eggs
Christmas Overnight Pickles

Oregano

Sage

Mint

Cilantro

Basil

Fresh Herbs for Drying

Herb:	Use in:	Complements:
Basil	Egg dishes, salads, tomato & cream sauces, pesto, vegetable soups, vegetable dishes	Beef, lamb, pork, veal, poultry, fish
Chervil	Egg dishes, creamed mixtures & soups, vegetable dishes	Poultry, fish & seafood
Cilantro*	Mexican dishes & sauces, Chinese & Italian dishes	Beef, lamb, pork, veal, poultry, fish & seafood
Dill weed	Soups & stews, sauces & butters, pickles, vegetable dishes	Beef, lamb, pork, veal, poultry, fish & seafood
Marjoram	Meatballs, meatloaf, salads, soups, stuffings, egg dishes, vegetable dishes	Beef, lamb, pork, veal, poultry, fish & seafood
Mint	Desserts, beverages, fruit compotes, jellies	Lamb, veal, fish
Oregano	Chili, spaghetti sauce, tomato dishes, soups, stews, vegetable dishes, pizza	Beef, lamb, pork, veal, poultry, fish & seafood
Parsley	Stuffings, sauces, soups, stews, vegetable dishes	Beef, lamb, pork, veal, poultry, fish & seafood
Rosemary	Egg dishes, vegetable dishes, stuffings, soups, stews	Beef, lamb, pork, veal, poultry, fish
Sage	Sausages, soups, stuffings, egg dishes, vegetable dishes	Pork, veal, poultry, fish
Tarragon	Egg dishes, meat sauces, poultry or fish sauces, salads, salad dressings, soups, stews	Beef, veal, poultry, fish & seafood
Thyme	Chowders, soufflés, omelets, vegetable dishes, stuffings, soups, stews	Beef, lamb, pork, poultry, fish & seafood

*also: Chinese or Italian parsley, fresh coriander

Fresh-dried Herbs

Whether you grow your own fresh herbs or buy them at the supermarket, you probably have more than you can use. Save your surplus herbs by drying them quickly in the microwave oven. Herbs dried in the microwave retain their fresh, bright color, fragrance and characteristic leaf shapes.

Make your own flavor combinations by mixing equal parts of fresh-dried herbs. For poultry, seafood or salad dressings, try tarragon, chervil and parsley. Complement meat with a mixture of thyme, sage and marjoram.

Drying Fresh Herbs in the Microwave

Wash and thoroughly dry one bunch of fresh herbs selected from chart (page 277). Strip leaves from stems. Discard stems and tear larger leaves in ½ to ¾-inch pieces. Loosely pack enough herbs to equal ½ cup. Place one paper towel on plate. Sprinkle herbs evenly over towel.

Place ½ cup cold water in 1-cup measure. Place water next to plate in microwave oven. Microwave at High for 3¼ to 4 minutes, or just until leaves begin to feel dry and papery, tossing with fingers after first minute, and then after every 45 seconds. Watch closely to avoid over-drying.

Remove herbs and sprinkle evenly onto another paper towel. (Repeat procedure for additional herbs, if desired.) Let air-dry for 24 hours to complete drying. Store in airtight container in cool, dark place when completely dry. Slightly crush dried herbs before measuring for use in recipes.

Italian Herbs

1 tablespoon dried parsley leaves (opposite)
1 tablespoon dried oregano leaves (opposite)
1 tablespoon dried basil leaves (opposite)
1 teaspoon dried thyme leaves, (opposite)
2 teaspoons dried marjoram leaves (opposite)
¼ teaspoon dried crushed red pepper

About ¼ cup

Combine all ingredients in small bowl. Mix well. Store in covered container in cool dark place. Slightly crush mixture before using. Use herbs on meats and poultry, and for seasoning Italian sauces and pizza.

Herb-seasoned Salt

2 tablespoons salt
1 tablespoon dried parsley flakes (opposite)
1 tablespoon dried basil leaves (opposite)
1 teaspoon dried dill weed (opposite)
½ teaspoon onion powder
¼ teaspoon garlic powder

About ¼ cup

Combine all ingredients in a small bowl. Crush mixture in mortar with pestle, or place mixture in blender and process until very fine. Serve as all-purpose seasoning.

Poultry Herb Medley

2 tablespoons dried rosemary leaves (opposite)
1 tablespoon dried marjoram leaves (opposite)
1 tablespoon dried thyme leaves (opposite)

¼ cup

Combine all ingredients in small bowl. Mix well. Store in covered container in cool dark place. Slightly crush mixture before using. Use medley on poultry, lamb or pork.

TIP: Dry ½ cup celery leaves in the same way as fresh herbs (opposite). Use dried celery leaves in soups, stews, main dishes and sauces.

279

Softening Butter

Butter and margarine melt and soften quickly because they have a high fat content, which attracts microwave energy. To soften butter without melting it: place butter in small bowl or on plate, and microwave at 30% (Medium Low) as directed in chart (below), checking after every 15 seconds.

Amount	Microwave at 30% (Medium Low)
2 tablespoons	15 to 30 seconds
¼ cup	15 to 45 seconds
½ cup	15 seconds to 1 minute

TIPS: Pack butter into crocks or butter molds for serving. Or use a pastry tube to pipe butter onto wax paper into individual butter pats. Chill until firm.

Use softened butter for spreads, for sweet and savory breads, or as a topping for hot cooked vegetables. For fluffy whipped butter, beat using an electric mixer.

How to Microwave Flavored Butters

Microwave ½ cup butter or margarine in small mixing bowl as directed in chart (above), or until softened.

Blend in additional ingredients for desired flavor (opposite).

Serve flavored butters as directed (opposite); store in refrigerator no longer than 2 weeks.

Flavored Butters

Flavor & yield	To ½ cup butter, blend in:	Serving suggestions
Almond-Peach Butter about ¾ cup	¼ cup ground almonds, 2 table-spoons peach preserves, 1 table-spoon Amaretto	Toast, Danish pastries, quick breads
Deviled Butter about ½ cup	1 teaspoon dry mustard, ¼ tea-spoon cayenne, ¼ teaspoon paprika, ⅛ teaspoon garlic powder	Meats, poultry, fish or seafood, hot cooked pasta, vegetables, cornbread
Fruit Preserve Butter about ⅔ cup	⅓ cup powdered sugar, 1 tablespoon of desired fruit preserves (straw-berry, blackberry, pineapple, etc.)	Toast, pancakes, waffles, French toast, croissants, quick breads
Honey-Pecan Butter about ¾ cup	¼ cup honey, 2 tablespoons chopped pecans, ⅛ teaspoon ground nutmeg	Toast, pancakes, waffles, French toast, quick breads
Lemon-Chive Butter about ½ cup	2 teaspoons freeze-dried chives, ½ teaspoon grated lemon peel, 6 drops hot red pepper sauce	Fish or seafood, hot cooked vegetables
Orange-Cinnamon Butter about ¾ cup	2 tablespoons packed brown sugar, 1 tablespoon orange juice, 1 tea-spoon grated orange peel, ¼ tea-spoon ground cinnamon	Toast, pancakes, waffles, French toast, quick breads
Parsley-Herb Butter about ½ cup	1 tablespoon fresh snipped parsley, 2 teaspoons finely chopped shallot, ¼ teaspoon dried marjoram leaves, ⅛ teaspoon dried thyme leaves	Steaks, dinner breads, hot cooked pasta, vegetables
Blue Cheese-Walnut Butter about ¾ cup	2 oz. crumbled blue cheese, 2 tablespoons chopped walnuts, ¼ teaspoon Worcestershire sauce, dash pepper	Steaks, savory crackers

Softening Cream Cheese

In small mixing bowl, microwave cream cheese as directed in chart (below), or until softened. DO NOT microwave cream cheese in the foil wrapper. For use in dips and spreads, blend softened cream cheese with favorite flavors, as directed in chart (opposite).

TIP: Cream cheese softens quickly in the microwave and spreads easily. Softened cheese is easier to blend in your favorite appetizer, main dish or dessert recipe.

Amount	Power setting	Microwave Time
1 pkg. (3 oz.)	High	15 to 30 seconds
1 pkg. (8 oz.)	50% (Medium)	1½ to 3 minutes

How to Microwave Flavored Cream Cheeses

Microwave 8 oz. cream cheese in small mixing bowl as directed in chart (above), stirring once or twice.

Blend in additional ingredients for desired flavor (opposite).

Serve flavored cream cheeses as directed (opposite); store cream cheese as recommended.

Flavored Cream Cheeses

Flavor & yield	To 8 oz. cream cheese blend in:	Serving suggestions	Store up to:
Cheddar & Chive Cream Cheese about 1¼ cups	½ cup finely shredded Cheddar cheese, 1 tablespoon sliced green onion, 1 teaspoon freeze-dried chives, ⅛ teaspoon garlic powder	Dip for vegetables; topping for hot cooked vegetables; spread for crackers, bread	2 weeks
Cocoa Cream Cheese Frosting about 1¼ cups	½ cup powdered sugar, 2 tablespoons cocoa, ½ teaspoon vanilla	Frosting for graham crackers, brownies, bars, cakes	2 weeks
Italian Herb Cream Cheese about 1 cup	2 tablespoons fresh snipped parsley, ½ teaspoon Italian seasoning	Spread for sandwiches or crackers; topping for hot cooked vegetables	2 weeks
Lemon-Basil Cream Cheese about 1¼ cups	2 teaspoons lemon juice, ½ teaspoon dried basil leaves (crushed), ¼ teaspoon garlic powder	Dip for vegetables; spread for bagels, French bread, cheese croissants	2 weeks
Mustard Relish Cream Cheese about 1¼ cups	2 tablespoons sweet relish, 1 tablespoon chopped onion, 2 teaspoons Dijon mustard	Spread for bagels, sandwiches, crackers	2 weeks
Orange Spice Cream Cheese about 1 cup	2 tablespoons sugar, 2 tablespoons orange juice, 1 teaspoon grated orange peel, ⅛ teaspoon ground allspice	Spread for fruit muffins, bagels, croissants, quick breads	2 weeks
Red Wine Onion Cream Cheese about 1¼ cups	2 tablespoons chopped onion, 2 tablespoons red wine, ⅛ teaspoon salt, dash pepper	Dip for vegetables; spread for crackers	2 weeks
Strawberry Cream Cheese about 1⅓ cups	½ cup fresh sliced strawberries, 2 tablespoons sugar, 1 teaspoon vanilla	Dip for fruit; spread for pound cakes, quick breads	3 days

Chocolate Pinwheel Spread

½ cup butter or margarine,
    softened (page 280)
1 pkg. (3 oz.) cream cheese,
    softened (page 282)
1 cup powdered sugar
¼ cup chocolate fudge topping
    Chocolate shot (optional)

One 6-inch roll

TIP: Serve spread with crois-
sants, pastries or quick breads.
Store remaining spread in refrigerator for no longer than
2 weeks.

How to Microwave Chocolate Pinwheel Spread

Blend butter and cream cheese
in small mixing bowl. Reserve ¼
cup of mixture in another small
bowl. Add powdered sugar to
larger portion of butter mixture.
Mix until smooth and creamy. Line
baking sheet with wax paper.

Spread sugar mixture on baking
sheet, forming 6 × 9-inch rectangle, about ¼ inch thick. Chill
for 15 minutes. Blend topping into
reserved ¼ cup butter mixture.

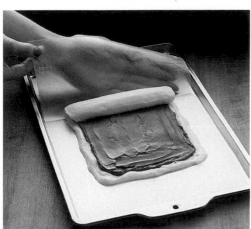

Spread fudge mixture evenly over chilled sugar layer. Chill for 1 hour to firm. Starting on short side, lift paper and roll until layer begins to roll tightly, enclosing fudge layer.

Lift and peel back paper while rolling, until roll is complete. Sprinkle with chocolate shot. Chill for at least 2 hours before slicing.

Mocha Variation: Follow recipe opposite, except blend 1 teaspoon instant coffee crystals with 1 teaspoon hot water and add to fudge-butter mixture.

Pickles, Relishes & Condiments

Putting up pickles and relishes once meant hours of effort at harvest time. With most ingredients available year 'round, modern cooks microwave small batches as they are needed. Experiment with a variety of pickles, your own homemade salsa, or trend-setting specialty mustards which add spice to meals and cost less than those purchased from gourmet food shops.

The recipes on pages 286-297 are packed into sterilized jars after microwaving. They are not pressure- or water bath-canned, so they do require refrigeration.

Mixed Pickle Relish

1   cup peeled, seeded and
      chopped cucumber
1   cup chopped onion
1   cup chopped red pepper
1   cup chopped green pepper
1   tablespoon pickling salt
⅔   cup sugar
½   cup white wine vinegar

2   teaspoons dry mustard
½   teaspoon grated fresh
      gingerroot
¼   teaspoon ground turmeric
⅛   teaspoon ground allspice
⅛   teaspoon cayenne
1   clove garlic, minced

1-pint jar

In colander, place cucumber, onion, red and green peppers. Sprinkle with salt. Toss lightly to mix. Let colander stand over bowl for 1½ hours, stirring occasionally.

Place salted vegetables in 1½-quart casserole. Add remaining ingredients. Mix well. Microwave at High for 20 to 30 minutes, or until mixture thickens slightly, stirring twice. Spoon mixture into sterilized 1-pint jar. Cover and refrigerate overnight before serving. Store relish in refrigerator for no longer than 1 month.

Christmas Overnight Pickles

1 large cucumber (¾ lb.) peeled and cut crosswise into 3 pieces
4 whole allspice
4 whole cloves
½ cup water
½ cup cider vinegar
½ cup sugar
¼ teaspoon salt
¼ teaspoon ground nutmeg
½ teaspoon red food coloring
½ teaspoon green food coloring

4 to 6 servings

How to Microwave Christmas Overnight Pickles

Scoop out and discard seeds from cucumber, slice hollow pieces into ¼-inch rings. Divide cucumber rings evenly between two plastic food-storage bags. Add 2 allspice and 2 cloves to each bag. Set aside.

Combine remaining ingredients, except food colorings, in 2-cup measure. Microwave at High for 2 to 5 minutes, or until mixture boils, stirring once to dissolve sugar and salt. Divide mixture into two portions. Stir red coloring into one portion. Stir green coloring into remaining portion. Cool slightly.

Pour red vinegar mixture over cucumbers in one food-storage bag. Pour green vinegar mixture into remaining bag. Tie securely and refrigerate bags overnight. Drain pickles before serving. Store in refrigerator for no longer than 3 days.

Pickled Garden Relish

Joan M. Romero
Los Angeles, California

3 cups fresh cauliflowerets,
   1-inch pieces
2 medium carrots, cut into
   2 × ¼-inch strips
¼ cup water
1 medium red pepper, cut into
   2 × ¼-inch strips
2 stalks celery, sliced ½ inch
   thick
⅔ cup whole green or black
   olives
¾ cup white wine vinegar
½ cup olive oil
2 tablespoons sugar
1 teaspoon salt
½ teaspoon dried oregano
   leaves
¼ teaspoon pepper

About 6 cups

In 1½-quart casserole, combine cauliflower, carrots and water. Cover. Microwave at High for 3 to 5 minutes, or until vegetables are hot, but still crisp, stirring once. Stir in red pepper, celery and olives. Set aside.

In 2-cup measure, blend vinegar, olive oil, sugar, salt, oregano and pepper. Pour vinegar and oil mixture over vegetables. Mix well. Re-cover. Chill for at least 8 hours or over-night. Drain before serving.

Cranberry Chutney ▶

Kathy Ferguson
Walnut Creek, California

A traditional family recipe for holidays.

```
 1  lb. frozen cranberries
 1  cup granulated sugar
 ½  cup packed brown sugar
 ½  cup golden raisins
2½  teaspoons apple pie spice
 ¾  cup water
 1  cup peeled chopped pear
 ⅔  cup chopped onion
 ½  cup chopped celery
 ⅓  cup chopped green pepper
```

4 cups

In 3-quart casserole, combine cranberries, granulated and brown sugars, raisins and apple pie spice. Stir in water. Cover. Microwave at High for 10 to 14 minutes, or until cranberries begin to open, stirring once or twice. Stir in remaining ingredients. Microwave, uncovered, at High for 22 to 30 minutes, or until mixture is desired consistency, stirring 2 or 3 times. Mixture can be stored in refrigerator or ladled into 2 hot sterilized pint jars. Seal and process according to canning directions. Serve as a relish with all meats.

Pepper Jelly

Doyle Henson
Blytheville, Arkansas

Complements the flavor of cooked meats.

```
½  small red pepper
½  small green pepper
2  seeded fresh jalapeño
   peppers, each 2½ inches
3  cups sugar
¾  cup white vinegar
1  pouch (3 oz.) liquid fruit
   pectin
```

3 cups

In food processor or blender bowl, combine red, green and jalapeño peppers. Process until finely chopped, stopping to scrape side of bowl if needed. Pour mixture into 2-quart measure. Stir in sugar and vinegar. Microwave at High for 5 minutes. Stir thoroughly to dissolve sugar. Microwave at High for 4½ to 6½ minutes, or until mixture comes to a full rolling boil. Microwave at High for 1 minute longer. Add pectin. Mix well. Mixture can be stored in refrigerator or ladled into hot sterilized jars. Seal and process according to canning directions. Serve with all meats.

Yellow Summer Squash Pickles

3 cups thinly sliced yellow
　summer squash
½ cup coarsely chopped red
　pepper
1 small onion, thinly sliced and
　separated into rings
8 whole peppercorns
1 large clove garlic, cut into
　quarters (optional)
1 cup white wine vinegar
⅔ cup sugar
2 teaspoons pickling salt
¼ teaspoon celery seed
¼ teaspoon mustard seed

　　　　Two 1-pint jars

In medium mixing bowl, mix squash, red pepper and onion. Divide mixture and pack evenly into two sterilized 1-pint jars. Place 4 peppercorns and 2 garlic quarters in each jar. Set aside.

Combine remaining ingredients in 2-cup measure. Microwave at High for 2 to 5 minutes, or until mixture boils, stirring once to dissolve sugar and salt. Pour mixture evenly into jars. Cover and refrigerate for at least 5 days before serving. Store in refrigerator for no longer than 1 month.

Pickled Eggs ▶

Juice from 1 can (16 oz.)
  sliced beets
Water
⅔ cup cider vinegar
3 tablespoons packed brown
  sugar
¾ teaspoon salt
6 whole cloves
6 whole allspice
6 whole peppercorns
1 medium onion, thinly sliced
6 hard-cooked eggs, peeled

6 servings

Add enough water to beet juice to measure 1 cup. (Reserve beets for future use, if desired.) In medium mixing bowl, combine beet juice mixture, vinegar, sugar, salt, cloves, allspice and peppercorns. Add onion. Cover with plastic wrap. Microwave at High for 6 to 8 minutes, or until onion is tender-crisp, stirring once. Add eggs. Cover and refrigerate for 1 to 2 days, turning occasionally to assure even-colored eggs. Drain and slice eggs. Serve on platter or in salads.

Pickled Green Beans

1 pkg. (10 oz.) frozen cut, or
  French-cut, green beans
1 small onion, cut in half
  lengthwise and thinly sliced
½ cup sliced black olives
1 cup white vinegar
⅔ cup sugar
2 teaspoons pickling salt
¼ teaspoon dried tarragon
  leaves or dried dill weed

Three ½-pint jars

In medium mixing bowl, microwave beans at High for 4 to 6 minutes, or until defrosted, breaking apart once. Drain thoroughly. Add onion and black olives. Mix well. Divide mixture and pack evenly into three sterilized ½-pint jars. Set aside.

Combine remaining ingredients in 2-cup measure. Microwave at High for 2 to 5 minutes, or until mixture boils, stirring once to dissolve sugar and salt. Pour mixture evenly into jars. Cover and refrigerate for at least 5 days before serving. Store in refrigerator for no longer than 1 month.

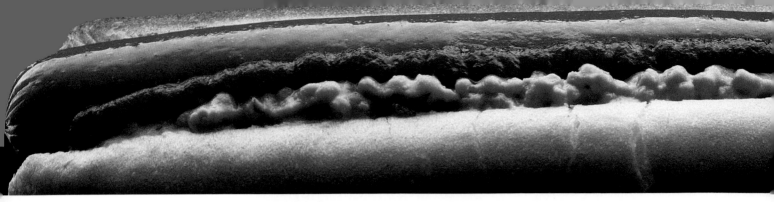

How to Microwave Basil-Onion Mustard

Basil-Onion Mustard

⅓ cup dry mustard
3 tablespoons mustard seed, slightly crushed
2 teaspoons dried basil leaves, divided
½ cup hot water
⅓ cup white wine vinegar
⅓ cup finely chopped onion
1 tablespoon sugar
2 teaspoons mixed pickling spices
1 teaspoon salt

¾ to 1 cup mustard

Combine dry mustard, mustard seed and ½ teaspoon basil leaves in small mixing bowl. Add water. Mix well. Cover and set aside for 1 hour. Combine remaining 1½ teaspoons dried basil leaves and remaining ingredients in 1-quart casserole. Mix well. Cover. Microwave at High for 3 to 4 minutes, or until onion is tender. Let stand, covered, until cool.

Strain vinegar mixture into mustard mixture using wire strainer, pressing with back of spoon. Discard onion solids. Stir mustard mixture. Microwave, uncovered, at High for 4 to 5 minutes, or until mixture thickens slightly, stirring once.

Spoon mustard into sterilized jar. Cover and refrigerate overnight before serving. Store in refrigerator for no longer than 3 months. If desired, mix vinegar or water into cooled mustard to thin.

Tarragon-Garlic Mustard: Follow recipe above, except substitute tarragon leaves for the basil, and 2 cloves garlic, (each cut into quarters), for the onion. Microwave as directed, or until garlic is tender.

292

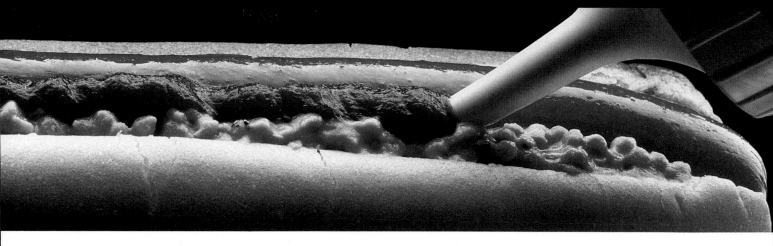

Home-style ▲ Brown Mustard

⅓ cup dry mustard
3 tablespoons mustard seed, slightly crushed
½ cup hot water
¼ cup plus 2 tablespoons cider vinegar
⅓ cup coarsely chopped onion
3 tablespoons packed dark brown sugar
1 clove garlic, cut into quarters
1 teaspoon salt
½ teaspoon dill seed
¼ teaspoon dried marjoram leaves
⅛ teaspoon ground allspice
⅛ teaspoon ground cinnamon
6 whole peppercorns

1 cup mustard

In small mixing bowl, combine dry mustard and mustard seed. Add water and mix well. Cover and set aside for 1 hour. In 1-quart casserole, combine all remaining ingredients. Cover. Microwave at High for 3 to 4 minutes, or until onion is tender. Let mixture stand, covered, until cool.

Using wire strainer, strain vinegar mixture into dry mustard mixture, pressing with back of spoon. Discard onion solids. Stir mustard mixture. Microwave, uncovered, at High for 4 to 5 minutes, or until mixture thickens slightly, stirring once. Spoon into sterilized jar. Cover and refrigerate overnight before serving. Store in refrigerator for no longer than 3 months. If desired, mix vinegar or water into cooled mustard to thin.

Homemade Catsup ▲

2 medium fresh tomatoes (about 1 lb.), seeded and chopped
¼ cup chopped onion
1 clove garlic, minced
2 teaspoons vegetable oil
1 can (12 oz.) tomato paste
⅓ cup red wine vinegar
¼ cup light corn syrup
1½ teaspoons paprika
¾ teaspoon salt
¼ teaspoon cayenne
¼ teaspoon Worcestershire sauce
⅛ teaspoon ground cloves

2½ cups catsup

In 2-quart casserole, combine tomatoes, onion, garlic and vegetable oil. Microwave at High for 7 to 9 minutes, or until onion is very tender, stirring once. Place mixture in food processor or blender and purée. Mix in remaining ingredients. Return to casserole. Cover with wax paper. Microwave at High for 15 to 25 minutes, or until mixture reaches desired thickness, stirring 3 times. Spoon catsup into sterilized jar and refrigerate overnight before serving. Store catsup in refrigerator for no longer than 1 month.

Salsa

1½ cups chopped onion
1 cup chopped green pepper
1 to 2 cloves garlic, minced
1 tablespoon vegetable oil
1 can (28 oz.) whole tomatoes
1 can (15 oz.) tomato purée
1 can (4 oz.) chopped green chilies, drained
2 teaspoons fresh snipped cilantro, or 1 teaspoon dried cilantro leaves
1 teaspoon salt
1 teaspoon packed brown sugar
1 teaspoon chili powder
1 teaspoon ground cumin
¼ teaspoon dried crushed red pepper

Three 1-pint jars

In 3-quart casserole, combine onion, green pepper, garlic and oil. Cover. Microwave at High for 3 to 4 minutes, or until vegetables are tender-crisp, stirring once. Stir in remaining ingredients. Microwave, uncovered, at High for 15 to 20 minutes, or until mixture is hot and flavors are blended, stirring twice. Spoon mixture evenly into three sterilized 1-pint jars. Cover and refrigerate overnight before serving. Store salsa in refrigerator for no longer than 2 weeks.

Hot Salsa: Follow recipe above, except substitute 1 can (3.5 oz.) jalapeños, drained and chopped, for green chilies.

Blueberry-Kiwi
Refrigerator Jam ▲

2 cups peeled, cored and sliced
  kiwi fruit
2 cups frozen blueberries
2 cups sugar
1 pkg. (3 oz.) lemon gelatin

Three ½-pint jars

In medium mixing bowl, combine
kiwi fruit, blueberries and sugar.
Mix well. Microwave at High for 15
to 25 minutes, or until fruit is very
soft, stirring 3 or 4 times. Add
gelatin, stirring until dissolved.
Divide mixture evenly between
three sterilized ½-pint jars. Cover
and chill until set, about 2 hours.
Store jam in refrigerator for no
longer than 1 month.

Blueberry-Kiwi Light Jam: Follow recipe above, except substitute 1 pkg. (0.3 oz.) low-calorie
lemon gelatin for the 3-oz. pkg.

Cherry-Almond
Refrigerator Jam

4 cups frozen pitted dark sweet
  cherries
2 cups sugar
1 pkg. (3 oz.) cherry gelatin
¼ teaspoon almond extract

Three ½-pint jars

In medium mixing bowl, combine
cherries and sugar. Mix well.
Microwave at High for 15 to 25
minutes, or until cherries are very
soft, stirring 3 or 4 times. Add
gelatin, stirring until dissolved. Stir
in almond extract. Divide mixture
evenly between three sterilized
½-pint jars. Cover. Chill until set,
about 2 hours. Store jam in refrigerator for no longer than 1 month.

Cherry-Almond Light Jam: Follow recipe above, except substitute 1 pkg. (0.3 oz.) low-calorie
cherry gelatin for the 3-oz. pkg.

Strawberry-Rhubarb
Refrigerator Jam ►

4 cups frozen cut-up rhubarb
2 cups sugar
1 pkg. (3 oz.) strawberry gelatin
2 teaspoons lemon juice

Three ½-pint jars

In medium mixing bowl, combine
rhubarb and sugar. Mix well.
Microwave at High for 15 to 25
minutes, or until rhubarb is very
soft, stirring 3 or 4 times. Add
gelatin, stirring until dissolved.
Mix in lemon juice. Divide mixture
evenly between three sterilized
½-pint jars. Cover. Chill until set,
about 2 hours. Store jam in refrigerator for no longer than 1 month.

**Strawberry-Rhubarb Light
Jam:** Follow recipe above, except substitute 1 pkg. (0.3 oz.)
low-calorie strawberry gelatin
for the 3-oz. pkg.

Pear Honey

 2 lbs. pears (4 medium),
     peeled and cored
2¼ cups sugar
 1 can (8 oz.) crushed
     pineapple
 1 tablespoon lemon juice
 ½ teaspoon grated lemon peel

Three ½-pint jars

Cut each pear into 6 pieces. Place in food processor or blender. Process until finely chopped. Place chopped pears in 3-quart casserole. Stir in remaining ingredients. Mix well. Microwave at High for 30 to 40 minutes, or until pears are translucent and very tender, stirring 2 or 3 times. Divide mixture evenly between three sterilized ½-pint jars. Cover and refrigerate overnight before serving. Store in refrigerator for no longer than 1 month.

Apple Butter ▲

 3 lbs. cooking apples, peeled,
     cored and cut into quarters
 ¼ cup apple cider
1½ cups granulated sugar
 ½ cup packed brown sugar
 2 tablespoons cider vinegar
1½ to 1¾ teaspoons ground
     cinnamon
 ¼ teaspoon ground allspice
 ⅛ teaspoon ground nutmeg

Three ½-pint jars

Place apples in 3-quart casserole. Add apple cider. Cover. Microwave at High for 18 to 23 minutes, or until apples are very soft, stirring once or twice. Place mixture in food processor or blender, and process until smooth.

Return apple mixture to 3-quart casserole. Stir in remaining ingredients. Microwave, uncovered, at High for 30 to 45 minutes, or until mixture is very thick, stirring 3 or 4 times. Spoon mixture evenly into three sterilized ½-pint jars. Cover and refrigerate overnight before serving. Store Apple Butter in refrigerator for no longer than 1 month.

Brandied Fruit

¾ cup water
½ cup packed brown sugar
⅓ cup granulated sugar
½ teaspoon ground cinnamon
⅛ teaspoon ground allspice
⅛ teaspoon ground nutmeg
½ to ¾ cup brandy
1 cup dried apricots
1 cup dried apples
1 cup pitted prunes
½ cup raisins
¾ cup drained maraschino
  cherries (optional)

1 quart fruit

In medium mixing bowl, combine water, sugars, cinnamon, allspice and nutmeg. Mix well. Microwave at High for 4 to 6 minutes, or until mixture boils and sugar dissolves, stirring once.

Stir in remaining ingredients. Microwave at High for 9 to 14 minutes, or until apricots and apples are tender, stirring once or twice. Cover and refrigerate for at least 3 days before serving. Store in refrigerator for no longer than 3 weeks. Serve fruit over plain cake or ice cream, if desired.

Microwaving Tips

The microwave oven's ability to soften and melt can simplify and enhance food preparation in many ways. Turn jelly or jam into a quick and colorful meat glaze or dessert topping. Restore hardened brown sugar, crystallized honey, even over-set gelatin.

Soften ice cream and blend with your favorite liqueur to create your own liqueur-flavored specialties or mold a dramatic ice cream dessert.

Miscellaneous Softening Chart (see photo directions)

Item	Microwave Time at High
Tostada & Taco Shells	
2 shells	15 - 20 sec.
4 shells	25 - 30 sec.
6 shells	30 - 45 sec.
8 shells	45 - 60 sec.
Tortillas, 4 to 6	20 - 40 sec.
Jelly & Jam	
¼ cup	30 - 45 sec.
½ cup	1 - 1¼ min.
1 cup	1½ - 2 min.
Ice Cream Topping	
¼ cup	25 - 35 sec.
½ cup	40 - 60 sec.
1 cup	1 - 1¼ min.
Peanut Butter	
¼ or ½ cup	30 - 60 sec.
Ice Cream	**50% (Med.):**
1 quart	30 - 60 sec.
½ gallon	1 min.
Overset Gelatin	**50% (Med.):**
3-oz. pkg.	1 - 1½ min.
6-oz. pkg.	1 - 2 min.

Warm Tostada & Taco Shells.
Place stack of shells on roasting rack. Microwave at High as directed in chart, left, until hot and slightly softened.

Melt Jelly & Jam. Place desired amount of jelly or jam in 2-cup measure or medium bowl. Microwave at High as directed in chart, left, or until melted, stirring every 30 seconds. Serve as dessert topping, as a glaze for meats, or use for sauces.

Soften Hard Brown Sugar. Sprinkle brown sugar lightly with water or add one apple slice to bag. Close bag loosely with string. Microwave at High 30 to 60 seconds, checking after half the time. Let stand 5 minutes to complete softening. If brown sugar begins to melt, remove from oven and let stand to complete softening. For amounts less than ½ lb., microwave at High until softened, checking every 15 seconds.

Soften & Warm Tortillas. Place four to six flour or corn tortillas between damp paper towels. Microwave at High 20 to 40 seconds, or until tortillas are warm to the touch.

Soften Ice Cream. To soften ice cream for scooping individual servings, or for layering in desserts, microwave in cardboard container at 50% (Medium) about 30 seconds. Scoop out desired amount; refreeze remaining ice cream in container.

Soften ice cream for filling pies or cakes, or for creating liqueur-flavored ice creams. Remove 1 quart ice cream from container. Place in medium bowl. Cut into quarters. Microwave at 50% (Medium) 30 to 60 seconds, or until softened.

Liqueur-Flavored Ice Cream. Stir ¼ cup liqueur into 1 quart softened ice cream, above. Place in freezer for 1 hour. Stir again, cover with foil, and store in freezer until serving time.

Flavor Combinations:
• Coffee Liqueur with chocolate, vanilla or coffee ice cream
• Crème de Menthe with chocolate ice cream
• Orange Liqueur with chocolate or coffee ice cream
• Raspberry Liqueur with peach or chocolate ice cream

Praline Ice Cream. Stir 1 cup crushed peanut brittle into 1 quart softened ice cream and freeze as directed for Liqueur-Flavored Ice Cream, above.

Warm Ice Cream Topping. Spoon desired amount of ice cream topping (butterscotch, fudge, chocolate, pineapple, caramel or strawberry) into 2-cup measure or small bowl. Microwave at High as directed in the chart (page 298) until heated. Stir. Serve over ice cream or cake.

Prepare Gelatin. Measure water as directed on package. Microwave 1 cup at High 2 to 3 minutes, or 2 cups 3 to 5 minutes, or until boiling. Stir in gelatin until dissolved. Add cold water.

Soften Overset Gelatin. If gelatin sets before you have added fruit, vegetables or nuts, resoften it. Microwave at 50% (Medium) 1 to 1½ minutes for 3-oz. package or 1 to 2 minutes for 6-oz. package, or until soft-set. Stir. Add desired ingredients. Refrigerate until firm.

Soften Crystallized Honey. Remove lid from glass honey bottle, or transfer from plastic container to measuring cup. Microwave at High 2 to 2½ minutes, or until clear, stirring every 30 seconds. Let cool.

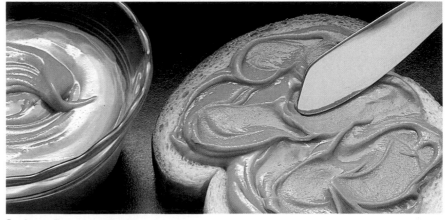

Soften Peanut Butter. To ease spreading, microwave ¼ or ½ cup peanut butter at High 30 seconds, or until easy to stir. For a dessert sauce, continue to microwave additional 30 seconds, or until of a thin consistency. Serve over chocolate ice cream.

Clean up quickly. Use paper-towel-lined paper plates for microwaving canapés or nachos.

Line layer-cake dishes easily. Cut a circle of paper towel to fit bottom of 9-inch round cake dish. Paper absorbs excess moisture and provides smooth surface for frosting cakes.

Prevent spatters. Cover sauces that tend to spatter with a dry paper towel while they microwave. The paper towel allows steam to escape from spaghetti or barbecue sauces, and at the same time prevents spatters and absorbs excess moisture.

Absorb excess moisture. Place a paper towel under bread products and microwave just until warm. Towel will help keep bottom of bread dry.

Degrease soups and stews. Lightly place a paper towel on the surface of soups and stews after microwaving to absorb grease rising to the top during cooking.

Keep toppings crisp. Use paper towel as a cover when casseroles have crisp toppings. Towel holds in warmth while absorbing steam to prevent topping from becoming soggy.

Absorb grease. Layer 4 paper towels in bottom of 1-quart casserole. Crumble 1 lb. lean ground beef in casserole. Cover with another paper towel. Microwave at High for 4 to 7 minutes, or until beef is no longer pink, stirring once or twice to break apart. Remove top paper towel. Lift bottom paper towels, shaking ground beef into casserole. Use ground beef in tacos, spaghetti or other ground beef recipes.

Steam-heat dinner plates. Moisten 4 paper towels and place 1 towel on each of 4 microwave-safe plates. Stack plates and place in microwave oven. Microwave at High for 2 to 3 minutes, or until plates are hot. Remove from microwave using oven mitts.

Catch drips by placing a sheet of wax paper under wire rack when cooling dipped chocolate candies.

Cover leftover foods with wax paper to hold in heat and moisture when reheating.

Wax Paper Tips

Wax paper is an excellent cover for fruits or other foods that do not require steam to tenderize.

Spread candies, mints, drop candies or caramel corn on wax paper or parchment paper to cool after microwaving.

Line dishes with wax paper for easy removal of food. Cut wax paper to fit bottom of loaf and cake dishes — especially good for upside-down cakes and quick breads.

Hold in warmth by covering frozen foods with wax paper while defrosting in the microwave.

Use wax paper to cover custards and egg-based dishes. It holds in heat and promotes more even cooking. Because some steam escapes, surfaces will collect less moisture than when covered with plastic wrap.

Foil Tips

Shield wing tips and leg ends of whole poultry with small amounts of foil to protect them during defrosting and microwaving.

Keep bread products drier and crisper when reheating. Cut a piece of foil smaller than portion to be reheated. Place foil on plate in microwave. Cover with a folded paper towel. Place food on folded paper towel to reheat in microwave.

Wrap baked potatoes and tent whole roasts with foil during standing time to hold in heat and complete cooking.

Cover corners of square dishes and the ends of loaf dishes to help cakes, brownies, bars and quick breads cook more evenly during microwaving.

Use foil to shield and protect protruding angles and edges of roasts that may overcook because they are exposed to more microwave energy.

Microwaving with Foil:

- Keep all foil at least 1 inch from oven walls.
- Area of food exposed should be at least three times the area covered by foil (e.g., two-thirds of whole roast should be exposed).
- Crinkles in foil can sometimes cause arcing. Smooth out foil to fit close to food.
- Frozen convenience foods that come in foil containers should be transferred to a microwave-safe dish for more even defrosting or cooking.

NOTE: Always follow oven manufacturer's directions in regard to use of foil.

Protect thinner parts of foods — such as tails of whole fish, turkey tenderloin tips, thin ends of fish steaks — with small pieces of foil to prevent these areas from overcooking.

In About 1 Minute...

Look at what you can microwave in a minute-plus. They're so easy, you'll hardly need any directions.

Scramble Eggs: Microwave 1 egg at High for 30 seconds to 1 minute, stirring once.

Heat Hot Chocolate: Microwave 1 cup at High for 1¼ to 2¼ minutes.

Heat Fudge Topping: Microwave ½ cup at High for 45 seconds to 1 minute.

Heat Frozen Burrito: Microwave 1 burrito (4 oz.) at High for 1 to 2½ minutes.

Reheat Pizza: Microwave 1 to 2 slices at High for 45 seconds to 1¾ minutes.

Reheat Burgers: Microwave 1 hamburger in bun at High for 45 seconds to 1½ minutes.

Heat Syrup: Microwave ½ cup at High for 30 seconds to 1 minute.

Heat Hot Dog: Microwave 1 hot dog in bun at High for 45 seconds to 1 minute.

Melt Cheese Dip: Microwave 1 cup at 50% (Medium) for 45 seconds to 1 minute, stirring once.

Soften Cream Cheese: Microwave 1 pkg. (8 oz.) at 50% (Medium) for 1½ to 3 minutes.

Defrost Orange Juice Concentrate: Microwave 1 can (12 oz.) at High for 1 to 2½ minutes.

Warm Up Fruit Pie: Microwave 1 slice at High for 45 seconds to 1 minute.

Combination Cooking Tips

Quick Broiler-browned Casseroles. Prepare gratins (crumb- or cheese-topped casseroles) in a broiler-safe dish or casserole. Microwave as directed, then place under broiler, 2 to 4 inches from heat, until browned, watching carefully. You can also use oven broiler for browning coffee cakes or crisps that use a brown sugar, crumb-type topping.

Fast Tortillas. Soften tortillas in vegetable oil on your conventional rangetop, according to package directions. Prepare filling and cook filled tortillas in your microwave for fast finishing.

Quick Pasta Meals. Prepare pasta on your conventional rangetop while your favorite red or white sauce, meat or vegetable mixture is in the microwave.

Deliciously Browned Meats. For an attractive appearance, quickly brown pork chops or chicken pieces in a small amount of vegetable oil over medium-high heat on your conventional rangetop. Place meat on a roasting rack or in a casserole, and microwave to finish recipe.

Speed Grilling. Microwave chicken or ribs until almost done, then finish on the barbecue grill for a true charcoal flavor. Meat will be fully cooked and juicier with less chance of overbrowning. To give barbecued leftovers just-grilled flavor, reheat in the microwave.

Meringue Pies. Speed up preparation of meringue pies by cooking pie crust and filling in the microwave oven. Top with prepared meringue. Bake in preheated 400°F conventional oven until meringue is lightly browned.

Quick Ranch Fries. Extra baked potatoes from your microwave can be peeled and sliced into wedges, then browned in butter on your conventional rangetop.

Crispy Baked Potatoes. Partially cook whole potatoes in the microwave, then place in preheated 400°F conventional oven and bake until skins are dry and crispy.

Defrosting Meat Chart

Type	Power Level	Time	Procedure
Beef, Pork & Lamb			
Large Roasts, Flat Roasts & Large Steaks	50% (Med.)	5½ to 9 min./lb.	Unwrap and place on roasting rack. Microwave for ¼ of time. Shield if needed. Turn meat over. Microwave another ¼ of time. Let stand 10 minutes. Microwave remaining time, turning over once, until cool but not icy and skewer can be inserted into center. Let stand 20 to 30 minutes.
Ribs & Chops	50% (Med.)	3 to 6½ min./lb.	Unwrap and place on roasting rack. Microwave for half of time. Separate, turn over and rearrange. Microwave remaining time until cool but not icy. Let stand 10 to 15 minutes.
Ground	50% (Med.)	4 to 6 min./lb.	Unwrap and place in 1-quart casserole. Microwave, removing defrosted portions to another dish. Let stand 5 minutes.
Cooked Cubed Meat (2 cups) (Beef, Pork, Fully Cooked Ham or Turkey)	50% (Med.)	4 to 6 min.	Unwrap and place in 1-quart casserole. Microwave for half of time. Remove defrosted portions to another dish. Microwave remaining time until cool but not icy. Let stand 5 minutes.

Defrosting Fish & Shellfish Chart

Type	Power Level	Time	Procedure
Fish			
Fillets, block	50% (Med.)	6 to 10 min./lb.	Unwrap and place in baking dish or on roasting rack. Microwave for half of time. Separate fillets as soon as possible. Microwave remaining time until fish is pliable but still icy. Let stand 10 minutes.
Fillets, individual	50% (Med.)	5 to 8 min./lb.	Unwrap and arrange on roasting rack. Microwave for half of time. Rearrange once. Microwave remaining time until fish is pliable but still icy. Let stand 10 minutes.
Steaks	50% (Med.)	4 to 7 min./lb.	Unwrap and place in baking dish or on roasting rack. Microwave for half of time. Separate and rearrange. Shield thin portions. Microwave remaining time until fish is pliable but icy in center. Let stand 5 to 10 minutes.
Scallops	50% (Med.)	4½ to 6 min./lb.	Unwrap and place in baking dish. Microwave for half of time. Separate scallops as soon as possible. Microwave remaining time until cold but not icy, stirring 2 or 3 times. Rinse with cold water. Let stand 5 minutes.
Shrimp			
Shelled, deveined	50% (Med.)	4 to 8 min./lb.	Unwrap and place in baking dish. Microwave for half of time. Separate shrimp as soon as possible. Microwave remaining time until cold but not icy, stirring 2 or 3 times. Rinse with cold water. Let stand 5 minutes.

Defrosting Poultry Chart

Type	Power Level	Time	Procedure
Chicken			
Whole	30% (Med. Low)	5 to 9 min./lb.	Unwrap and place breast-side down in baking dish. Cover with wax paper. Microwave for half of time. Turn breast-side up. Shield if needed. Microwave remaining time. Remove giblets. Let stand 5 to 10 minutes until cool but not icy.
Quarters, Legs, Thighs, Wings	50% (Med.)	4 to 6½ min./lb.	Unwrap and place in baking dish or on roasting rack. Microwave for half of time. Separate pieces. Arrange with thickest portions toward outside. Microwave remaining time. Let stand 10 to 15 minutes until cool but not icy.
Boneless Breasts	50% (Med.)	5½ to 8 min./lb.	Unwrap and place in baking dish or on roasting rack. Microwave for half of time. Separate pieces. Microwave remaining time until pliable but cold. Let stand 15 to 20 minutes.
Turkey			
Whole, boneless, 4 lbs.	50% (Med.)	7½ to 9½ min./lb.	Unwrap and place on roasting rack. Microwave for half of time, turning over once. Let stand 15 minutes. Remove gravy packet. Turn turkey over. Microwave remaining time, turning over once. Let stand 20 minutes until cool but not icy.
Bone-in Breast	50% (Med.)	3½ to 5½ min./lb.	Unwrap and place skin-side down on roasting rack. Microwave for half of time. Remove gravy packet. Turn skin-side up. Shield if needed. Microwave remaining time. Rinse in cool water. Let stand 5 to 10 minutes until cool but not icy.
Tenderloins	50% (Med.)	4 to 6 min./lb.	Unwrap and place on roasting rack. Microwave for half of time. Shield thin portions. Microwave remaining time. Let stand 10 to 15 minutes until cool but not icy.
Cutlets	30% (Med. Low)	7 to 11 min./lb.	Unwrap and place on roasting rack. Microwave for half of time. Separate and rearrange as soon as possible. Microwave remaining time, until pliable but still icy. Let stand to complete defrosting.
Ground	50% (Med.)	4 to 6 min./lb.	Unwrap and place in casserole. Microwave, removing defrosted portions to another dish. Let stand 10 minutes.
Cornish Hens	50% (Med.)	5 to 7 min./lb.	Unwrap and place breast-side down in baking dish. Cover with wax paper. Microwave for half of time. Turn breast-side up. Shield if needed. Rearrange hens. Microwave remaining time. Remove giblets. Let stand 5 minutes.

Microwaving Vegetable Chart

Vegetable	Amount	Microwave Time at High	Standing Time, Covered	Procedure
Artichokes				
Fresh	2	5½-8½ min.	3 min.	Trim and rinse artichokes. Wrap in plastic wrap.
	4	9½-14½ min.	3 min.	Arrange in oven with spaces between.
Frozen	9 oz. pkg.	5-6 min.	2 min.	1-qt. covered casserole with 2 tablespoons water. Stir after 2 minutes.
Asparagus				
Fresh	1 lb.	6½-9½ min.	3 min.	12 × 8-in. dish with ¼ cup water. Rearrange spears once.
Frozen	10 oz. pkg.	5-7 min.	3 min.	1-qt. covered casserole with 2 tablespoons water. Stir once.
Canned, spears & cuts	10 oz. can	2-4 min.		1-qt. covered casserole. Drain all but 1 tablespoon liquid. Stir once.
Beans				
Fresh, Green & Wax	1 lb.	7-13 min.	3 min.	Cut into 1½-in. pieces. 1½-qt. covered casserole with ¼ cup water. Stir once.
Frozen, Green & Wax	9 oz. pkg.	6-7 min.	3 min.	1-qt. covered casserole with 2 tablespoons water. Stir once.
Frozen, Lima	10 oz. pkg.	4-7 min.		1-qt. covered casserole with 2 tablespoons water. Stir once.
Canned, Green & Wax	15½ oz. can	2-4 min.		1-qt. covered casserole. Drain all but 2 tablespoons liquid. Stir once.
Canned, Lima	15-16 oz. can	2-3 min.	1 min.	1-qt. covered casserole. Drain all but 2 tablespoons liquid. Stir once.
Canned, Pork & Beans	16 oz. can	3-4 min.		1-qt. covered casserole. Stir after first 2 minutes.
Beets				
Canned	16 oz. can	2-3 min.		1-qt. covered casserole. Drain all but 2 tablespoons liquid.
Broccoli				
Fresh, spears	1½ lbs.	8-12 min.	3 min.	12 × 8-in. dish with ½ cup water. Cover with plastic wrap. Rotate dish ½ turn once.
Frozen	10 oz. pkg.	5-7 min.	3 min.	1-qt. covered casserole with 2 tablespoons water. Stir once.
Brussels Sprouts				
Fresh	4 cups	4-8 min.	3 min.	1½-qt. covered casserole with ¼ cup water. Stir once.
Frozen	10 oz. pkg.	5-7 min.	3 min.	1-qt. covered casserole with 2 tablespoons water. Stir once.
Cabbage				
Shredded	1 lb.	7½-13½ min.	3 min.	¼-in. wide shreds. 1½-qt. covered casserole with 2 tablespoons water. Stir once.
Wedges	1 lb.	12½-15½ min.	2-3 min.	12 × 8-in. dish with ¼ cup water. Cover with plastic wrap. Rearrange wedges and rotate dish once.
Carrots				
Fresh, slices, ⅛-in.	2 cups	4-7 min.	3 min.	1-qt. covered casserole with 2 tablespoons water. Stir once.
Frozen, sliced	2 cups	4-7 min.	3 min.	1-qt. covered casserole with 2 tablespoons water. Stir once.

Vegetable	Amount	Microwave Time at High	Standing Time, Covered	Procedure
Cauliflower				
Fresh, whole	1 lb.	5½-7½ min.	3 min.	Wrap in plastic wrap. Turn over after 3 minutes.
Fresh, flowerets	2 cups	4-7 min.	3 min.	1-qt. covered casserole with 2 tablespoons water. Stir once.
Frozen	10 oz. pkg.	5-7 min.	3 min.	1-qt. covered casserole with 2 tablespoons water. Stir once.
Corn				
Fresh, husked	2 ears	4½-10 min.	5 min.	12×8-in. dish with ¼ cup water. Cover with plastic wrap. Turn over and rearrange once or twice.
	4 ears	7½-16 min.	5 min.	
Frozen, cob	2 small ears	5½-7½ min.	3 min.	12×8-in. dish with 2 tablespoons water. Cover with plastic wrap. Turn over and rearrange once.
Frozen, whole kernel	10 oz. pkg.	4-6 min.	3 min.	1-qt. covered casserole with 2 tablespoons water. Stir once.
Canned, whole kernel	16 oz. can	2-3 min.		1-qt. covered casserole. Drain all but 2 tablespoons liquid. Stir once.
Okra				
Frozen, whole	10 oz. pkg.	5-6 min.	2 min.	1-qt. covered casserole with 2 tablespoons water. Stir every 2 minutes.
Frozen, sliced	10 oz. pkg.	5-7 min.	2 min.	1-qt. covered casserole with 2 tablespoons water. Stir every 2 minutes.
Canned	14½ oz. can	3-4 min.		1-qt. covered casserole. Drain all but 2 tablespoons liquid. Stir once or twice.
Peas, Black-Eyed				
Frozen	10 oz. pkg.	8-9 min.	2 min.	1-qt. covered casserole with ¼ cup water. Stir every 2 minutes.
Peas, Garden				
Fresh	2 cups	5-8 min.	3 min.	1-qt. covered casserole with ¼ cup water. Stir once.
Frozen	10 oz. pkg.	4-6 min.	2 min.	1-qt. covered casserole with 2 tablespoons water. Stir once.
Canned	16 oz. can	2-3 min.		1-qt. covered casserole. Drain all but 2 tablespoons liquid. Stir once.
Pea Pods				
Fresh	¼ lb.	2-4 min.	2 min.	1-qt. covered casserole with 2 tablespoons water.
Frozen	6 oz. pkg.	3-4 min.	2 min.	1-qt. covered casserole with 2 tablespoons water. Stir once.
Potatoes				
Baked	2 med.	5-7 min.	5-10 min.	Prick potatoes. Place on paper towel. Turn over and rearrange after half the cooking time. Let stand wrapped in foil.
	4 med.	10½-12½ min.	5-10 min.	
Boiled	4 med.	7-9 min.	3 min.	Peel and quarter potatoes. 1- to 1½-qt. covered casserole with ¼ cup water and ½ teaspoon salt. Rearrange once. Drain.
Spinach				
Fresh	1 lb.	5-8 min.	3 min.	3-qt. covered casserole with 2 tablespoons water. Stir once.
Canned	15 oz. can	3-4 min.		1-qt. covered casserole. Drain all liquid. Stir once.
Squash				
Acorn Squash, fresh	1	8½-11½ min.	5-10 min.	Cut in half; wrap with plastic wrap. Rotate and rearrange halves after half the cooking time.
	2	13-16 min.	5-10 min.	
Zucchini, fresh ¼-in. slices	2 cups	2½-6½ min.	3 min.	2-qt. covered casserole with 2 tablespoons butter or margarine. Stir once.
Frozen, mashed	12 oz. pkg.	5½-8 min.		1-qt. covered casserole. Break apart after 2 minutes, then stir at 2 minute intervals.
Sweet Potatoes				
Baked (5-7 oz.)	2 whole	5-9 min.	3 min.	Wash, prick, place on paper towel. Rearrange once during cooking.
	4 whole	8-13 min.	3 min.	

Conversion Tables for Metric Measurements

Liquid Measures

[1 liter = 10 deciliters (dl) = 100 centiliters (cl) = 1,000 milliliters (ml)]

Spoons, cups, pints and quarts	Liquid ounces	Metric equivalent
1 tsp	1/16 oz	1/2 cl; 5 ml
1 Tb	1/2 oz	15 ml
1/4 c; 4 Tb	2 oz	1/2 dl; 59 ml
1/3 c; 5 Tb	2 2/3 oz	3/4 dl; 79 ml
1/2 c	4 oz	1 dl; 119 ml
1 c	8 oz	1/4 l; 237 ml
1 1/4 c	10 oz	3 dl; 296 ml
2 c; 1 pt	16 oz	1/2 l; 473 ml
2 1/2 c	20 oz	592 ml
3 c	24 oz	710 ml; 3/4 l
4 c; 1 qt	32 oz	1 l; 946 ml
4 qt; 1 gal	128 oz	3 3/4 l; 3,785 ml
5 qt		4 3/4 l
6 qt		5 3/4 l
8 qt		7 1/2 l

Conversion formula: To convert liters to quarts, multiply the liters by .95; quarts to liters, multiply the quarts by 1.057.

Weight

American ounces	American pounds	Grams	Kilograms
1/3 oz		10 g	
1/2 oz		15 g	
1 oz		30 g	
3 1/2 oz		100 g	
4 oz	1/4 lb	114 g	
5 oz		140 g	
8 oz	1/2 lb	227 g	
9 oz		250 g	1/4 kg
16 oz	1 lb	450 g	
18 oz	1 1/8 lb	500 g	1/2 kg
32 oz	2 lb	900 g	
36 oz	2 1/4 lb	1000 g	1 kg
	3 lb	1350 g	1 1/3 kg
	4 lb	2800 g	1 3/4 kg

Conversion formula: To convert ounces into grams, multiply the ounces by 28.35; grams into ounces, multiply the grams by .035.

Temperatures

Fahrenheit	Celsius
32°F*	0°C
60°F	16°C
75°F	24°C
80°F	27°C
95°F	37°C
150°F	65°C
175°F	79°C
212°F**	100°C
250°F	121°C
300°F	149°C
350°F	177°C
400°F	205°C
450°F	232°C
500°F	260°C

* water freezes   ** water boils

Conversion formula: To convert Fahrenheit into Celsius, subtract 32, multiply by 5, divide by 9. To convert Celsius to Fahrenheit, multiply by 9, divide by 5, add 32.

American Equivalents

Weights and Measures

a few grains = less than 1/8 teaspoon
60 drops = 1 teaspoon
1 1/2 teaspoons = 1/2 tablespoon
3 teaspoons = 1 tablespoon
2 tablespoons = 1/8 cup or 1 fluid ounce
4 tablespoons = 1/4 cup
5 1/3 tablespoons = 1/3 cup
8 tablespoons = 1/2 cup
10 2/3 tablespoons = 2/3 cup
12 tablespoons = 3/4 cup
16 tablespoons = 1 cup
3/8 cup = 1/4 cup plus 2 tablespoons
5/8 cup = 1/2 cup plus 2 tablespoons
7/8 cup = 3/4 cup plus 2 tablespoons
1 cup = 8 fluid ounces
2 cups = 1 pint or 16 fluid ounces
2 pints = 1 quart or 32 fluid ounces
4 cups = 1 quart
4 quarts = 1 gallon
8 quarts = 1 peck
4 pecks = 1 bushel
16 ounces = 1 pound

1 gram = 0.035 ounces
1 kilogram = 2.21 pounds
1 ounce = 28.35 grams
1 pound = 453.59 grams
1 teaspoon = 4.9 milliliters
1 tablespoon = 14.8 milliliters
1 cup = 236.6 milliliters
1 liter = 1.06 quarts or 1,000 milliliters

General Guidelines for Microwave Cooking at High Altitudes
(3000 to 7500 feet)

If you live at a high elevation, you may need to adjust your microwave cooking methods, since the thinner air and lower air pressure affect cooking in several ways. Water and liquids boil at lower temperatures (about 2°F lower for each 1000-foot rise in elevation) and longer cooking may be necessary, except for candy. Water and liquids evaporate faster and may need to be increased. Foods cool more quickly. Cakes and breads rise higher, are more crumbly and can even fall due to excess leavening action. Since the air is less humid, dry ingredients are drier and additional liquids may be needed; for moistness, tightly wrap baked goods. Always make a note of problems with finished dishes so you can change the recipe next time.

These guidelines are intended for use with the recipes in *More Joy of Microwaving* only. Other recipes may require different adjustments. For more information contact your County Extension Agent.

High Altitude Adjustments

Appetizers and Sandwiches
No change usually necessary. Check cheese toppings before completed cooking time. Double wrap sandwiches in paper napkins for heating.

Beverages and Soups
Stir more to dissolve dehydrated items. Watch milk-based liquids to prevent foaming over; slightly reduce time. Increase ingredients and steeping time for better-flavored coffee and tea. Increase soup simmering times to tenderize meats and vegetables.

Breads, Quick
If sugar and oil are less than ½ cup: Reduce leavening about ⅛ teaspoon per teaspoon to prevent bitter taste; increase liquid 1 to 3 tablespoons for each recipe, and add 1 to 2 teaspoons more oil. If bread has more than ½ cup oil and sags in center: Reduce oil 2 to 5 tablespoons per recipe and add 1 to 3 tablespoons flour, plus follow directions above for leavening and liquid. If sugar is about 1 cup or more: Follow cake recipe suggestions below. In all recipes: Use large eggs; finely chop all nuts and fruits and dust them with flour; measure moist fruits. Use 9 × 5-inch loaf dish or muffin liners filled only ½ full. Plan on 1 to 4 extra muffins. Watch baking time; use doneness test.

Breads, Yeast
Use less flour in last addition. Conventional rising times will be 5 to 15 minutes shorter; let rise until just double. Watch baking time; use doneness test.

Cake Mixes
Contact food companies for high altitude plus microwave directions, or use conventional high altitude directions: Watch baking time and add 1 to 2 minutes if cake falls; elevate if bottom isn't completely cooked and, if too crumbly, add 1 extra tablespoon flour next time.

Cake Recipes
Select recipes designed for microwaving; they need less adjustment than conventional ones. Measure accurately. In all recipes: Use large eggs; finely chop all nuts and fruits and dust them with flour; measure moist fruits. *Measure* fruits, e.g. use "½ cup," not "1 medium" banana. Use high-sided or next larger size dishes, and 14-cup ring pans. Grease generously and use extra coating crumbs. For heavy batters: Fill baking dish or cupcake liners a scant ½ full; fill only ⅓ full for light batters. Plan on extra cupcakes. Increase 50% (Medium) bake time by 1 minute; increase 100% (High) time as necessary. Reduce sugar 1 to 2 tablespoons for each 1 cup in recipe, and leavening ⅛ teaspoon per 1 teaspoon. Add 2 to 4 tablespoons flour and 1 to 4 tablespoons liquid per recipe. In rich cakes, reduce shortening or oil 2 to 5 tablespoons per recipe.

Candies and Syrups
For each 1000 feet of elevation above sea level, subtract 2°F from the temperature on the candy thermometer. The cold water test is unchanged and reliable. Use a large cooking dish and watch for boil-overs.

Casseroles
If recipes contain milk, increase dish size to prevent bubble-overs. Vegetables may require slightly more liquid and longer cooking for tenderness. If thick, check center bottom for doneness; if not completely cooked, elevate dish on saucer. Watch for drying out of top.

Convenience Foods
Contact company for specific directions; expect slight time increases.

Egg Dishes
Quiches and custards may need to be elevated and time increased 2 to 4 minutes at 50% (Medium).

Frostings
Confectioners' sugar is drier, so 1 to 2 tablespoons extra liquid may be needed.

Meats, Fish and Poultry
Cooking will be similar in time, except large pieces may take longer, and poultry may take 3 to 5 minutes more at High. Use doneness tests suggested. If, after standing time, meat is cool, reheat a short time. Moist cooking of less-tender cuts requires 5 to 35 minutes more time. Use tight coverings or bags and watch liquid level; add more if necessary. Increase first cooking period at High from 8 to 10 minutes. Should be fork tender before standing time. Ground meats and poultry may require 1 to 1½ minutes more cooking time per pound at High.

Pies and Puddings
In crusts, 1 to 3 teaspoons more water may be needed. Fresh fruit should be thinly sliced and the baking time increased to reach tenderness. Above 6500 feet, slightly precook fruit in separate bowl. Cornstarch fillings: See "Sauces," below.

Reheating
Watch moisture levels; if dry add 1 teaspoon water before heating. Or cover with damp paper towel, then wax paper.

Rices, Grains and Pasta
More liquid (2 to 4 tablespoons per ½ cup water in recipe) and longer time will be needed. The first cooking at High should be increased from 5 to 8 minutes. In addition, instant rices need a short (1 to 2 minutes) boiling time before standing to rehydrate properly. Watch cooked breakfast cereal to prevent foaming. Use larger bowls to prevent boil-overs for all these foods.

Sauces, Sweet and Savory
Watch for thickening, stir more often and continue to boil for correct time. If recipe calls for 4 tablespoons cornstarch, reduce to 3 tablespoons and add 2 tablespoons flour for proper thickening.

Vegetables
Follow directions for vegetable size, etc. Thoroughly prick whole vegetables. Fresh: Add 1 to 2 tablespoons extra water and check for doneness after standing time. For whole vegetables increase time about ½ to 1 minute per piece. Let stand and check. Frozen: Add 1 extra tablespoon water. For vegetables in cheese sauce, make sure center is hot. For blanching, increase time about 1 minute for 5000 feet. In soups and stews, increase liquid and time for correct tenderness. Dried beans require overnight soaking and greatly increased cooking time and liquid; above 7500 feet conventional cooking methods are recommended. Above 7500 feet many vegetables (fresh or frozen) may boil dry and cook faster, so check them before they are due to be done.

Index